Peter Wynne-Thomas has been Nottinghamshire CCC archivist and librarian for some forty years and is currently serving as the club's President. Honorary Secretary of the Association of Cricket Statisticians and Historians for thirty-two years, he is the author of many books relating to cricket's history. His *Nottinghamshire Cricketers 1821-1914* won the Cricket Society Book of the Year award in 1971 and he was commissioned by Her Majesty's Stationery Office to write *The History of Cricket* in 1997.

# ARTHUR CARR

## THE RISE AND FALL
## OF NOTTINGHAMSHIRE'S
## BODYLINE CAPTAIN

PETER WYNNE-THOMAS

*Chequered Flag* PUBLISHING

First published in the UK by Chequered Flag Publishing 2017
PO Box 4669, Sheffield, S6 9ET
www.chequeredflagpublishing.co.uk

A CIP record for this book is available from the British Library

ISBN 9780993215292

Photo credits
Duncan Anderson: pp.4, 114, 148
Nottinghamshire CCC: pp.40, 64, 78, 96, 128, 170, 194, 212,
236, 258
June Prescott: pp.16, 52
Sherborne School: p.28

# CONTENTS

# ARTHUR CARR'S FAMILY TREE

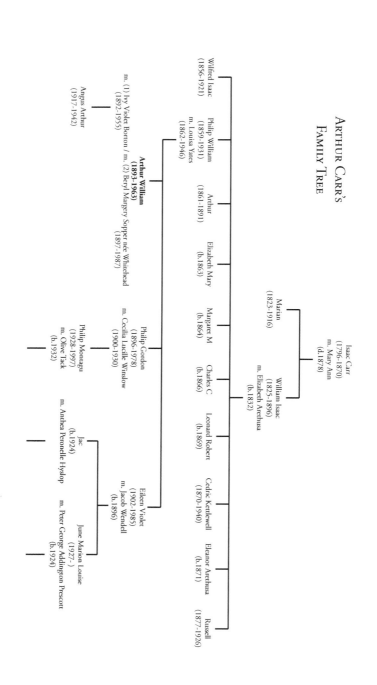

Isaac Carr
(1796-1870)
m. Mary Ann
(d.1878)

Marian
(1823-1916)

William Isaac
(1825-1896)
m. Elizabeth Arethusa
(b.1832)

Wilfred Isaac
(1856-1921)

Philip William
(1859-1931)
m. Louisa Yates
(1862-1946)

Arthur
(1861-1891)

Elizabeth Mary
(b.1863)

Margaret M
(b.1864)

Charles C
(b.1866)

Leonard Robert
(b.1869)

Cedric Kettlewell
(1870-1940)

Eleanor Arethusa
(b.1871)

Russell
(1877-1926)

**Arthur William
(1893-1963)**
m. (1) Ivy Violet Borton /
(1892-1955)
m. (2) Beryl Margery Sopper née Whitehead
(1897-1987)

Philip Gordon
(1896-1978)
m. Cecilia Lucille Winslow
(1900-1930)

Eileen Violet
(1902-1985)
m. Jacob Wendell
(b.1896)

Angus Arthur
(1917-1942)

Philip Montagu
(1928-1997)
m. Olive Tack
(b.1932)

Jac
(b.1924)
m. Anthea Petronelle Hyslop

June Marion Louise
(1927- )
m. Peter George Addington Prescott
(b.1924)

# Introduction

There's a breathless hush in the close to-night –
Ten to make and the match to win –
A bumping pitch and a blinding light,
An hour to play and the last man in.
And it's not for the sake of a ribboned coat,
Or the selfish hope of a season's fame,
But his Captain's hand on his shoulder smote,
'Play up! And play the game.'

'Vitaï Lampada', Sir Henry Newbolt's poem of 1897, is now much derided. Yet it summarised the philosophy of Arthur Carr, a future Nottinghamshire and England cricket captain, when it was acquired unconsciously both through his prep school and his public school. Their teachings were based on Thomas Arnold's muscular christianity which reached its zenith during the Edwardian era.

There was no side to Arthur Carr. He brought his honesty and forthrightness to every aspect of his life. The wealth of his father presented him with an independence, allowing him to adopt what he believed to be the right course and pursue it regardless of the opposition. If his life had been portrayed by Hollywood, the only actor designed to take his role must surely be Gary Cooper.

Carr loathed London and all its trappings – for him it was a case of the grass beneath his feet (or his horse's hooves) rather than the pavement. He had excelled at every sport to which he put his hand, right from his days at Hazelwood, but most especially to cricket. That was the game that was to consume his life from the moment he became captain of Nottinghamshire in 1919 until the people who had covered him in praise for years deserted him in 1935. The peculiar county captaincy system in vogue during the first half of the twentieth century, I have dwelt upon in the course of the narrative.

Carr was rescued fortuitously from his wilderness years by the outbreak of the Second World War, when he found himself back in uniform and stationed at Catterick. He fought in France through most of the Great War, but for this second conflict he was used to improve the physical fitness of new recruits. He went to a local dance and fell in love with Beryl – a controversial story which will be told in detail – but they, by all accounts, lived happily ever after. Yet it was a retirement spent more involved in horse racing and hunting than cricket, since the former England captain was effectively ostracised from Trent Bridge for his input into the biggest cricket controversy of the century: Bodyline.

Arthur Carr's prowess as a schoolboy sporting star was fictionalised in Alec Waugh's novel, *The Loom of Youth.* In the process of researching this biography, I have read the biographies of both Alec Waugh and his brother Evelyn. The authors of those biographies had access to a veritable treasure trove of diaries, letters and other written material which poured from the pens of these two brothers. In complete contrast, Arthur Carr was not a person who wrote letters other than those which were short, succinct and conveyed the information he wished to deliver in as few words as possible. From what is known of his conversation, it was conducted in the same vein.

There exists Carr's own ghosted autobiography, written in haste directly after the tragic events of 1935, some of which first appeared in a series of newspaper articles. Carr's book certainly conveys a flavour of his personality. Yet I hope that the details set out in this present work provide a more rounded picture and do justice to a man whom I grew to like and admire as I dug through numberless old newspaper files, minute books and other scraps. Discussions with the few relatives who have first-hand knowledge of him have been invaluable, but alas it has proved too late to talk to the county cricketers who were his colleagues.

ENGLAND'S TEST TEAM
Left to Right (Standing) KILNER, LARWOOD, TATE, WOOLLEY, ROOT, SUTCLIFFE.
Left to Right (Sitting) STRUDWICK, A.P.F.CHAPMAN, A.W.CARR, (CAPT.) HOBBS, HENDREN.

The highlight of Carr's cricket career, captaining the likes of
Sutcliffe and Hobbs for England – but have his achievements
been tainted by Bodyline?

# 1

## BEGINNING WITH AN ENDING

### 1938

Bulcote Manor,
Nottinghamshire,
Telephone: Burton Joyce 32
8 January [1938]

Dear Brown,

I shall be much obliged if you will tender my resignation to your Committee. It is quite impossible for me to attend meetings in the winter owing to my hunting and this summer I expect to be continually away from home. I hope the Club will have a very successful season.

Yrs sincerely,
AW Carr

The recipient of this letter, HA Brown, was the Secretary of Nottinghamshire County Cricket Club, a post he had held since 1921, when he had been temporarily appointed due to the sudden departure of the previous occupier of the post, FS Ashley-Cooper, after less than a year at Trent Bridge. Brown, generally known as Captain Brown, had little knowledge of cricket and had come up to Nottingham from his London home purely to resolve some problems which had arisen with the local Boys' Brigade which met in a hall on Trent Bridge Cricket Ground. He unravelled the problems which threatened to engulf the brigade and he proved eminently suitable for the position of County Secretary, which was unexpectedly been thrust upon him. Brown's temporary post as Secretary was quickly made permanent and he was destined spend the rest of his working life in Nottingham – he finally retired as Secretary in 1959 at the age of sixty-nine.

Carr, in his letter, writes about 'your Committee', which in 1938 comprised eighteen members of the County Cricket Club elected by an adult membership of some 4,000. The nominal head of the Club in 1938 was the President, who that year was Sir Julien Cahn, a wealthy businessman. Cahn had been a member of the Committee for over ten years and was the club's most generous benefactor. His fortune meant that he wielded great influence in Nottingham cricket and business circles. The 1938 Chairman of the Committee was a Nottingham lawyer, Sir Douglas McCraith, who had played club cricket with the leading Nottingham team, Nottingham Amateurs.

Trent Bridge Cricket Ground in the Nottingham suburb of West Bridgford had been created by William Clarke, the landlord of the adjacent Trent Bridge Inn, in 1838. Since 1840 it had been the principal ground used by the County Cricket Club. Great celebrations were planned in 1938 to mark the centenary, the arrangements being made by AW Shelton, another member of the Committee and in terms of years served the senior member. He ran a local estate agency and land surveying business.

The writer of the resignation letter, Arthur Carr, had been a highly successful captain of the county team since his appointment by the Committee, in 1919, but from about 1927 his relationship with the Committee had steadily declined. In contrast his standing with his fellow county players and the general Nottinghamshire membership had grown progressively over his sixteen seasons as captain. In 1934 the committee had relieved him of his position in very acrimonious circumstances, but the membership had elected Carr to the County Cricket Club Committee, most of whom felt uncomfortable at his presence. It is in the circumstances not surprising that, when his letter was submitted to the next meeting of the Committee on 10 January 1938, the minutes contain the following note: 'A letter was received from Mr AW Carr resigning his membership of the Committee. It was resolved that this be accepted and the original letter be placed in the Minute Book.'

In fact so relieved were the members that the above last sentence is, it is believed, without precedent. Very rarely were letters of any sort inserted into the Minute Book and although Committee members were resigning fairly regularly, usually for business reasons or ill health, no one else's such letter written during the inter-war period survives even in the extensive Trent Bridge archives. The club's Annual General Meeting was held just over a fortnight later, but the minutes of that AGM contain no mention of Carr not standing again. The chairman had no wish to refer to Carr during the meeting for fear the many Carr admirers might reignite the fuse which caused such dire consequences in 1934.

On a personal level, in sending the letter, Carr was shutting the door on a thirty-year chapter of his life. It was a chapter which had begun, one might justifiably state, just by accident. His father, a wealthy stockbroker, had a desire to enhance his fox hunting hobby by joining England's premier hunt, the Quorn, based near the Leicestershire town of Loughborough.

Since the eighteenth century, if not before, the Carr family had been based in the Home Counties and their lives revolved round the City. Certainly during the nineteenth century, the Carr family members had no known connections with the Midlands. Arthur Carr's father's keenness to join the Quorn happened, by chance, to find a small estate available for sale just across the northern border of Leicestershire, in the adjoining county of Nottinghamshire.

Over the last fifty years the regulations regarding the qualification of a cricketer to play for a specific county have become so elastic as to be almost non-existent, but while Lord Harris's word was law, the regulations were there to be administered without fear or favour. A man could only play for the county of his birth or the county in which he genuinely resided. These simple rules appear to have been kept for as far back as county cricket has been recorded, though it was not until 1873 that the rules were laid down in writing, after several players had chosen to play for both the county of their birth and the one in which they resided.

Although Arthur Carr was only fifteen when the family moved to Nottinghamshire, he had already resided in three other counties: Surrey, Kent and Essex. In addition he was currently at school in yet another county: Dorset. So in effect he had a permanent right to play for Surrey and then a right in turn to play for first Kent and then Essex.

Unlike the majority of counties, both major and minor, Nottinghamshire and Yorkshire County Cricket Clubs both had their origins in principal cricket clubs of manufacturing towns, run by lower middle-class tradesmen as opposed to the more common evolution where the landed gentry set up a club and brought in some paid players when and as necessary.

The schoolboy Arthur Carr, hailing from a very wealthy family background, was faced with a situation when he joined Nottinghamshire that was vastly different to the position he would have held had he joined Surrey, Kent or Essex.

The first reference to a match between two specific counties is in 1709 when Kent opposed Surrey in Dartford. Early eighteenth-century patrons or organisers of counties in the south-east of England were in the case of Surrey, the Prince of Wales; of Kent, the Duke of Dorset's family from Sevenoaks;

and of Sussex, the Duke of Richmond at Goodwood. County teams in the north of England developed a hundred years later. The Nottingham Club simply renamed itself Nottinghamshire when in 1835 the club first opposed Sussex. It is the Sheffield Club which developed the first organised Yorkshire County side. The southern county sides were a mixture of amateur and paid players invariably captained by an amateur. The Nottinghamshire and Yorkshire elevens were led by a professional and were usually made up of professionals with an occasional amateur. It was in the 1880s that Yorkshire and Nottinghamshire fell in line with the rest of the counties and appointed an amateur as captain, but in the case of Nottinghamshire the professional ethos remained robust. It was as if the infamous strike of Nottinghamshire professionals in 1881 was still bubbling just below the surface even at the time when Carr had his debut for Nottinghamshire Second XI in 1909. Carr in his autobiography noted: 'Before I took over the captaincy [of Nottinghamshire] busy people told me all sorts of disturbing things about the Nottinghamshire team and its players. For one thing, I was warned that they did not want "any b--------amateurs" in the side and would set about getting me out of it.'

The wealthy Nottingham manufacturer, John Dixon, had been the first amateur in 1889 to captain Nottinghamshire and a few local amateurs had from time to time flitted in and out of the side during the 1890s. In 1900, the Cambridge blue and son of a local clergyman, Arthur Jones, had succeeded Dixon and the Nottinghamshire Cricket Committee made a determined effort to recruit young public school cricketers: VH Cartwright (Rugby), Hon Mervyn Herbert (Eton), AE Hind (Uppingham), Rev H Staunton (Dunstable), EG Allen (Lancing), GT Branston (Charterhouse), RE Hemingway (Rugby), WD Barber (Eton), WG Heymann (Haileybury), CR Morris (Oakham), NVC Turner (Repton) and RHT Turner (Repton) were a dozen such young trialists, each given a few matches in the decade, most played much amateur club cricket in the county, but apart from Trevor Branston none had a regular place in the county side and he soon had to retire to earn a living. Carr initially followed their path. The Nottinghamshire committee were happy therefore to give sixteen-year-old Carr a handful of games with the county second XI in 1909, which joined the Minor Counties Championship at the start of that season. Carr was to play a few matches each season up until the outbreak of the First World War following at the same time what seems to have been a desultory army career.

Many first-class county cricketers were among the soldiers killed during the First World War, just as many were so badly wounded that a career in county cricket was no longer possible. Carr was fortunate to survive his years in France without serious injury. The generosity of his father allowed him to accept the offer to captain Nottinghamshire when peace returned. Carr was to lead his county for sixteen seasons and a total of 397 first-class matches. Carr was never one for records as such, so he would not have been particularly interested to know that only one other captain in the whole history of first-class cricket had exceeded his total. That was the redoubtable Lord Hawke as Yorkshire's supremo (for Lord Hawke was more than just a county captain!)

Like the Yorkshire captain, Carr was utterly devoted to the county of his adoption, but his approach to the task was to be in complete contrast to the way his Lordship ran things. Nottinghamshire was Carr's county and Nottinghamshire County players under him were his responsibility. That finite desire regardless of any consequences to promote what he felt was in the best interest of Nottinghamshire and its players was to prove his nemesis. Lord Hawke's diplomacy among his equals would mean that he ruled Yorkshire cricket until he died in 1938.

Viewed from a purely cricketing angle, Carr had impeccable credentials when appointed captain, both as an individual player on the field, as will be amply demonstrated in the chapters that follow, and as a batsman. He was a brilliant outfielder in his younger days, the reports of his time in South Africa make that fact plain. Later he rarely missed chances in the slips – the palaver over the catch he dropped in the 1926 Test at Headingley tells its own story. It is truism to state that a captain can only really exercise his authority over his players if he is able to set an outstanding example in the field. Nottinghamshire were particularly blessed by having AO Jones as their leader for fifteen seasons, then Carr's sixteen seasons following directly on.

Reading through the detailed press reports of matches in which he captained Nottinghamshire makes transparent that Carr's analyses of match situations, his field placings and his tactics on bowling changes were as good, if not better, than any of his contemporaries. The way he nursed Harold Larwood in order to ensure that Larwood's quite extraordinary gift was not frittered away is a lesson for all captains. Would it be too much to say that Carr could have handled Larwood and indeed Voce much better on their tours of Australia than the captains the MCC appointed? Admirers of Jardine might differ on this point. It was Carr's dream to lead England in Australia, a dream never realised.

So far as his batting ability went, he never really had much opportunity at Test level, except on the matting wickets in South Africa on which he floundered, despite his friend Bill Fender's coaching and guidance. At county level Carr was a formidable striker of the ball – no cricketer hit more sixes in first-class cricket for Nottinghamshire than Carr. It's often forgotten that in Carr's day there were no sightscreens at Trent Bridge and the ground's reputation for featherbed wickets did not come to the fore until the later 1930s. His aggressive batting frequently turned round games that appeared to be drifting away.

The final aspect of Carr's captaincy was his relationship with his players. County sides in his day were almost without exception led by an amateur. At Trent Bridge the amateurs occupied a separate dressing room, on a separate floor, to the professionals. Many amateur captains remained aloof from the men under them, remote figures who came and went. They were often direct from Oxford or Cambridge and led the county side for two or three seasons, their fathers then told them to get 'proper' jobs; father wasn't going to support them any longer. In other instances, though this practice became more common after the Second World War, they were 'shamateurs', a class always resented by the ordinary professional. Several counties gave their amateur captain the post of secretary to the county club, but with an assistant secretary who relieved the captain of most of his secretarial duties. Carr was most fortunate in that his father agreed to give him an allowance which allowed him to play cricket, for the county club offered no more than standard expenses, and Carr was therefore in a totally independent position.

There are quite well publicised examples of professionals who effectively didn't see eye to eye with the captain and/or the Committee and either finished with the game as an occupation or moved to another county, not easy in the days of strict qualification rules. Carr led Nottinghamshire for sixteen seasons, the only player who left Nottinghamshire having established himself in the side during Carr's reign was Garnet Lee, but his move was not due to Carr's actions; a talented all-rounder, Lee just couldn't find a permanent place in the batting line-up of Gunn, Whysall, Walker, Carr, Hardstaff and Payton which had established itself in 1921. A simple example of Carr's concern for his players came in 1929. The Nottinghamshire Committee shared out the money donated by the public to mark the

Championship success between the professionals depending on their ability and the number of matches they played. Carr saw the list and wrote to demand that a sum be given to Syd Copley. Copley had not appeared in a single game, but had fielded brilliantly when acting as sub. That's the sort of detail which made Carr the captain he was. The story of Carr looking after the destitute family of a soldier in his regiment who was killed in the Irish Easter Uprising of 1916 is another example from his time as an officer in the First World War.

Tact, however, was not his forte. In theory the Nottinghamshire County Cricket Club Committee was his master, but Carr was not the type of individual to butter up the landed gents and business men who formed that Committee. Today the players and their captain are effectively controlled by 'cricket managers' and, in the case of the more notable, by agents pulling strings. Carr decided he was in total control of the professionals at Trent Bridge (unlike other counties, Nottinghamshire did not have an influx of amateurs each vacation who took places in the county team in the 1920s and 30s). From Carr's viewpoint the pros, mainly hard-bitten miners from the Nottinghamshire coalfield, were his personal responsibility, just as the soldiers under him during the First World War had been. Of course the Nottinghamshire Committee were happy to go along with him in the good times and share the plaudits and bouquets. When the brickbats arrived, the ordinary members and the professionals stayed with him, but one by one the Committee deserted him. Thus it was that his final letter of resignation was glued in the Minute Book. Like the skulls of men had been stuck on the spikes of London railings, the Committee wanted to be certain Carr was gone and would not return.

A short paragraph from a player who appeared against Carr's Nottinghamshire side of the 1920s: Robertson-Glasgow of Somerset became a well-known journalist, writing cricket essays for *The Observer* and other newspapers and periodicals.

His pieces are among the finest of his day and many were gathered together and reprinted in book form. He wrote a piece on Carr which closes: 'but Carr, though he himself would not care, deserves to be remembered as a mighty man in cricket, one who smote the ball and the enemy; a tremendous opponent, and, if a personal touch be allowed, a most exhilarating friend.'

It was not Robertson-Glasgow's habit to express his personal feelings for a player for, of the many essays he wrote describing mainly his contemporaries, very few contain such a sentiment. The fact that Robertson-Glasgow employs the adjective 'exhilarating' to describe Carr's friendship is significant. June Prescott, Arthur's niece who knew him in the last thirty years of his life, describes him as having a dry sense of humour, a twinkle in his eye, but a man of few words. The ladies seem to have been attracted to him, but he was not one for town life and the attractions that go with it, such as the theatre, cinema. Carr even comments in his autobiography that the wireless goes a long way. His life revolved around cricket and horses and people who cared for either were his preferred companions. The few letters written by Carr that survive demonstrate his manner of being succinct and just to the point – literature was not an interest, beyond that connected to his own sports.

The Carr family were more usually associated with horse racing than cricket – here a young Arthur rides one of the family stock

# 2

# FAMILY MATTERS

## 1893-1907

Arthur William Carr was born in The Cottage, London Road, Mickleham, Surrey, on 18 May 1893 and was christened after his late uncle Arthur and his grandfather William. His father, Philip William Carr, though also born in Surrey (in Croydon in 1859) seems to have had no particular attachment to that county. The family's allegiance, if they had one, was to the City of London and the Stock Exchange, the place that generated the family's wealth. Away from his City office, Philip William Carr's interest was principally in horses, both racehorses and those used for hunting, for he enjoyed riding to hounds. Gregory Blaxland's *Golden Miller* provides a colourful snapshot of Philip Carr in his latter days: 'Philip Carr was an enormous man, big of body, big of heart, and red of face, who strode through life with Rabelaisian verve. He took great interest in his horses, and Mrs Tidey [the housekeeper] had to bring out her kitchen table to enable him to mount a hack to see them work.'

If Philip Carr sounds like a Dickensian character gleaned from *Pickwick Papers*, families in Victorian novels more often than not also hid some dark secret, only whispered about and certainly not in front of the children – until in the course of the tale a terrible past is uncovered. It is impossible to know what details young Arthur as a schoolboy knew about the uncle after whom he was named. Over a century has passed by since then, but the secret behind Uncle Arthur's demise remains just that – a secret. Is it a pure coincidence that, less than six months after Arthur's death, his parents and those offspring still at home moved from Upper Tooting across the river to Ingatestone in Essex, unless it was to try and forget the tragedy? Yet, would Philip name his first child after his late brother if the death had been anything other than a simple accident?

Uncle Arthur was born at his parents' house in Croydon in 1861; by 1890 the family had moved to Upper Tooting, but Philip and Arthur, both stockbrokers in the City, still resided with their parents, as did most of their other younger siblings. In July of the following summer, Philip, Arthur and two of their brothers went down to Hove on a short holiday. They stayed in a small guest house, intending to play golf on the local course. This long weekend break had been a custom with the brothers for several years. What was supposed to be a happy few days by the seaside turned into tragedy. On Sunday morning, 12 July, Arthur was found fatally injured on the ground at the rear of the Hotel Metropole in Brighton. He was rushed to Sussex County Hospital, but died during the short journey.

A coroner's inquest heard that Joseph Norton, a porter at the hotel, heard a noise at the rear of the building at about 2.30 am, went outside and found the deceased lying on the ground seriously injured. A police surgeon was summoned to the scene, called a cab and conveyed Arthur Carr to the Sussex County Hospital, but he died before the destination was reached. Carr had fallen a distance of about eighty feet from a fourth storey bedroom window. Arthur and Philip had taken a room at the hotel on Saturday evening. Philip, the main fam-

ily witness, stated at the inquest that his brother was in particularly good spirits having played a good round of golf on
Saturday and that they intended to go swimming on Sunday.
He was sure that the fall was a complete accident. However a
night porter stated he overheard the deceased at about 1.40
am, cry out, 'Kill me, I cannot breathe, give me chloroform.'
The press report in the *Sussex Agricultural Express* noted that
the jury at first could not agree, but the eventual verdict was
that, 'Deceased died from injuries caused by the fall from his
bedroom window, but under what circumstances there was no
evidence to show.' The death certificate confirmed this. The
present-day members of the family to whom the writer has
spoken can offer no explanation, so the reader must ponder
the possible options unaided. What nephew Arthur thought,
when at some stage of his life he was told is unknown – it is
not a detail that is mentioned in his book *Cricket With The Lid
Off,* or in any of the personal reminiscences which appeared in
the press during the 1930s.

Philip Carr was a partner in the firm of WI Carr, Sons
and Tod. The firm had been established by William Isaac Carr,
Philip's father. William had been given his second name, Isaac,
from his own father, Isaac Carr. The latter was a wealthy City
merchant, born in Middlesex in 1796; he had married Mary
Ann Moore at St Michael's, Queenhithe, London, in 1823.
Family tradition has it that the Carrs originally came from
Yorkshire, but it has been difficult to confirm this, Carr being a relatively common name. Apart from William Isaac, the
couple had a daughter, Marian (or Marianne). Isaac Carr died
in Cheam, Surrey, in 1870, leaving about £45,000.

Until 1882 the business was known as Moore, Carr and Co.
In January of that year the partnership was dissolved by mutual
consent and changed to WI Carr and Sons. *The London Gazette*
of 20 January 1882 published the following notice: 'Notice is
hereby given, that the Partnership heretofore existing between

us the undersigned, William Isaac Carr, Robert Tunstall Moore and Wilfred Isaac Carr, carrying on business as Stockbrokers at 2 Royal Exchange buildings in the city of London, under the style Moore, Carr and Co, has been dissolved by mutual consent; and that the said business will in future be carried on by the said William Isaac Carr, the said Wilfred Isaac Carr and the undersigned Philip William Carr, under the style of WI Carr and Sons, by whom all outstanding transactions will be settled. (signed) WI Carr, Wilfred I Carr, Philip W Carr, RT Moore'

Philip Carr was only aged twenty-two at the time the partnership was formed; Wilfred, his eldest brother, was twenty-six. William Isaac Carr himself was fifty-seven and it would seem that he was intent on ensuring the future of the firm as a family business. The family was certainly a large one, Wilfred and Philip had eight other siblings. Arthur (b 1861) was the third eldest, then followed Elizabeth Mary (b 1863), Margaret (b 1864), Charles (b 1866), Leonard Robert (b 1869), Cedric Kettlewell (b 1870), Eleanor Arethusa (b 1871) and Russell (b 1877). In the 1881 census, all but one were living at home at 4 St John's Park, Greenwich with William Isaac and wife Elizabeth Arethusa, nee Kettlewell. The absentee in 1881 was Charles, who was set on a military career.

Turning from his paternal to his maternal roots, Arthur's mother, Louise Yates Smith, was Scottish. Louise was born in Broughty Ferry in 1862, a place described around the time of her arrival as 'the richest square mile in Europe'. Until the First World War, Broughty Ferry was a separate burgh, but today is a mere suburb of Dundee. The ferry disappeared when the Tay Bridge was built and Broughty Ferry, originally a small fishing village, became a seaside resort with a smart esplanade. Forfarshire Cricket Club was based in the town, indeed it still is. With St Andrews and a number of other courses not too distant, golf dominated every other sport in that part of Scotland and in the 1880s the game had a particular boom period.

Louise played golf and she later said that she met her future husband, Philip Carr, on the golf course. One assumes that he, perhaps with one or two of his brothers, had gone to the east coast of Scotland on a golfing holiday, maybe to try and forget the Brighton tragedy. Talking to her niece many years later, Louise reminisced that she had one or two suitors before settling on Philip Carr – she was after all twenty-nine and the term 'old maid' was threatening, when she wed.

The couple married in Broughty Ferry on 4 January 1892. The *Dundee Courier* carries a 750-word report on the marriage, which indicates the status of the Smith family in the community at that time. A paragraph in the report gives a flavour of the event: 'Miss Smith, who was a very lovely bride, wore a bridal robe of white satin, the court train edged with a ruche of white tuile. A ruff of white ostrich feathers was worn at the throat and a small wreath of orange blossom held the veil in place. The large bouquet was of white flowers with streamers. There were six bridesmaids – Miss Annie Smith (sister of the bride), Miss Ellan Carr (sister of the bridegroom) Miss Mamie Carter and Miss Winnie Smith (nieces of the bride), Miss Olive Carr and Miss Dorothy Donald (niece of the bride).'

The bride was given away by her brother, Charles Smith; her father, also Charles Smith, was deceased. Her mother wore a black gown, as did the bridegroom's mother. The report notes that the bridegroom was accompanied by his groomsman, but does not mention his name – one assumes he would have been one of Philip's brothers. The report also gives descriptions of the dresses worn by some twenty ladies, but does not indicate the ladies' relationship to either bride or groom. The ceremony was performed by the Rev Mr Lawrence, in whose church it took place, assisted by the Rev Mr Carter, brother-in-law of the bride.

The couple moved into The Cottage, Mickleham, soon after their marriage; there seems to be no extant detail of where the honeymoon was spent. Their new home had been previously owned by Samuel Woods; he, like Arthur Carr's father and grandfather, worked as a stockbroker on the London Exchange. The village of Mickleham formed part of the Norbury Park, which estate had been purchased in 1880 by another London financier, Leopold Salomons, founder of the Employers' Liability Assurance Co.

What in 1800 had been the agricultural village of Mickleham was, when the Carrs arrived, becoming part of the 'stockbroker belt'. The expansion of the railway network during the second half of Queen Victoria's reign meant that businessmen could travel with ease into the City from desirable villages described by travel writers and estate agents as being in 'leafy Surrey'. There was no longer a need to live within carriage distance of the office – in the case of Mickleham they caught the train from the adjacent Box Hill Station, which lies at the foot of that notable Surrey landmark. Salomons later bought Box Hill to preserve it from developers. The so-called 'cottage' which the Carrs leased was in reality a substantial house set in a large garden. Today it is used as one of the boarding houses of Box Hill School, an independent senior school opened in 1959 on the principles of Gordonstoun, with the main school building housed in Mickleham Hall, just across the road from what is now termed 'The Old Cottage'.

Philip and his wife Louise were not long in Mickleham; less than three years after Arthur was born the family moved to Dennett's Lodge, Crockham Hill, Westerham, Kent, a much larger property and, in October 1896, Arthur's brother, Philip Gordon, was born. Dennett's Lodge included a large set of stables and a lodge housing the coachman and his family, as well as several grooms. Basil Briscoe, who trained Philip Carr's racehorses after the war, commented that Philip Carr had had horses for forty years, which was a slight overstatement since that would put Philip as an owner of horses in 1890, two years prior to his marriage. It seems more liking that his serious ownership of horse flesh began at Dennett's Lodge.

Philip's father, William Isaac, died at home in 1898. The value of his estate at the time of death was £149,736 18s 11d gross, a very substantial sum. The family were then living at Trueloves, Ingatestone, Essex. His widow was left the estate and horses and carriages as well as £5,000. Each of his nine surviving children also received £5,000.

Philip's third child and the only sister to Arthur and Philip Gordon (usually referred to in the family as Gordon, to differentiate from father Philip) was born at Dennett's Lodge in 1902 and christened Eileen Violet. Philip and Wilfred were now in charge of the family stockbroking business. Young Arthur, now eight, could not help but be interested in horses and racing, as well as riding to hounds. There is no direct evidence of the Carr family being interested in cricket, but Philip Carr could hardly have failed to observe how fellow members of the Stock Exchange loved the game. *The Stock Exchange in the Year 1900* gives an overview of the development of the Stock Exchange to that date and then goes into detail on the various sports in which members participate. The paragraph on cricket is the most detailed and lists the current members who are active cricketers. The list is a formidable one: The Hon Ivo Bligh, CJ Burnup, S Christopherson, AP Lucas, A Lubbock, G MacGregor, S W Scott, AE Stoddart, G Strachan, C Boyle, KJ Key, HDG Leveson Gower, GJV Weigall and RS Lucas are included in the roll call. The author of the volume considered that an eleven could be picked 'at a very short notice, that would challenge the best the MCC could field'. Certainly the names given all played first-class cricket and about half of them played Test cricket for England.

It is not known whether Arthur Carr was educated at home until the age of ten (his sister Eileen was taught by tutors at home throughout her early years) or if he attended a local private school, but in the autumn of 1903 he was enrolled as a pupil at Hazelwood School at Wolf's Hill near Limpsfield in Surrey, but no great distance from Dennett's Lodge. However no sooner had Arthur left the bosom of his family than his father decided to up sticks and move across the Thames estuary to Essex, specifically to a larger estate, Newton Hall near Great Dunmow. Having received the large legacy from his father and with the firm of WI Carr, Sons and Tod continuing to thrive, Philip Carr's move to Great Dunmow must have been greatly influenced by the fact that it was only twenty or so miles for Newmarket, the centre of the horse racing fraternity. Philip Carr does not seem to have appeared in the winner's enclosure too often, Basil Briscoe's *The Life of Golden Miller* comments that Philip Carr brought his stockbroker's mind to the racecourse and bought and sold his racehorses when a profit could be made out of them from the sale itself, rather than waiting for the hoped for prize money.

By the time Arthur William Carr began his formal schooling, a standard regime had been established in prep schools and public schools throughout Britain and in similar establishments had been set up throughout the major countries of the Empire. The ideals set out by Thomas Arnold during his reign as headmaster of Rugby School from 1828 included the prefectorial system and also what came to be described as 'muscular christianity', where the playing of organised team games, cricket in particular, was fused together with academic subjects which in the 1830s centred on Greek and Latin. To understand how the education system of the day moulded the actions Carr took through his adult life it is necessary to realise that Hazelwood and Sherborne (Arthur's main public school) embraced the ethos of muscular christianity during Carr's time and prowess on the sports field was considered as vital to adult life as success in the classroom.

As a boarding prep school, Hazelwood had been founded in a brand new building by the Cambridge cricket blue, Edward Peter Baily. Many, perhaps the majority, of prep schools began life in former large residential houses then, if they flourished, moved out to a small country estate, large enough to provide playing fields. Whether, by coincidence or not, the land on which Hazelwood was sited belonged to the Leveson-Gower Titsey Estate. The two Leveson Gowers who played in first-class cricket were still schoolboys when Baily founded his school, but the Leveson Gower father was keen on cricket and a cricket field was laid out at Titsey.

Headmaster Baily set out from the start to have a school that was as interested in sport as in scholarship. This certainly showed early on. Despite a roll call of just forty pupils, by 1906, when both Baily and Carr left the school, it had reared nine captains of public school cricket elevens.

The preparatory school system had come into being to give younger boys a flavour of life in a boy's boarding school – in many cases it was more than a flavour, simply replicating public school life. EP Baily had founded two very small prep schools during the 1880s before launching Hazelwood. The Independent Association of Preparatory Schools was founded in 1892 and twelve years later this led to the Common Entrance exam. With a standardised exam system, the prep schools became uniform in their teaching and friendly cricket and football matches between adjacent rival schools nurtured a sporting competitive spirit.

There seems to be no written evidence of Arthur Carr playing cricket before he entered Hazelwood, even if he had, the one patently obvious fact in his book *Cricket With The Lid Off* is that he considers Hazelwood and EP Baily as his introduction to the finer points of the game and his great love of cricket. The book's first illustration facing the title page is Carr being coached in the nets by Baily (actually just outside the nets, so that the latter did not obscure the camera shot). The first illustration in the main body of the book is Carr in front of the scoreboard which displays his 167 – a record score for the school achieved in 1906. Two fellow pupils who were to become notable cricketers were Tommy Jameson, who played in the Harrow XIs of 1909 and 1910 and for Gentlemen v Players on four occasions, but as a regular serving army officer his county career (with Hampshire) was very restricted; and Dick Twining, who played for Eton and then for Oxford, captaining the University in 1912. Like Jameson, his county cricket (for Middlesex) was restricted, initially through injuries received in the First World War and then through the demands of business. Like Carr he lost his son in the Second World War during the North Africa campaign.

The move to Great Dunmow was primarily to further father's enthusiasm for horse racing, but as it coincided with Arthur's introduction to serious cricket playing, the move also meant that the boy's summer holidays could be spent watching his new county, Essex. Carr writes: 'The Essex ground at Leyton was my first happy hunting-ground. I used to spend days there, armed with apples and packets of sandwiches, watching the cricket, worshipping at the shrine of great players and – oh, yes – badgering them for their autographs.'

Essex played all their home games on the Lyttelton Ground at Leyton. It was never the most attractive of venues. Small boys worried little of the architectural niceties or even the utilitarian standards of such venues, they came to see their heroes – the hardness of the benches were of no consequence. Carr possibly attended all three home games played during that summer holiday – against Middlesex, Nottinghamshire and Lancashire – one loss and two draws. Essex ended the season last but one in the Championship table. In 1905 all four of the summer holiday fixtures at Leyton were drawn, but in 1906 Essex did beat Middlesex and Sussex, with Buckenham taking respectively eight and seven wickets. Buckenham was the county's outstanding bowler that year with 113 Championship wickets. It proved to be his best summer and he was considered one of the most deadly fast bowlers of the day. He was, however, let down by the poor close to the wicket catching of the team.

Claude Buckenham was Carr's hero, who notes: 'My youthful ambition was to be a fast bowler. Like most little boys, I had to "be" someone in my mind and I began by "being" Buckenham, the then Essex fast bowler. I did get plenty of wickets in small-boy cricket, but I am afraid that if I had been dependent upon my bowling for a cricketing career the answer would have been "so much for Buckenham".'

Four years later, amusingly, the notes appended to Carr's word pic for the Sherborne XI include 'A useful fast bowler, but cannot last long.'

Arthur Carr left Hazelwood at the end of the summer term and joined Eton for Michaelmas 1906. His Uncle Wilfred had been at the college in the 1870s. Arthur's cricketing ability would not be put to the test at his new school, since at the end of the Lent term 1907, he was ordered to leave. Not only did he do no work, he also was a trouble maker and reported for betting and smoking, although the rumour that he was expelled for dallying with one of the female domestic staff at Eton has no substance to it. According to Old Etonians, the females employed were selected so they were most unlikely to attract young blood!

Carr sits behind the gym shield at Sherborne School,
the location of his early sporting endeavours

# 3

# THE LOOM OF YOUTH

## 1907-1910

Why Arthur's father decided to send him to Sherborne following his son's abrupt departure from Eton is not known, but one suspects that this Dorset school was selected because of its relative isolation; geography keeping at least some of life's temptations away from his wayward son. The only obvious family connection to the county of Dorset was Arthur's Uncle Cedric, who was eleven years younger than brother Philip. Cedric had married Norah Magor, heiress to a tea fortune, in 1901. They set up a horse training establishment to Tarrant Gunville, a small village near Blandford Forum, less than twenty miles to the east of Sherborne. Uncle Cedric is not mentioned in Arthur Carr's autobiography, although none of his uncles feature, so Cedric's non-appearance cannot be taken as any indication that Arthur had nothing to do with him. Cedric's only son, Richard, was not born until 1910, seventeen years after Arthur. Anyway, he had no known cricketing interest, being initially an actor on the West End stage and after the Second World War running a small motor car repair business in West London.

Tradition has it that Sherborne School was created when Aldhelm left Malmesbury Abbey to found a new See based at Sherborne. This occurred in 705; some 150 years later another tradition has King Alfred being educated at Sherborne, though the single scrap of evidence to support this is that Alfred, aged fifteen, is reported as being in the town on Good Friday 864. It would be wiser in these circumstances to place the date of the present school's foundation as 1550. The school buildings advanced north from the Abbey itself. School House, of which Arthur Carr became a member, was built in 1860 – by a coincidence, the railway reached Sherborne in the same year and the numbers attending the school grew, with boys coming from many parts of southern England. The first reference to cricket at the school had been in 1805, but the first known inter-school fixture was not reported until 1846, against Bruton. The first extant team photograph dates from 1861 and the present pavilion on the Upper, the school's principal playing field, from 1877.

In 1907 Sherborne School was not flourishing. There were some 200 pupils, whereas ten years previously there had been about 300. The Headmaster, the Rev FB Westcott, was no diplomat. The famous story of him addressing two parents to whom he took a dislike only in classical Greek is believed to be true. Luckily for Arthur the Head was a very keen sportsman – whilst at Cambridge he had been awarded a cycling blue (according to the Sherborne history, riding a penny-farthing!) and at Sherborne Westcott would run up and down the touchline urging the rugby team on in quaint English, Latin or Greek, depending on his mood. Carr became captain of the rugby XV, although Westcott was nearing the end of his sixteen years as Headmaster by the time of Carr's arrival.

A colourful picture of Carr and life at Sherborne before the First World War is portrayed in *The Loom of Youth*, Alec Waugh's novel, published in 1917. When Waugh joined the school, Carr was in his final year and was looked up to as the greatest schoolboy sportsman of his generation. Waugh's novel features Carr as the character Lovelace ma, one assumes Lovelace mi is Carr's young brother, Gordon. Gordon was an exact contemporary of Alec Waugh in his Sherborne days and one wonders if Gordon, consciously or not, had some role in the stories that unfold in what is, theoretically, only a novel. Carr notes in *Cricket With The Lid Off*: 'I was at school with Alec Waugh, and although I doubt if I should know him if I met him now I have always blushingly understood that I am supposed to be Lovelace, the cricketer in his story ... if Lovelace was really intended as a portrait of me it was a prophetic one.'

Apart from scenes involving Lovelace on the cricket and rugger fields, it is worth commenting that Waugh has Lovelace devoted to horse racing, spending his time studying *The Sportsman* and keeping meticulous ledgers on the form of individual horses and riders. Lovelace would announce at the end of term how much money he would have won, had he actually placed the bets, which he had penned in his ledgers. As it happens, after the Second World War Carr's life would indeed revolve round the racing scene to the exclusion of much else.

The games master at Sherborne during Carr's days was GM Carey. Carey had been educated at Sherborne and was in both the cricket XI, where he was the leading bowler in 1891 with 45 wickets at 10.39 runs apiece, and in the rugger XV. Carey went up to Exeter College, Oxford, gaining a rugger blue in his first year as a forward. He appeared in the 1892 cricket freshman's match, opening the bowling, but this proved to be his sole outing in any major cricket match at the university.

Carey features strongly in Waugh's novel, thinly disguised as Buller or The Bull, and Waugh makes derogatory comments about his attitude to games and life in general; however when writing his autobiography many years later Waugh backtracked, surprisingly noting that Carey 'stands for all the things I admire'.

An amusing aside: AG MacDonell had his 'autobiographical' novel *England Their England* published in 1933. As with Alec Waugh's book the characters are recognisable despite the fictitious names. In MacDonell's book Alec Waugh is featured as Bobby Southcott, the talented batsman of Squires' side. Alec Waugh did gain a place in the Sherborne XI of 1915. *Ayres' Cricket Companion* covering that season describes Waugh as: 'Has good eye and wrists, and, though unorthodox in his methods, has been very useful to the side and often made runs. Hits very hard when set. A moderate field.'

Waugh had left the school for the Inns of Court OTC prior to the following summer. It was while awaiting posting overseas that he wrote his novel. Waugh was to write extensively through his adult life, having numerous books published, but he is nowadays only really recalled simply as the elder brother of Evelyn Waugh, one of the outstanding novelists of the twentieth century – Evelyn, though educated at Lancing and Oxford, had no interest in cricket, but he is through marriage related to the Carr family.

Carr gained a place in the rugby XV of 1909-10 and his player profile read: 'Has the making of a centre three-quarter – for he has good hands and can kick well – but he must go harder both in attack and defence if he is ever to be made.' His second year in the XV noted: 'Possessing most of the qualifications essential for a really good centre, has not yet become one. Lacks unaccountably the sense of the joy of battle – and his wing has suffered accordingly.'

It was in his third year of 1911-12 that he captained the XV, the report noting: 'Captained his side well under conditions frequently depressing. Possessing strength, pace and good hands, he has great possibilities as a centre three-quarter if he unlearns completely a tendency to slowing up and grows stronger in defence. Screw kicks beautifully.' It was during the winter holidays of 1911-12 that Carr made four rugby appearances for Leicester, against Birkenhead Park, Glasgow University, London Welsh and Gloucester, all home matches between 26 December and 13 January. Leicester obtained three wins, only losing to Gloucester. It is most probable that Carr's predecessor as the Nottinghamshire cricket captain, AO Jones, recommended Carr to the Leicester club. Jones captained the Tigers for nine seasons and only retired from playing in December 1910 – he took up the role as a rugby referee, in which post he officiated in five rugby internationals.

Apart from rugby and cricket, Carr was a member of the Sherborne gym team, being one of the five-man team that represented Sherborne in the 1911 Aldershot inter-schools competition. For some years he held the school record for hurdles, achieving this feat in 1910.

As it was expected that he would leave Sherborne to follow an Army career, he was a keen member of the Officer Training Corps, finishing in his final year as a Lance-Corporal in C Company, No 1 Section under Lieutenant G O'Hanlon. There were seventeen privates in the Section, with only Carr as a non-commissioned officer. Geoffrey O'Hanlon was one of the masters. Carr is listed in the corps as Carr ma, also in the same section is Carr mi, Gordon, Arthur's young brother. Gordon was also in School House, which was run by the Headmaster and physically attached to the headmaster's house. Carr ma began his school career in Form IVB and ended in the Army Class VA – the Army Class form master was none other than sports master GM Carey.

In 1908 the Carr family moved house (or rather mansion) yet again, to Rempstone Hall, Nottinghamshire, situated on the road out of the village leading to Kegworth, the latter village being over the border in Leicestershire. The Carr family had no known connection with Rempstone, or indeed Nottinghamshire. Philip Carr moved his family there only so he could join the Quorn Hunt.

The Hall's extensive grounds, including a cricket pitch used by the village team, looked across the fields to Leicestershire. According to the records held by the present secretary of the Quorn, Carr paid the princely sum of £75 for his first season in 1908/09. Philip also built a range of stabling with a stable yard and living accommodation to the west of the main house, creating a second entrance on to the road, together with a lodge. It would seem that some if not all his racehorses were stabled at the Hall rather than at a trainer's establishment. A newspaper search of the 1911 racing results reveals that three horses ran that year under Philip Carr's ownership: Two Bells, Ahoy and Mamby.

Rempstone Hall had been built in 1792 in the contemporary Georgian style. It has twelve bedrooms and the usual reception rooms. A handsome frontage with two wings that are separated by a columned loggia looks south over the garden and fields, the ground falling gently away, and the Leicestershire border is seen in the distance. The two entrances are off the Kegworth Road. The lodge at the original entrance, first met when approaching from the main village, is matched by the one erected by Philip Carr. The immediate predecessors to the Carrs at the Hall were an extended Martin family. In speculating as to how Philip discovered the property, there is a possible Eton connection, the grandson of the 1891 owner was a contemporary of Cedric Carr at the College – a mere coincidence?

The Carrs must have moved into their new residence in the summer of 1908. The *Essex County Chronicle* of 15 August reports the presentation of 'a handsome red morocco-bound volume containing signatures of friends and well-wishers in Dunmow and district to Mr and Mrs Philip Carr'.

The book contained 220 signatures and there was an address thanking the Carrs for all that they had done for Dunmow during their five years of residence. It had been hoped that Mr and Mrs Carr would go down to Dunmow where a public presentation would have been arranged, but owing to the Carrs 'very retiring nature, they preferred not to face the ordeal of meeting their friends under circumstances which would be very trying'.

The press article, describing the event, included letters from both Mr and Mrs Carr, the one written by Mrs Carr being particularly poignant: 'Dear Sir – No words can convey what we feel over this great token of affection; it has touched us very deeply. There was a wonderful understanding between us, the people of Dunmow and the farmers round. We knew them and they knew us and it will ever be a lasting regret we could not have lived and died amongst them. Yours truly, LB [sic] Carr.'

When Arthur Carr first arrived at Sherborne the cricket professional at the school was Tom Bowley, a Nottinghamshire-born cricketer who had played first-class cricket for Surrey. A fast bowler, he had appeared in the Easter Colts trials at Trent Bridge for three successive years, but having failed to break into the very strong Nottinghamshire eleven, went first to Northamptonshire and then Surrey. Obtaining a post at Sherborne in 1894, he qualified for Dorset and played for that county until 1903. Bowley's contacts in Nottingham meant that he made the county club aware of the promising young player, now resident in that county. The first local score published in the press containing Arthur Carr's name is Gentlemen of Leicestershire v Burghley Park on 22 August 1908. Carr was just fifteen.

Carr made his debut for Nottinghamshire Second XI in the Minor Counties Competition the following August, hitting 102 not out in his second appearance, against Cheshire. He and Charles James added 275 for the first wicket. Nottinghamshire' success that summer in the competition enabled the county to top the Northern Division. Glamorgan were the opponents in the semi-final knockout stage where James was dismissed without scoring and Carr scored only 8, but the Nottinghamshire captain, the Rev H Staunton, was not happy with the batting conditions and wrote to the MCC and the MCCA complaining that the Glamorgan groundsman had interfered with the pitch. The authorities clearly felt Nottinghamshire' grievance was unjustified and Glamorgan went through to the final.

Of those early contemporaries, Charles James had been a member of Nottinghamshire playing staff since 1904, but never obtained a regular place in the first XI. He left Nottinghamshire in 1910 to become a pro in Northumberland and after the war became groundsman for Sir Julien Cahn. The Rev Staunton was part of the Staunton family who resided at Staunton Hall in south Nottinghamshire. He was to volunteer as an Army Chaplain, after some years as an incumbent in parishes in Nottinghamshire; Staunton went with his Indian regiment to the Persian Gulf and died in Mesopotamia in January 1918.

Carr obtained his place in the Sherborne XI in 1909 and finished second in the batting averages, though he owed his high average to an innings of 133 played late in the season. Carr opened the batting, hitting 303 runs at an average of 27.54. The school's fixture list contained just two major matches against good quality public schools each summer: Tonbridge and Radley. The rest of the programme was a mix of local amateur teams plus the Old Boys. The Sherborne school magazine player profile for 1909 on Carr noted: 'Plenty of defence and has scoring shots everywhere. He is a little too apt to throw his wicket away through lack of restraint. A sound field in the country and a good slip.' *Wisden* noted that the side had 'two most promising players in Carr and Mason, respectively, batsman and stumper.'

During the school holidays Carr played for Rempstone against Wymswold; unfortunately the former were utterly outclassed, Wymeswold scoring 139, Rempstone 18, Carr contributed 2.

The summer of 1910 saw Carr topping the school averages, hitting 638 runs, average 45.41 – he had overtaken Read who, though second, saw his batting average drop to 19.00. In addition Carr took most wickets for the school – 32 at an average of 15.06. There was no match against Radley due to illness, but against Tonbridge he made 75 and Sherborne achieved a respectable draw. *Wisden* noted 'Carr, if a bit reckless, is an excellent bat'. *The Shirburnian* commented: 'Very good bat, with any number of good shots, his best being his drive, which is very powerful. His fault is his great recklessness, getting himself out by treating full tosses and long hops too carelessly. A good field anywhere, at his best in the slips. A useful fast bowler, but cannot last long.'

On Saturday 20 August 1910, a match was played at Rempstone between the village team and CW Wright's XI. It is worth publishing the score in detail, over the page.

Note that Arthur Carr is joined by his brother, Gordon, and his father, Philip. In his autobiography, Carr commented that his father and brother were not cricket people. Gordon left Sherborne too early to find a place in the XI. In a brief note in *The World of Cricket* dated 1 August 1914, Tom Bowley stated that 'Carr, a brother of AW, can get runs and would get more if he didn't move his feet so much.' After the war Gordon was reported to be a useful but occasional club cricketer.

| Rempstone | | CW Wright's XI | |
|---|---|---|---|
| G Hibbert b Copley | 9 | D McCraith b AW Carr | 16 |
| F Bexby b Copley | 0 | F Copley run out | 1 |
| AW Carr b McCraith | 31 | CW Wright b AW Carr | 3 |
| PG Carr b McCraith | 3 | FW Copley b Stevenson | 22 |
| A Chapman c H'head b McC'th | 13 | P Kent c Inwood b Stevenson | 14 |
| PW Carr b McCraith | 2 | A Morris b PG Carr | 5 |
| J Watkin b Head | 0 | - Head b Stevenson | 4 |
| F Watkin C Morris b Head | 4 | - Hollinshead not out | 0 |
| W Inwood not out | 5 | AW Wright b AW Carr | 0 |
| G Stevenson c Kent b Head | 0 | - Garwood b AW Carr | 0 |
| G Gaylor b Copley | 13 | - Smith c Chapman b Stevenson | 9 |
| Extras | 10 | | 9 |
| Total | 90 | | 84 |

The opposition that the Carrs faced were led by the former Nottinghamshire and England cricketer Charles Wright and includes Douglas McCraith. Wright was one of the trustees of the county club. An outstanding player in his school days at Charterhouse and then at Cambridge, Wright was an intermittent member of the Nottinghamshire side from 1882 to 1899. By the time of the game at Rempstone he was handicapped having lost the sight of an eye in a shooting accident. McCraith was the solicitor who would be Chairman of the Committee when Carr sent in his resignation letter all those years later. It would have been interesting to know what McCraith thought of Carr the Sherborne schoolboy, when the two first met at that village game in 1909! He must have noticed that the boy Carr made the highest score and took four wickets, including that of Charles Wright.

Young amateur and senior professional –
Arthur Carr and John Gunn

# 4

# Disappointing Debut

## 1910-1914

It was during the week that followed the game against Wright's XI, in August 1910, that Nottinghamshire County Cricket Club gave Arthur Carr his debut in Championship cricket. *Wisden* commented in their seasonal review, 'and, though he [Carr] did not greatly distinguish himself, I hope that they will not lose sight of him.' The match was against Gloucestershire at the County Ground in Bristol. The pitch was all in favour of the bowlers, especially the two left-armers, Charlie Parker and George Dennett, opening the home attack. Sixteen wickets fell on the first day. Ted Alletson had been omitted from the Nottinghamshire side to make way for Carr. Rather surprisingly, AO Jones dropped himself down the order and debutant Carr was asked to open with George Gunn. Parker dismissed the seventeen year old twice, for 1 and 0. Happily for Nottinghamshire the pitch also suited Topsy Wass, who picked up 13 wickets for 108 and Nottinghamshire won by five wickets. If it hadn't been for long rain delays on the second and third days, the game would have been completed in a day and a half.

Charlie Parker was an incredible bowler; only Rhodes and Freeman took more wickets in first-class cricket, but he played just a single Test match for England and is now largely forgotten except in Bristol. It was no disgrace to lose your wicket to such a cricketer.

Carr later told how Jones had consoled him and told him not to be too disappointed. Jones had been born in Shelton, a small south Nottinghamshire village, where his father was the rector. His father died when Jones was only two, but Arthur Jones, thanks to the generosity of other family members was educated at Bedford Modern School and Jesus College, Cambridge. An excellent sportsman, he made his debut for both Cambridge and Nottinghamshire in 1892, was appointed Nottinghamshire captain in 1900 and captained England in the 1907/08 series against Australia. It is said that he owed both his Cambridge blue and his England Test caps to his astonishing fielding ability, but for Nottinghamshire, in addition to fielding, he was a prolific batsman and at the time of Carr's debut held the county record for highest individual score.

The Nottinghamshire CCC Committee minutes for the meeting directly after Arthur Carr's debut for Nottinghamshire First XI contains the following item: 'The following correspondence was read: From PW Carr re his son's expenses in the Gloucester match, give same as a donation to the Club.'

Philip Carr's gesture must have impressed the Committee and membership. At the county club's Annual General Meeting on 5 February 1913, held in the Exchange Hall, Philip was to be nominated as President for 1913 by the retiring incumbent, the Duke of Portland. The nomination met with the approval of the meeting. If the minutes of the meeting are a reflection of the matters discussed, it is unlikely the gathering lasted above fifteen minutes. Philip Carr was to attend only one Committee meeting during his year in office. As was the custom he donated £100 to the club, in effect paying the wages of two young players for the season. The 1914 AGM was not held until 24 March. A note stated, 'PW Carr regretted his inability to be present as he was going abroad.' The chair was taken by TS Pearson-Gregory, who nominated Sir Jesse Boot as the new President. The finances in those final pre-war years were not healthy; £172 was lost in 1912 and a further £253 in 1913.

The 1911 census has Philip Carr, his wife, Louisa, and two children, Gordon and Eileen, plus a butler, a footman, a cook, a ladies maid, a kitchen maid and two housemaids as residents at Rempstone Hall. Arthur was not on the Rempstone census return, being included in the list for Sherborne School. His brother Gordon, who had been at Hazelwood School, would move on to Sherborne in September of 1911 and thence to RM Sandhurst in 1914. Eileen was educated at home by a governess, one of the neighbours' children, Joan, acted as a classmate.

Carr hit two centuries in the same year as the census, his final season for Sherborne, 225 v Bruton Nomads (the next highest scorer for the school made 35 and the total was 323-7 dec) and 165 v Wells Clergy. Mainly due to these scores he acquired 749 runs with an average of 62.42; Mason, the captain, was second with 240 runs, average 20.00. Carr scored 80 in the principal inter-school game against Tonbridge but the match was lost by ten wickets. Again the match against Radley was cancelled due to illness. Carr's twelve wickets cost him 30 runs apiece. *Ayres' Cricket Companion* noted 'A really brilliant bat and a valuable field'. The school magazine's appraisal was more down to earth: 'A very fine bat. Excellent shots all round the wicket, his driving being brilliant. Has far more defence and steadiness than he had last year, but lacks grit in an uphill fight. Bowls well for a short time, but his action is too strenuous for him to last long; should never bowl more than five overs at a time. Brilliant, but not safe, in the field.'

As a result of his school form, Carr received the following postcard from EG Wynyard, on behalf of the MCC: 'If invited by the Committee of the MCC to represent the Public Schools at Lord's, would you care to play and would your people have any objections?'

Carr was delighted to accept. Wynyard captained the MCC side, which contained a collection of cricketers who had been occasional first-class players, aside from Wynyard himself and Goldie who scored a century in the game. The single professional was White of Hertfordshire. Of the eleven Public School men only Carr himself and his opening partner DJ Knight were destined to make a name for themselves on the cricket field, though Max Woosnam (Winchester) became the ultimate amateur sportsman. Carr scored 2 in his single innings and bowled fourteen expensive overs for a single wicket. The game was a high-scoring draw.

DJ Knight wrote about the match in a piece some years later: 'He [Carr] was my captain at Lord's in the year 1911, when we both, as youngsters, underwent together our first baptism of fire at the headquarters of cricket ... When I first saw him and studied him (as a matter of fact, when we were going out to open the innings), I noticed the strong, determined set of the jaw and chin and the almost uncanny massiveness of the shoulders and arms. He seemed old beyond his years – already a full-grown man – and he faced the fiery ordeal before him with the most refreshing coolness and imperturbability, which I shall not soon forget. To come straight from the intimate and friendly associations of your school ground to the vast arena at Lord's and to face bowlers of long tried merit and, what is far worse, the super-critical attitude of the veteran inmates of the Pavilion, constitute for any boy a supreme and arduous trial, before which the stoutest heart must inevitably quail.'

Immediately prior to the match at Lord's, Carr played three games for Old Shirburians with quite astonishing success, scores of 147, 40, 125, 91 and 51. Maybe this glut of runs went to his head and he foolishly lost it (though not according to Knight's account of the Lord's game). He played four matches for the Old Boys the following August, hitting three fifties and then 211 against Exmouth at Exmouth.

For financial reasons, Nottinghamshire had resigned from the Minor Counties Championship after the 1910 season. Carr was selected for the final four first XI matches of the summer of 1911, again opening the batting with George Gunn. Carr commented about George: 'George Gunn was another marvel, with an amazing eye, an amazing pair of feet and a bat which he used as if it was a walking stick. When George felt like it he made bowling just what it pleased him to be, strolling about the place and up and down the wicket as if the whole thing were the simplest child's play in the world. How George Gunn, in his prime, would have laughed at leg theory. I once saw Macdonald, then playing for Lancashire, have a go at him with the new ball and with six men plastered on the leg side. I have seldom seen any batsman make any bowler look such a damned fool.'

Carr made two reasonable innings of 40 in these games and *Wisden* noted, 'AW Carr of Sherborne School, showed capital form in an innings of 47 towards the end of the season. A good deal should be seen of him, if he can spare the time for county cricket.'

Carr states that he was sent down from Oxford after two terms for not doing a stroke of work. I have yet to discover which college he attended at the university; Sherborne, who have extensive archives, have no details of Carr going up to Oxford. One assumes that his stay at Oxford was during the first two terms of the 1911/12 academic year.

During the summer of 1912 Carr played in all but one of the Nottinghamshire Championship matches between 4 July and 9 August. In all these games he opened the batting with

George Gunn, but in none of his eight innings did he register a 50. *Wisden* made the following comment on Carr and his fellow amateurs who had had trials with the first XI that year: 'In addition to AO Jones, at different times, Nottinghamshire had three amateurs in the team. AB Crawford is just a hard hitter and nothing more, but HA Hodges and AW Carr have some pretensions to class, and should be heard of again. Unfortunately, GT Branston, who has little liking for county cricket, could not be induced to play.' Both Crawford and Hodges lost their lives in France during the Great War.

It is most curious that Carr never played in any Club and Ground matches for Nottinghamshire during the seasons from 1908 through to 1912, then only once in 1913. In 1914, however, he appeared in several matches. Maybe by that stage his father had given up any hope of Arthur taking any serious occupation!

Carr's great innings in County Championship cricket prior to the war was made against Leicestershire at Trent Bridge in August 1913. On the first day rain delayed the start until 3 o'clock. Nottinghamshire batted and lost the wicket of George Gunn during the curtailed period of play, but then reached 144 for one, Carr being 52 not out and Garnet Lee 62 not out. On Tuesday morning the pair tore the bowling apart. Their partnership realised 333 in just over three hours, at which point Carr was lbw to Coe for 169. His innings included twenty fours and only one mistake. Nottinghamshire won by an innings and 126 runs; in Leicestershire's second innings Carr's bowling, rather despised at Sherborne, took Leicestershire's first two wickets, those of Whitehead and King, who were their county's top two batsmen that summer.

A notice in *The London Gazette* of 26 September 1913 read: 'SPECIAL RESERVE OF OFFICERS. Cavalry. *20th Hussars,* Arthur William Carr, late Cadet Lance-Corporal, Sherborne

School Contingent, Officers Training Corps, to be Second Lieutenant (on probation). Dated 27 September, 1913.'

The 20th Hussars had been based in Colchester since 1911 and it can be no coincidence that Carr rode his only winner in a National Hunt Race on the old course at Chelmsford, riding Cruckawnabarna during the autumn of 1913. When asked by a reporter many years later what he was doing watching races at Chelmsford, he remarked that it was on this racecourse that he rode his only winner and therefore he was sentimentally attached to the place. The 20th Hussars was one of three units that made up the 5th Cavalry Brigade, the others being the Royal Scots Greys, based at York and 12th Royal Lancers base in Norwich.

At the beginning of the 1914 season it appeared that AO Jones had recovered sufficiently to resume the captaincy, having missed much of 1913 through illness, Dr GO Gauld captaining the county in his absence. Gauld, originally from Aberdeen, ran a medical practice in Nottingham and played good class club cricket in the local district. The 1914 programme of county matches had not been long running when it became quite clear that Jones had been seriously weakened by his illness. He was forced to drop out of the seventh match. Iremonger, as senior professional, led the side against Lancashire at Trent Bridge. Jones was selected for the next game against Middlesex, but did not appear and Gauld was brought back as an emergency captain. A note in the Nottinghamshire Minute Book reads: 'The question of payments to AO Jones during his illness at the present time was considered. The Secretary was instructed to give him sums as thought necessary, but such money not to be charged to the match account.'

Philip Pearson-Gregory, son of the former Middlesex cricketer and current Nottinghamshire Committee member TS Pearson-Gregory, was persuaded to lead Nottinghamshire in the next two matches, against Sussex and Yorkshire. Gauld returned for the eleventh match against Derbyshire. According to the Minute Book, GT Branston was included in the Sussex match team but did not appear; Branston was picked to captain the side against Derbyshire as Pearson-Gregory was not available. Carr was also included in the Nottinghamshire team for that game but did not come. Against Kent at Tunbridge Wells, Gauld was selected as captain, but was absent. It is quite obvious that the Nottinghamshire cricket sub-committee who chose the eleven, usually a week prior to the date of the game, were not communicating with their amateurs in a coordinated manner.

Carr was also selected for the Kent fixture and found himself leading Nottinghamshire for the first time. The low-scoring match was won by 32 runs. For the following match against Yorkshire at Headingley, Pearson-Gregory was chosen as captain but failed to turn up; Carr led the side for a second time. Nottinghamshire lost the match. *The World of Cricket* commenced its report with the sentence, 'Toujours l'audace is evidently AW Carr's motto.' He put Yorkshire in and saw them dismissed for 75. Nottinghamshire gained a first innings lead of 86. Yorkshire scored 286 in their second innings, setting Nottinghamshire 201, which they fail to achieve. The report ends with, 'Carr's bold policy may seem to lack justification on the result; but that is not the view which those who like to see reasonable risks taken will adopt. The rain on Tuesday night was not his fault.' Nottinghamshire' target of 201 had to be achieved on a damaged wicket, on the last day. However it is clear from the Nottinghamshire Minute Book that rain was not Carr's sole problem. The minutes read: 'AW Carr came before the Committee and made a statement regarding the conduct of J Gunn, Iremonger and Oates on the "field" during the match at Leeds. A very lengthy discussion took place on the subject, it being finally resolved the Committee be adjourned until later in the afternoon, the three players in question to then come before the whole Committee or sub-committee as might be decided upon.'

Due to the outbreak of war it was not until 14 September that any definite decision was taken regarding Carr's complaint. By then John Gunn had again been reported for unbecoming conduct and was severely reprimanded. The offence was bad temper and intemperate language following a questionable umpiring decision. There can be little doubt that the vagaries of the amateurs who were selected for the side due to Jones' illness had an unsettling effect the professional players. They probably wondered why the Committee, clearly at sixes and sevens, didn't take the bold step of appointing Iremonger as captain for the rest of the summer. As it was both the Committee and the players didn't seem to know who would captain the team in a given match until the day of the fixture.

Carr had surely proved his credentials as captaincy material, both by his act in putting Yorkshire in to bat and then reporting his unruly senior professionals to the Committee – bearing in mind that it was only his second match in charge, that he was only twenty-one and that his total experience of Championship cricket amounted to nineteen matches. Gauld resumed command for the next game against Gloucestershire; Carr made Nottinghamshire's highest score in the first innings, 68, including thirteen fours. Gauld remained captain, though Carr also played in the next match against Kent at Trent Bridge.

*The Loom of Youth* provides the story of Carr's last match and his final pre-war innings. It was during Nottinghamshire's traditional August Bank Holiday game at Surrey, usually considered the major annual inter-county fixture at The Oval. Waugh's somewhat inaccurate fictionalised account runs:

> On the Tuesday Gordon went to the Oval; Lovelace major was playing against Surrey. In the Strand he ran into Ferrers. 'Come on, sir I am just off to the Oval to see Lovelace's brother bat. Great

fellow! Captain of the House my first term.' 'Right you are. Come on. There's a bus.'

For hours, or what seemed like hours, two painfully correct professionals pottered about, scoring by ones and twos. Gordon longed for them to get out. A catch was missed in the slips. 'Surrey are the worst slip-fielding side in England,' announced Gordon fiercely. The Oval crowd, always so ferociously partisan, moved round him uneasily.

At last a roar went up, as Hitch knocked the leg stump flying out of the ground. Then Lovelace came in. He looked just as he had looked on the green Fernhurst sward, only perhaps a little broader. He was wearing the magenta and black of the School House scarf. He was an amateur of the RE Foster type – wrist shots past cover, and an honest off-drive. A change came over the play at once. In his first over he hit two fours. There was a stir round the ground. His personality was as strong as ever.

A boy ran on the field with a telegram for him.

'I bet that means he has got to join his regiment,' said Gordon, 'and it also means we are going to fight.'

Lovelace shoved the telegram into his pocket, and went on batting just as if nothing had happened, just as if he did not realise that this was his last innings for a very long time. He hit all round the wicket. At last a brilliant piece of stumping sent him back to the pavilion amid a roar of cheering.

'My word, Mr Ferrers, there goes the finest man Fernhurst has turned out since I have been there. And, my word, it will be a long time before we turn out another like him. There will be nothing to see now he has gone.'

They wandered out into the Kennington Road, excited, feverish. They had lunched at Gatti's, went into *Potash and Perlmutter* and came out after the first act. 'This is no time for German Jews,' said Ferrers, 'let's try the Hippodrome.'

It was an expensive day. They rushed from one thing to another. The strain was intolerable. After supper they went to the West End Cinema, and there, just before closing time, a film, in which everyone was falling into a dirty duck-pond for no ostensible reason, was suddenly stopped, and there appeared across the screen the flaming notice:

ENGLAND HAS DECLARED WAR ON GERMANY. GOD SAVE THE KING.

For the pedantic, the corrections required to Alec Waugh's tale of the Surrey game are as follows: Carr was not stumped but caught Platt, bowled Kirk for 30 – he batted at number five. The four professionals who preceded him were George Gunn (31), Garnet Lee (6), Joe Hardstaff (42) and when he came to the wicket to join John Gunn, the total was 110 for three. He helped John Gunn add 54 runs and his 30 included five fours. This all occurred on the second day. The third day was almost totally washed out, Jim Iremonger, who took over as the captain when Carr left on the second evening, had little to do.

Curiously in the Nottinghamshire match in the last three days of that week, against Hampshire at Trent Bridge, one of the Hampshire bowlers, Dr Basil Melle, was called up during the first day when Nottinghamshire were batting. He had opened the Hampshire bowling but left at lunchtime having bowled six overs. Nottinghamshire allowed Hampshire's twelfth man to bat in place of Melle.

For King and country –
brothers Gordon and Arthur in uniform

# 5

# OFF TO WAR

## 1914-1918

Though the First World War took four years of his life, Carr makes only a brief reference to those traumatic times in his autobiography: 'A queer thing this immunity to pain and a queerer thing still that I went through the War on and off from the time of the retreat from Mons and did not even get a Blighty wound. The worst that happened to me all through the War was that a horse fell on me and broke my right foot.'

Since Carr was in the Army Reserves and his father a City stockbroker, the family were probably more aware of the coming conflict than much of the British population. The Archduke Franz Ferdinand and his wife was assassinated in Sarajevo on 28 June, which event led to Austria declaring war on Serbia and, as Lloyd George noted, the governments of Europe stumbled and staggered into war.

If Carr in retrospect is very off-hand regarding the war, *The World of Cricket* provides a more vivid picture in its first issue after war was declared:

> The days of waiting are past. Great Britain is at war, and the people are glad thereof – glad with no riotous gladness, with no cocksure

assurance, but soberly, sternly glad. It is not that we wanted war; but we could not brook dishonour. We had to stand by our friends, and to bear England's old, great part – that of the nation towards which the little peoples looked as a shield and buckle against the arrogant tyranny of the continental despots. That crowned madman, William of Hohenzollern, has committed the greatest crime against civilisation of which any ruler has been guilty since the days of Napoleon. Through his restless ambition and insane lust for dominion the whole continent is likely to be shortly in the throes of a desperate struggle. The nations which now hold aloof will be dragged into the cockpit. Little Holland, full of stolid courage, remembering her great struggle of old against the might of Spain; little Denmark, the blood of the sea-kings in her people's veins, peaceful though they are today, with an old score to settle with the Teuton tyrant; gallant Italy, who will never fight on the same side as the hated Austrian white-coats, who so long held her in chains; free Switzerland, indomitable among the mountains – these and others can scarcely stand aside. The might of Germany will go down ringed by hostile steel. The enemies she has raised up by her wanton aggressions will see to it that at the end of the war there shall be no more a German Empire, that no Hohenzollern shall ever rule again.

Already the army of cricket has had heavy demands made upon it for that other and greater army. Apart from the service players who hold their own so well in county matches, Territorials and others have answered the call. PF Warner, NJA Foster, AT Sharp, BG von B Melle, AW Carr and Sir AW White were some of the earliest to be called upon.

County cricket did carry on for a few weeks, but the usual end of season festivals were cancelled and Surrey's ground at The Oval was quickly taken over by the Army. Surrey played two home matches at Lord's but cancelled their final two county fixtures. Surrey in fact led the Championship table. In the opinion of some the competition should have been declared void, but this idea was a minority one and Surrey were declared County Champions. Nottinghamshire had a poor summer ending in tenth place with only five wins. In 1913 the county had been fifth. The best bowler, Jim Iremonger, stood twenty-sixth in the table of regular first-class players. Fred Barratt in his debut season captured 100 wickets with his fast bowling, but was below Iremonger – poor fielding, with the enthusiasm of Jones absent, did not help the attack. The Trent Bridge Pavilion and the adjacent Ladies' Pavilion were converted into a military hospital in the autumn of 1914. No county cricket was played during the seasons from 1915 to 1918 and many local clubs disbanded for the duration.

Although Carr was in the 20th Hussars based at Colchester he was seconded to the 5th (Royal Irish) Lancers; one of six such officers, including one from the Medical Corps and another from the Veterinary Corps. The 5th Lancers had found themselves short of officers. Carr therefore travelled from The Oval to the Marlborough Barracks in Dublin, taking the train to Holyhead and the ferry across the Irish Sea. On 15 August the regiment marched through the city to the North Wall Quay, cheered by enthusiastic Dubliners – a week earlier a soldier would have scarcely dared walk down a Dublin street for fear of his life. Before embarkation the regiment was given a short speech by the Lord Lieutenant of Ireland. It proved difficult to truss up and hoist the horses on board the 6,560-ton SS *Kingstonian*, whose hold had been specially converted to accommodate this unexpected cargo. In total some 9,300 men and 9,800 horses from eighteen British cavalry regiments were taken to France at this stage of the war.

On the seventeenth the ship arrived at the French port of Le Havre. On the nineteenth the regiment boarded three trains, the men in carriages, the horses in box cars. The journey to the front took a whole day, arriving at Jeaumont near the France-Belgium border. Fourteen French soldiers were attached to the regiment to act as interpreters. After a night's rest, they moved to Bray, ten miles east of Mons. Carr was involved in forward patrols to locate the Germans and then was one of the cavalry who formed a screen whilst British troops dug in along the Mons Canal. The Battle of Mons commenced on 23 August; facing the German First Army, the strongest of their units, the combined French and British troops had little hope of defending their positions. The Germans broke through the French defences adjacent to the British lines and the 5th Lancers together with the infantrymen had no option but to retreat. The Allies in these circumstances did well to maintain a cohesive front as they fell back. Carr was involved in the rearguard actions through to 17 September, including the battle on the Aisne River, when he was injured near Soissons. His charger was shot in the head and, rearing up, fell over on to him. Carr lay for three hours with the dead horse on top until he was rescued. Prior to this event Carr had, for several days and nights, been out in pouring rain without a greatcoat. The accident allied to this brought on an attack of fever, to which he nearly succumbed. He was brought home to Rempstone Hall.

The Rempstone Hall of autumn 1914 was a far different place to its peacetime equivalent. Arthur was on military service; Gordon left school at the end of the 1914 summer term and got himself to Sandhurst. That left Eileen, aged fourteen, as the only young person in residence. All the suitable horses, including Eileen's favourite pony, had been commandeered by the army. The grooms were left with a few old nags to feed and water. The Quorn Hunt, together with all the hunts in England, had effectively disbanded and was destined not to resume until the end of hostilities. Likewise the village cricket team followed the general trend and closed down for the duration.

Eileen remembered driving her father to Loughborough station to catch the London train – the groom being unwilling and no one else being available – so she put up her hair in order to look much older than her fourteen years. Philip probably spent more time in the family's London house and attending to business at the Stock Exchange than travelling back and forth to Rempstone, especially now he was deprived of his horses and the opportunity to hunt.

Carr gave a graphic account of the early fighting and this was reported in the *Leicester Chronicle*: 'The regiment was sent out to attack a position and found themselves with hostile forces also on both flanks. Without hesitation the Lancers rode first at one flank and then at the other, and, having disposed of these, then went forward and captured the position in front of them. Referring to the destructiveness of the German shell fire, he saw that one "Jack Johnson" killed thirteen horses and four men, wounding three others. Chasing Uhlans was the only amusement of his regiment and there was not much amusement even in that as the Germans always bolted unless in very superior numbers.'

The 5th Lancers after the retreat from Mons were mainly involved in training behind the lines. This, however, was not a holiday; for along time after the retreat, it was anticipated that the infantry would break through the enemy lines and at that moment the cavalry would exploit that initial success. The 5th Lancers were therefore kept at the peak of fitness with continuous military exercises. Carr returned to France as soon as he was fit. In April 1916 he was at the regimental horse show in St Pierre and won the charger class, he also was the captain of the regimental football team. Although these breaks from military duties were welcome, a number of cavalry regiments were dismounted and the men sent to fight in the trenches, though only as a temporary measure when the infantry was short of men. In the minds of those who retained their horses there was the gruesome thought that cavalry charges against machine gun fire could only have one result. Carr is not mentioned again in the regimental history until September 1916, when the 5th Lancers were in the battle of the Somme, the first occasion when a formation of tanks was to be used. The tanks were to break through the German lines and it was intended that the cavalry should take advantage of the breach in the German lines and advance through the gap. However the tanks suffered serious mechanical failure, no breach was achieved and therefore the anticipated cavalry charge did not take place. Lieutenants Fleur and Carr went out on patrol and came under fire; three cavalrymen were wounded. Carr was mentioned in dispatches during this engagement.

There is an interesting piece of reminiscence concerning Private Arthur James Scarlett of the 5th Lancers, who had remained behind at the regimental HQ in Ireland. He was killed in Dublin during the Easter Rising on 24 April 1916, when he was one of a group of mounted soldiers who cantered up Sackville Street. On reaching Nelson's Pillar they were greeted by a hail of bullets from rebels occupying the Post Office. Three other soldiers and two horses were killed in the action. His widow and three children, who were Londoners, were moved into one of the lodges at Rempstone Hall, a move was facilitated by his commanding officer, 'a member of the Carr family'. How long the Scarlett family stayed in Rempstone is not mentioned, but 'some years ago' there was a lady living in Rempstone who remembered the family being in the lodge. One assumes that Arthur Carr, being an officer in the 5th Lancers, must have had a hand in helping the impoverished London family.

The first months of 1917 saw the regiment again training, the Germans having retreated to the Hindenburg Line. On 10 February 1917, whilst on leave, Arthur Carr married Ivy Violet Borton at St Saviour's Church, Chelsea. The witnesses were Stanley Crayshay (presumably a friend of Carr's) and the bride's parents, Col Charles Edward Borton and Amy L Borton.

Charles Borton, Arthur's new father-in-law, was born in Kingston, Canada, in 1857 and on the 1891 census was serving with the Norfolk Regiment at Thorpe, near Norwich, his rank then being a captain. At one time he used the surname 'Nunn' (the names Nunn and Borton are shown on the 1891 census). Ivy Borton was born in Billericay, Essex in 1892 and was the adopted daughter of Col Borton.

It would appear to be a shotgun wedding since Ivy Carr gave birth to a son, Angus Arthur, on 14 September 1917 at The Bungalow, The Beach, Shoreham-by-Sea. Sussex. Family tradition has it that Ivy sneaked into the barracks at Colchester and seduced Arthur, but that sounds a trifle one-sided! In the latter part of 1917, Carr, back in France, had several bones in his foot broken when his horse trod on him. This seems to be the end of his active service in France and by the Armistice he was on special duties at the War Office in Whitehall.

Carr was not the only member of his family to see action. His brother, Gordon, was commissioned as a Second Lieutenant in the 7th (Princess Royal's) Dragoon Guards on 16 December 1914. He then underwent training at Camberley and was stationed at Tidworth, going to France in 1916, aged eighteen. Gordon spent nine months in hospital during 1918 and was ordered an open-air cure for six months before joining the regimental depot at Dunbar. The most likely cause of his hospitalisation would seem to be the effects of a gas attack, though another version is that he was buried when a shell exploded near him and was dug out only just in time. He was invalided out of the army in December 1918. His experiences in France were to have a serious effect on his later life, but as soon as he was well enough Gordon took a position in the family firm of WI Carr and Sons and moved to London.

In the winter of 1918/19 the cricket authorities at Lord's, and indeed the first-class county clubs, were anxious to return county cricket and the Championship back to its pre-war standing as soon as was practical. The newspapers were filled with suggestions as to how the game could be improved. In order to encourage scoring, for example, boundaries ought to be shortened, the batting side should be penalised if they allowed a maiden over to be bowled, county sides should be restricted to three or four professionals, even left-handed batsmen should be banned and county matches should be of two days duration with play continuing until 7.30 p.m. This last idea, against the wish of MCC, was approved. The county programme was not set out until 5 February 1919, when the idea that the Australian Services should run a programme of first-class matches had not yet been agreed. In the end the first-class programme meant that all MCC major matches and the Australian games should be of three days duration, in contrast all the Championship games were restricted to two days.

Less than a month after the Armistice, EV Lucas writing in *Punch* summed his thoughts on the game: 'Cricket is an intricate, vigilant and leisurely warfare, and the fact that every moment of it is equally fraught with possibilities and openings for glorious uncertainty makes it peculiarly the delight of intelligent observers, none of whom finds dullness in the spectacle of a batsman, no matter how stubborn, defending his wicket successfully against eleven opponents. Nor does it occur to them to ask him for gallery effects. First-class cricket calls for such very special gifts of temperament and skill that only the fittest survive; and all their actions are worth study.'

Despite the turmoil which engulfed much of Europe and the militant attitude of the British trades unions, whose membership boomed, the ultra-conservative controllers of county and international (i.e. Empire) cricket were anxious to return the game to its pre-war format as rapidly as possible. In Britain there was full employment in 1919, but even so it was estimated that on average 100,000 workers were on strike every day throughout the year. Although the following comment hardly affects Arthur Carr, very little in top class cricket was destined to change for the next fifty years – nostalgia and the notion that Edwardian cricket was the 'Golden Age' were a potent force.

Although several counties who had played first-class cricket in 1914 had doubts if they could produce a team to compete in 1919, in the event only Worcestershire withdrew. There was no competition held for the minor counties. Among the first-class counties, Nottinghamshire were fortunate that all their major professional cricketers of the pre-war era were available, though James Iremonger and Tom Wass, aged forty-three and forty-five respectively, were considered too old. Their places were taken, after some early season trials, by the brothers Billy and Ben Flint, both miners from Underwood. Billy Flint was the better known, having played football for Notts County since 1908 – he continued to play for them until 1926. Aged twenty-nine, he seemed too old to start a county career, but was to appear in 145 matches for Nottinghamshire between 1919 and 1929. Ben Flint was three years his junior. His county cricket career only lasted two seasons and just thirteen first-class matches. His best known connection with cricket is as the father-in-law of the England Ladies captain, Rachel Heyhoe-Flint. She married Derrick Flint, who had a short professional cricket career with Warwickshire.

The principal gap in the Nottinghamshire First XI was the captaincy. AO Jones had never recovered from the illness that laid him low during the summer of 1914 and died of consumption on 21 December of the same year. If he had returned to health, he would in any case, at forty-six, have been too old to resume first-class county cricket. As was detailed in the description of Nottinghamshire's 1914 season, the county struggled to find a regular stand-in leader to replace Jones. Three amateurs who had had occasional matches for the county immediately prior to the outbreak of war had been killed in France: Crawford, Hodges and Hemingway. Of the others, the only ones who seem to have been considered were the two Repton schoolboys, the Turner brothers, plus Pearson-Gregory, Branston and Arthur Carr. Branston's record was clearly the best, but he definitely ruled himself out. Pearson-Gregory also declined and the Turners were too busy working in the family business. The Nottinghamshire Committee, having taken soundings, decided to invite Carr.

With the very notion of employing a professional as captain was an anathema to all county cricket committees, one of the more bizarre ideas for changes put forward in 1918/19 was to restrict counties to a maximum of three or four professionals. How the counties would be able to find the amateurs needed doesn't seem to have been considered by the promoters of these proposals – when the minor counties, who in fact operated with only two or three professionals, resumed competitive cricket in 1920, several counties could only manage to play six games. In 1919 professionals received £20 for Test matches, amateurs received their railway fare and £1.10.0d per day.

Carr's father effectively agreed to make him an allowance to enable him to look after his young family in the style to which they were accustomed and to play as an amateur, provided, says Arthur, that he went on to captain England!

Stalwarts of the middle order –
Wilf Payton and Arthur Carr stride to the crease

# 6

# FRESH START

## 1919-1920

Ten of the fifteen counties who took part in the 1919 County Championship appointed new captains, five retained their 1914 skipper. Of the fifteen captains, all of whom were still genuine amateurs rather than shamateurs, only four were destined to last more than a few summers: Carr, Daniell of Somerset, Douglas of Essex (who began his leadership in 1911) and the redoubtable Lord Tennyson of Hampshire.

Johnny Douglas was very much an earlier version of Carr. He excelled at all sports whilst at school and as a boxer gained an Olympic gold medal. His academic achievements were little better than Carr's and he never went to university. His father made a fortune in the timber business and more or less saved Essex County Cricket Club by taking on part of the mortgage on the County Ground at Leyton in 1907/08, when the club was in deep trouble financially. Douglas was also to captain England, but unlike Carr he also had the highest honour of all, captaining England in Australia. A row with the Essex Committee ended his captaincy as well as his county career in 1928. Lionel Tennyson, the poet's grandson, had a style of leadership which was also in the mould of Douglas and Carr. He led England in three Tests, all in 1921 against Australia. His two autobiographies, *From Verse to Worse* and *Sticky Wickets*, amply illustrate his attitude to life.

The other long-serving skipper, John Daniell, was not as talented as the other three but was a very brave fielder at silly-point and in mid career switched from a hard-hitting devil-may-care batsman to one who battled with much more patience – probably due to the unknown quantity of the rest of his eleven, who seemed to vary alarmingly from match to match! Somerset's difficulties in fielding eleven cricketers of first-class standard are well told in Robertson-Glasgow's writing. Daniell's language was robust, but he treated all the players equally, so they tolerated the colour of it. Daniell never played Test cricket though, unlike Carr and Douglas, he did manage to stay friends with those who administered Somerset cricket; indeed he took over as Honorary Secretary when money was even shorter than usual.

The newly appointed 1919 captains, and in particular Carr, initially relied on the wise heads of long-serving professionals. Carr emphasised this point in several public speeches. In 1919, the running of county cricket clubs continued in the same style as in pre-war times. The era when each county employed a 'cricket manager' who oversaw a first team squad of professional players was still half a century away. The county coach dealt purely with the youngsters on the ground staff, he certainly did not travel away with the first team and even for home matches he was often with the county Club and Ground side, rather than at headquarters. The captain controlled his players, and though each eleven was theoretically picked by a sub-committee of the county club, the captain had a major say in the selection.

A separate treatise could be written analysing the county captains who led the first-class counties in the inter-war period.

A number of them were no more than enthusiastic club players with sufficient resources to have the time to spend their summers with the county side. A few still came from the landed gentry, as had been the case before the war, and treated the professionals under them as they would their domestic servants. Carr was to be a complete contrast; he had a special rapport with his players.

If John Gunn and Tom Oates, the two players who had been reported to the Committee by Carr after the 1914 Yorkshire match, bore any ill-feeling towards their new official leader, it certainly did not resurface when Championship matches resumed. Carr had captained the county side a mere three times before the war, but the experience of managing men as an officer in France for three years must have made him aware of the best way to handle his band of players. Most players accepted the way things were and had been in living memory: the divide between amateurs and professionals was still distinct. Although the chasm between to the classes of cricketers had been quite clear at Lord's for a hundred years, the role of full-time county professionals at Trent Bridge was still relatively new – until 1897 Nottinghamshire had paid their players on a match-by-match basis and only that year had begun to employ five or six young hopefuls on a weekly wage through the season. A number of Nottinghamshire professionals worked at Lord's for MCC on a weekly basis, with a clause allowing them to play for their county if and when required. In 1919 Tom Oates and Joe Hardstaff of the current Nottinghamshire team were the only ones in the employ of MCC. Back in the 1880s, perhaps half the Nottinghamshire team were at Lord's and regularly played or umpired in MCC out-matches.

Very few professionals moved counties because of the strict qualification rules. Free spirits did not last long – SF Barnes, briefly of Warwickshire and Lancashire, was a prime current example; Cec Parkin of Lancashire would be another a few years later. It was perhaps due to the leadership skills of AO Jones and of Carr that there seem to be no such examples of players rebelling against the system at Trent Bridge in the first three decades of the twentieth century. A great rebellion had occurred in 1881 with Alfred Shaw and Arthur Shrewsbury leading a strike against the amateur officials who controlled the County Cricket Club. Rightly or wrongly the players caved in and the Nottinghamshire Committee had won the day.

The County Cricket Club in 1919 was governed by a Committee of twelve, each man being elected by the votes of the adult male members of the club. The nominal leader of the club was the President, who in 1919 was Sir Jesse Boot – he had replaced Arthur Carr's father in February 1914 and, though the Presidency was an annual appointment, had been retained in the position due to the war. There were three trustees: W Hollins, Sir WH Tomasson and former Nottinghamshire cricketer CW Wright. The trustees had originally been appointed when the county club took a long lease on the Trent Bridge Cricket Ground and the Trent Bridge Inn in 1881. The trustees had bought the freehold of the ground and pub in December 1918 and in March 1919 sold the freehold of the inn to the Ind Coope brewery. Two trustees, Wright and Tomasson, also held the post of Honorary Treasurer and Honorary Secretary to the club and attended Committee meetings. The day-to-day running of the club was in the hands of the paid secretary, Henry Turner, who was now aged seventy-five and had held the position since 1895. He was also a local businessman, being Managing Director of the Wilford Brick Company. Turner's connection with cricket administration stretched back to 1872 when he was elected Secretary of the prestigious Notts Castle Cricket Club. Their ground in the Meadows, just across the River Trent from the County Ground, had in the past been used to stage Notts County FC matches.

Acting as both head groundsman and coach was Walter Marshall. A long-standing friend of Henry Turner, Marshall had played for Notts Castle and in three first-class matches for Nottinghamshire. He had taken on the job of groundsman in 1895, combining with that of coach when the groundstaff was formed in 1897. In 1919 he moved into the living accommodation in the main Trent Bridge pavilion, remaining there until he died in 1943 aged eighty-eight.

Those then were the County Cricket Club officials, but who were the men Carr had to lead in that first post-war summer? Senior man was John Gunn. An all-rounder in his earlier days he was, in 1919, regarded principally as a batsman. His bowling had become slower as the years progressed, but now and again he still took useful wickets – in 1921 he obtained 49 at a reasonable average; in 'retirement' in club cricket for Sir Julien Cahn's team he was to baffle many a local batsman. In 1919 he was aged forty-two and the days when he was an outstanding cover-point were fast disappearing. The wicketkeeper, Tom Oates, was almost a year older than John Gunn, but had not gained a regular place in the county side until 1902 when he was twenty-six, replacing Jack Carlin – both Oates and Carlin were fellow miners from Eastwood. He usually batted at number nine and recorded fifteen half-centuries in his 453 completed innings for the county.

The two middle-order batsmen, Joe Hardstaff and Wilf Payton, were both born in 1882, but Hardstaff had become a permanent member of the county side in 1904, whilst Payton had secured his place a year later. Hardstaff was a miner from Kirkby-in-Ashfield, Payton was a trained engineer and had supervised work in a munitions factory during the war, he then opened a flourishing sports outfitters in Beeston. Hardstaff had gone to Australia with the 1907/08 MCC side and played in all five Tests with considerable success. He was on the shortlist for the 1911/12 tour but missed out. Though he appeared several times for Players v Gentlemen, he was never selected for a home Test match, but he did umpire in seventeen Tests between 1928 and 1935, after which his career as a Test umpire ended abruptly when his son began to play for England.

The two most successful bowlers in 1919 were to be Len Richmond and Fred Barratt. Barratt was yet another miner from the Nottinghamshire coalfield. A tall, well-built man, he was designed in the tradition of fast bowlers who come to the wicket as batsmen purely to hit sixes. Barratt took over 100 wickets in his debut season. Len Richmond, from George Parr's old home village of Radcliffe, was twenty-eight. Often known as 'Tich' – he was about 5 feet 6 inches in height – his leg-breaks and googlies rivalled 'Tich' Freeman of Kent in those early post-war summers, but he became increasingly rotund and being both a very moderate batsman and fielder lost his place in the side. Like John Gunn, he found a secure berth with Sir Julien Cahn.

Garnet Lee from Calverton had joined the Nottinghamshire playing staff in 1905, but did not gain a regular place in the county side until 1911. From 1913 he was the usual partner with George Gunn opening the Nottinghamshire innings, and was used in that role in 1919. From 1925 he was to have nine productive seasons with Derbyshire, both with the bat and the ball. George Gunn, who was to top the first-class batting averages in 1919, has previously been described. Added to those eight were the two Flint brothers, neither of whom gets even a mention in Carr's autobiography and then Carr himself, the eleventh player.

This group of players were the senior capped cricketers. Their salary arrangements had been rather haphazard but, in 1921, the club put salaries on a more formal footing; the capped players' annual pay was made up of the following elements:

Winter pay, 32 weeks @ £2: £64 per winter
Groundstaff pay, 20 weeks @ £3: £60 per summer
Home matches, 14 @ £9: £126 per season
Away matches, 14 @ £11: £154 per season
Railway fares: £24 per season
Gross total: £428
Less £1 for each home match: £14
Net total: £414

Young players on the ground staff received varying amounts, Larwood in 1923 accepted £2 per week, Syd Copley £1 10s but only during the twenty weeks of the season. There is no information as to the amount Arthur Carr received as an allowance from his father. The single clue is the fact that the press stated he received £6,000 a year, an amount he denied, but an intelligent guess is that he received maybe £3,000 or in cricketer's terms £30 a week – the players averaged £8, though most if not all of them would have had additional employment in the winter. It is unclear from the accounts how much the county club paid Carr in expenses, but probably something similar to that received by amateurs playing in Test matches. Half of those listed worked as miners. Miners' wages in the early 1920s were about £6 per week, though there were quite dramatic fluctuations. The Sankey Report, which suggested that the mines should be taken into public ownership, was endorsed by Lloyd George, but there was no way he could get a bill though the ultra Conservative majority in the House of Commons. The result was continuous unrest in the mining industry through the 1920s, but a number of Nottinghamshire miners who were potential county cricketers thought themselves better off in the coal industry.

For spectators attending games at Trent Bridge, the accommodation in 1919 was unchanged from pre-war days, indeed unchanged since the first Trent Bridge Test in 1899, save that

Notts County FC had moved out in 1910, taking their main stand with them. The wartime hospital authorities had added the Ulster Room to the rear of the Ladies Pavilion which the County Cricket Club adapted into a members' dining room.

Nottinghamshire finished that first post-war season third, the best record since winning the Championship in 1907. Carr was helped enormously by fielding an almost unchanged side. George Gunn had his finest year ever and the other batsmen played their roles adequately; only one Championship game was lost. The away win against Yorkshire was well deserved and definitely not helped by luck. Carr hit a typical 50. In the days immediately prior to this great victory, Carr had played at Lord's for the Gentlemen v Australians and after a shaky start had 'driven Gregory's fast bowling with refreshing vigour'. He scored 51 and the Gentlemen beat the touring side by an innings and 133 runs. In a programme of thirty-two matches it was one of only four defeats the Australians suffered.

As a result of this innings, Carr was picked for the principal match of 1919, Gentlemen v Players at Lord's. He hit an energetic 40 in the Gentlemen's total of 322 for 8 declared and there was a distinct possibility of a Players' defeat but Hobbs and George Gunn put on 134 before the first wicket fell and thus secured an honourable draw. Carr's only other non-Nottinghamshire first-class game of 1919 was also at Lord's for the Army against the Navy. Lieutenant Carr hit 52 in the presence of King George V and the Army proved much too strong for the sailors, winning by an innings.

Carr's two hundreds for Nottinghamshire were both against Sussex, the first being at Hove when his 104 came in ninety minutes. Sussex, batting first, collapsed for 101. Scoring rapidly Nottinghamshire gained a substantial lead, Carr wanted to declare but left his decision too late – a new rule meant that a declaration on the first day had to allow for 100 minutes playing time to remain. Barratt had a timely explosion, hitting 82 in fifty minutes and on the second morning Nottinghamshire won by an innings and 175 runs. In the return at Trent Bridge, Sussex again lost by an innings, Carr making 112 in even time.

The *Wisden* summary of Nottinghamshire season stated: 'AW Carr was more than anyone else the aggressive force on the side. He is a natural hitter, and he wisely plays the game that suits him. Not many batsmen in present day cricket drive fast bowling as he does. Like most hard hitters he had, perhaps more than his fair share of luck, but the chances he gave were seldom easy.'

Tragedy struck the County Cricket Club at the end of August. The Secretary, Henry Turner, was driving his horse and trap over Trent Bridge when the horse took fright and Turner was thrown out. He died at his home in Wilford a few days later as a result of the accident. Known by players as 'Wiggy' Turner for obvious reasons, he had been just the person to bridge the gap, or chasm, between the professionals and the committee.

When the season closed Carr returned to military duties, having been granted leave of absence for the summer. In November 1919 his regiment left England for service in India. Carr, however, remained behind, stationed at the Lancer depot at Woolwich. He lived at his father's London residence, 13 Great Stanhope Street, Park Lane. On 26 March 1920, Carr resigned his commission and was placed on the Reserves List of Officers. It is not clear exactly when the Carr family left their Nottinghamshire home at Rempstone for good. Photographs show the family, including Arthur's wife, Ivy, at Rempstone in 1917. Having had most of his horses taken by the military and with hunting very restricted, it is assumed that Philip Carr spent much of his time in London. Great Stanhope Street, near the southern end of Park Lane, vanished under one of the hotels built facing Hyde Park in the inter-war period and by the early 1920s the Carrs had moved to Upper Brook Street, still off Park Lane, the street connecting to Grosvenor Square.

When Philip Carr began to rebuild his stable of horses in the post-war period, they were centred on training stables in the Newmarket area. It therefore made sense to seek a suitable residence within a reasonable distance of horse racing's historic centre and the Carrs, now just Philip and Louisa, moved to Hemingford Park Hall near St Ives in Huntingdonshire. The estate agent's brief particulars when Hemingford was offered for sale again in 2009 provide a flavour of the place: 'Grade II listed, includes a thatched Lodge, Cottage, coach house, stables and barns with 71.51 acres of timbered parkland. Estimated price £4,500,000.' It proved to be Philip Carr's final change of address. Until Arthur Carr bought his own house, it is believed that his wife and son spent much of their time at Ivy's sister's home near Malvern.

Much to the relief of cricketers and cricket watchers, the experiment of two-day Championship cricket was abandoned for 1920. The players hated the long hours, which still meant that six of the seven matches played at Trent Bridge ended as draws. Since the summer had been on the whole dry and fine, the draws could not be attributed to adverse weather conditions. The Nottinghamshire Committee report commented: 'Mr AW Carr captained the side with great judgment and his fine free cricket was most popular.' The number of Nottinghamshire Championship matches for 1920 was increased from fourteen to twenty.

The county had relied on two main bowlers in 1919, Richmond and Barratt. In 1920 Sam Staples was introduced into the eleven, but he did little more than replace John Gunn's spin of pre-war days. Staples, a miner from Newstead Colliery, was twenty-seven and had learnt his cricket with the colliery team. He earned an England Test cap in 1927/28 and but for illness might have appeared in more than three internationals. His county career was eventually cut short by sciatica. John Gunn's batting bloomed in 1920 and he scored more runs than brother George. 'Dodge' Whysall, who had had a regular place in the 1914 Nottinghamshire team, returned to the club in 1920 and took over from Garnet Lee as George Gunn's opening partner. Whysall in 1920 was living at Carcroft, near Doncaster, employed as a miner, but moved to Mansfield, opening a sports outfitters in the town. He had originally joined the playing staff in 1907, aged nineteen, as a batsman-wicketkeeper, but with regular keeper Oates rarely absent, was not often seen behind the stumps. It came as a complete surprise to the press when Whysall was selected for the Test side to tour Australia in 1924/25 as the team's reserve wicketkeeper. Whysall did play in three Tests on that tour, but purely as a batsman.

Carr had a poor season with the bat, only saved by a brilliant 105 not out against Surrey in August. It was a low-scoring match, apart from Carr no other batsman on either side produced an individual 50. Nottinghamshire in the final innings required 272 for victory in 260 minutes and the odds were all in Surrey's favour. HJ Henley reported: 'The turning point came in the hour when Carr and Payton put on 91 for the fifth wicket, a stand which brought the total within 40 runs of victory. Carr's century was the first scored against Surrey this season, and he made his 105 in a little over three hours. At 22 he might have been caught at short leg – a very hard chance – but he did not look like erring afterwards. A want of restraint used to be the failing of Carr, but there was no sign of that yesterday. He drove as hard as ever on the off-side – thumping drives of the kind that suggest muscle rather than wrist. He made his runs in a variety of ways on the leg side, but sandwiched between the hefty-looking blows was a well-considered defence. He always picked exactly the right ball for his forcing strokes ... it was appropriate that the Nottinghamshire captain should make the winning run after playing so gallant an innings.'

Nottinghamshire won by three wickets – Surrey's first defeat at The Oval, their tenth game there in 1920 – and Surrey were at that point third in the Championship table. In all, Nottinghamshire won ten Championship games (there was no first-class touring side that summer) and ended a modest seventh. The Nottinghamshire Committee report repeats Carr's great judgment as captain, but does not mention his batting, simply adding, 'the County is indebted to him for the time and trouble he gave to the side.' Carr played in all twenty Nottinghamshire first-class matches. In addition he was chosen for the Gentlemen v Players at The Oval, though not at Lord's, and for an unrepresentative North of England side at Hastings versus South – the match clashed with the Scarborough Festival and Nottinghamshire provided six of the North side. Carr achieved little in either game. MCC selected the England team which toured Australia in the winter of 1920/21, Carr does not seem to have been considered for this disastrous venture.

It was during 1920 that Lord Harris had been engaged a careful check to make certain all county cricketers were properly qualified for the county for which they played. Lord Harris had been educated at Eton and Oxford, having obtained a place in the cricket XI at both establishments, and had a long but interrupted career with Kent, captaining the side in the 1870s and 80s. He led England in the first home Test match – against Australia in 1880, and by 1920 was the supremo at Lord's. He certainly raised the standard of Kent cricket and as Governor of Bombay for five years in the 1890s did much to improve and promote cricket in India.

Walter Hammond turned out for Gloucestershire in 1920 though he was born in Kent (Harris's own county) and fell foul of his lordship's sweep. Carr also came under scrutiny. Harris wrote to the Nottinghamshire Secretary doubting Carr's qualification as he no longer lived in the county. The Nottinghamshire Secretary replied pointing out Rule 5 of the regulations: 'A player who had played for a county for five consecutive seasons was qualified for that county in perpetuity, unless he played for another county.' Carr had played 1910 to 1914 inclusive. This response must have rather knocked the stuffing out of Harris.

Frank Mann, Carr's first international captain

# 7

# MCC CALLING

## 1921-1923

The Australian tourists visited England in 1921, the first official side since 1912. On that earlier trip the team had been weakened by internal politics and the results were unimpressive, but the 1921 team, which had crushed England in Australia in the winter of 1920/21, was a different combination. The first Test match commenced at Trent Bridge on Saturday 28 May in front of a crowd of 21,000. The fast bowlers, Jack Gregory and Ted McDonald, dismissed England for 112. Australia reached 167 for six by the close. On Monday the tourists were all out for 232 and then dismissed England a second time for 147, leaving themselves only 28 to win. These they made in thirty-seven balls without losing a wicket. No less than 22,000 turned out to witness England's embarrassment. The tourists stayed in the Victoria Station Hotel while a miners' strike was in progress. Macartney, in his autobiography, notes that all the hotel guests were given candles when they retired to sleep, in order to light the bedrooms. Len Richmond was Nottinghamshire's sole representative in the match, like his colleagues he failed to achieve much. *The Cricketer*, reporting the game, advocated a clean sweep when picking England's squad for the second Test – in fact there were six changes, including Richmond. He was never to represent England again.

A month later the Australians returned to Trent Bridge to play the county team – the old tag 'you ain't seen nothing yet' would speedily prove accurate. 10,000 spectators attended on the Saturday, a number less than anticipated as the admission charge at 2/- was double that for an ordinary county game. Warren Bardsley, captaining the side in the absence of Warwick Armstrong, won the toss and decided to bat. At lunch the score was 154 for one, by tea it was 484 for four, Charlie Macartney not out 308, his partner Nip Pellew not out 88, of which 24 had come off Arthur Carr's single over – six fours. At close of play Australia were 608 for seven. Macartney was dismissed for 345 scored in three hours and fifty-three minutes. On Sunday the Nottinghamshire and Australian players were entertained to lunch and a tour of Sherwood Forest by the Duke of Portland. Bardsley decided to bat on when Monday's play began – all out 675. Nottinghamshire, with the pitch still in good order, were dismissed for 58 and 100. Carr was the only batsman to show much fight, having a match aggregate of 45 – the next best aggregate was 24 by Whysall. Macartney's innings remains a record both for the Trent Bridge ground and against Nottinghamshire. The Nottinghamshire defeat – an innings and 517 – is another record for the county.

Nottinghamshire could at least offer some excuses for the debacle – the players had been at Southampton on Wednesday, Thursday and Friday. Phil Mead, the Hampshire batsman, scored 280 not out in his county's second innings, which meant that Nottinghamshire required 286 in less than three hours. The score fell dramatically to 51 for six. Whysall made 97 not out and, for the loss of two more wickets, Nottinghamshire won with fifteen minutes to spare. The team then faced a tedious train journey back to Nottingham for Saturday's play against the Australians with little time for sleep prior to facing Macartney's onslaught. Fred Barratt was unable to bowl after tea due to a strain and Tom Oates was unable to bat in either Nottinghamshire innings due to a damaged thumb.

Having disposed of the most depressing Trent Bridge episodes of 1921, a calmer survey of the season now follows. Nottinghamshire fielded an unchanged first XI for 1921. Eleven players appeared in at least twenty-two of the twenty-five first-class games – four other players filled in the very occasional gaps. Unlike 1919, the value of possessing an unchanged team all season went unrewarded. As a group the players were, of course, two years older, which meant the fielding in general creaked that little bit more, but there was an obvious need for a stronger attack.

Carr must have been pleased to find his name included in a cartoon in *The Cricketer* on 21 May, prior to the selection of the side for the first Test at Trent Bridge, featuring thirteen 'young bloods' – nine of them amateurs. Four of the players, C Hallows, VWC Jupp, DJ Knight and A Sandham, did make their Test debut in the current season, but it cannot be said that any of the four made much impression. Three made their Test debut in the next England series (in 1922/23) – AW Carr, AER Gillgan and GTS Stevens – whilst two more, APF Chapman and H Sutcliffe, first appeared for England in 1924. The remaining three, H Ashton, MB Burrows and C Tyson, never wore an England cap.

In attempting to reverse the continuous success of the 1921 Australians, no less than thirty players represented England in the five-match Test series, to no avail. *The Cricketer* may have hailed Carr as one of the 1921 young bloods, but when reviewing Nottinghamshire at the season's close, the magazine's anonymous writer noted: 'AW Carr, the only amateur in the side, had a difficult task, which he faced with pluck and determination and he ought to be a much more successful batsman than he is, for when he makes runs he gets them very well, his driving being a conspicuous feature of his play. His defence however needs improving.'

Carr played in all twenty-five Nottinghamshire first-class matches, but was not chosen for any representative games. The county won the same number of matches, ten, as the previous year, but fell from seventh to eighth. The county did win the prime Trent Bridge Championship fixture – the Whitsun Bank Holiday game with Surrey – despite the visitors' secret weapon: Surrey gave a first-class debut to TJ Moloney.

The report contains the following paragraph: 'The score stood at 170 for 5 when Mr Moloney was put on. He is a lob bowler who bowls leg theory, and bowls it accurately, too. He varies the flight of the ball excellently and bowls an exceedingly good full toss at an awkward height. His field is placed as follows: Four men on the leg boundary, and four men forming an inner ring on the leg side, one man on the off-side at mid-off The attempts of the last few men in the Nottinghamshire side to play him were ludicrous and evinced much laughter from the crowd, who showed their unmistakeable delight at seeing a lob bowler go on. At any event bowling as he did wide on the leg side, very few runs were scored off him and in desperation several of the batsmen lashed out at his full pitches, with dire results, for they placed them right down the throats of the fieldsmen on the boundary. Payton was taken in this way by Mr Reay at fine leg; Barratt was caught at deep square leg by Shepherd; whilst Whysall attempted to execute an overhead tennis-serve shot through the unguarded covers and only succeeded in plunking the ball into Ducat's hands at mid-off. Richmond literally was halfway up the pitch to one ball, missed it and scampered back more or less alongside of it, just in time to get into his ground. Both Richmond and Strudwick (the wicketkeeper) finished up lying full length on the ground. Rarely has such comic bowling been seen in first-class cricket.'

Moloney finished with figures of 7-1-11-3. Sadly Carr had been dismissed first ball by Hitch and so did not have to tackle Moloney. Despite the lobs, Nottinghamshire's winning margin was seven wickets.

The batting was both strong and consistent, but the bowling relied too much on Richmond's leg breaks and googlies. Carr hit 204 against Essex and 102 against Sussex, his only three figure innings of the summer – both innings were scored against counties whose attack lacked their principal bowlers. Carr explains his success against Essex: 'As every cricketer knows, you can sometimes perform amazing feats at the game when you are "under the influence". There came a period during one season (1920) when, for the life of me, I could do nothing with the bat …. So one day in that dismal period I suddenly made up my mind to see what effect a night out would have on my batting average. I had been very good for a long time and it was not paying. When I awoke next morning I had what is commonly known as a "hang over". … I said to myself, "What you want is a hair of the dog that bit you, my good fellow – that's your only hope to-day." So, believe me, I went to the Pavilion bar and drank off three double whiskies and soda almost before you could say knife and, believe me or believe me not, when it came to my turn to bat I was in such form that I proceeded to make a double century!'

He had played six successive innings without reaching 50 and his 204 was the only three-figure knock in the match. This is the earliest direct reference to Carr's enthusiasm for the odd drink, but the tradition of cricketers drinking at the close of play is a proud one. Trent Bridge cricket ground was, of course, founded in the field behind the Trent Bridge Inn.

Carr was persuaded by a businessman to take the Nottinghamshire side on a four-match tour of Scotland as soon as the Championship programme ended. The trip ended at Greenock on 15 September, by which time the organiser had quit and taken what profits there were with him (Carr states he disappeared to Canada) and Tom Oates, the Nottinghamshire wicketkeeper, had become so fed up he'd gone home.

The Nottinghamshire Committee were conscious of the relative lack of success and appointed as coach James Iremonger, pre-war Nottinghamshire all-rounder, replacing Walter Marshall, who had had the dual role of coach and head groundsman. Marshall remained as head groundsman. An all-round sportsman, Iremonger had made his soccer debut for Nottingham Forest in 1895/96 and represented England in three internationals in 1901 and 1902. He first played for Nottinghamshire as a cricketer in 1897 and for some ten seasons was used almost entirely as a batsman, but, having reached 1,000 runs eight times in the nine seasons between 1901 and 1909, he was employed as a medium fast bowler, taking 90 wickets in the three successive seasons, 1911, 1912 and 1913; it was therefore as an all-rounder that he was picked for the MCC side that toured Australia in 1911/12. Charlie Barnett, Gloucestershire and England batsman, recalled his coaching experiences during his early days of county cricket, illustrating the esteem in which players held the Nottinghamshire coach: 'I had hours of coaching from Charlie Parker: at times the air was blue, but it was all worth it. Whenever I went to Trent Bridge, I used to beg a net from Jim Iremonger. He was much quieter, but his "Stand still, boy" carried dreadful authority.' Iremonger became more famous in the public's eyes as the mentor of Harold Larwood and Bill Voce; although in 1921 they were still to be brought on to the Nottinghamshire groundstaff.

Despite Carr's lack of runs in 1921, less than either of the Gunns and Payton and Whysall, he was chosen for the MCC side to tour New Zealand in the coming winter. The rest of the team were JC Hartley (Sussex), LHW Troughton (Kent), MB Burrows (Surrey), R St L Fowler (Hampshire), WAC Wilkinson (Oxford University), GF Earle (Surrey), WDV Dickinson

(Army), WGLF Lowndes (Hampshire), CH Gibson (Sussex), and Hon CN Bruce (Middlesex). The team, described as 'a good one, strong on all points', was due to sail on 23 October. The trip was cancelled when the list of cricketers was sent to the New Zealand Cricket Council. Although the side was restricted to amateurs, the New Zealand authorities felt that it was too powerful and would fail to attract large crowds because the local provincial sides would be overwhelmed and the NZCC would not receive enough gate money to pay the tourists' expenses.

After two seasons when all the pundits declared that the Nottinghamshire team lacked any real bite in its attack and the batting on the whole was becoming geriatric, the county surprised everyone, including themselves, by ending the 1922 season as runner up to Yorkshire and nearing the close of the summer, by some quirk of the current points system, Nottinghamshire might have taken the title. The side was virtually identical to the sides of 1920 and 1921 save that Frank Matthews, the tall fast bowler from Willoughby-in-the-Wolds, who had been very expensive in the few matches in which he appeared in 1921, took 37 wickets at 18 runs apiece adding an extra element to the attack.

The editor of *Wisden* was not amused by Nottinghamshire's high standing in the Championship table: 'Not having an arithmetical mind and, moreover, being quite unable to associate cricket with the niceties of decimal fractions, I have no suggestion to offer with regard to the method of deciding the Championship ... A very small accident would, on the present percentage plan, have placed Nottinghamshire at the head of the list, though their record could not bear comparison with that of Yorkshire or Surrey. The fact that they stood above Surrey in the final table was sufficiently ridiculous. Never having made a fetish of the Championship I should personally prefer a far more elastic method of deciding the matter, letting the

MCC place the first half dozen counties on the general play of the season, but it seems to be agreed that we must have a plan that admits of the positions of the counties being easily followed week by week.'

Sydney Pardon had been editor since 1891 and had been working on the Almanack in 1888 when the system the Pardon brothers created to decide the county league table caused ructions and led to a basic alteration.

Nottinghamshire began in tremendous form, winning all six of their initial matches, though this was a rather deceptive set of victories since by coincidence the opponents were mainly the weaker counties. The Championship table on 31 May showed Lancashire and Nottinghamshire with six wins out of six. Yorkshire stood third with five wins out of six and Surrey fourth with four wins from five matches. Defeat came in the seventh match. Carr made a determined effort for victory when Nottinghamshire required 295 in the final innings. His score of 82, made without a chance, was the highest individual total in the whole match, but none of his colleagues could survive for long – he was in for two and a half hours. Looking back on the campaign, the crucial Championship match was played at Trent Bridge at the end of July against Yorkshire. Nottinghamshire gained a first innings lead of 35, but the batting failed in the county's second innings, enabling a Yorkshire victory by five wickets.

Carr came second to Hardstaff in the Nottinghamshire batting table – Hardstaff's average however was enhanced due to the number of his not out innings. Of Carr's three Championship hundreds, his 103 against Lancashire at Trent Bridge was perhaps the most outstanding. The press report commented: 'He started quietly before lunch, but afterwards played fine, forcing cricket and quite dominated the game. He reached fifty in just over an hour, and completed his hundred in as many minutes, altogether collected 103 out of 156. He gave chances in the long field when 5 and 89, but for all that his display, which included fifteens fours, was brilliant.' Nottinghamshire won by 117 runs. In the Old Trafford match against Lancashire, Carr had scored 41 when he was struck on the foot by a fast ball from James Tyldesley. In great pain he backed towards the wicket; realising his position he attempted to leap over the stumps, but dislodged a bail in the process and was given out 'hit wicket'. Since he had completed his stroke before disturbing the bail, Nottinghamshire supporters felt the umpire was at fault in his ruling. Carr was not a fan of James Tyldesley, suggesting that he had bowled 'bodyline' before the war. Carr commented: 'James Tyldesley, a strong, thick-set man, bowled pretty fast and every time one of his short ones hit me on the body – and a number of them did hit me – Dick Tyldesley, standing at short leg, turned round and said loudly: "Well bowled, Jim."'

Carr's batting exploits over the season were recognised by his selection for the MCC tour to South Africa and by both *Wisden* and *The Cricketer*. The editor of the former chose Carr as one of the five Cricketers of the Year. The final six lines of the editor's appreciation of Carr reads: 'In 1921 he got on very much better and last summer, as everyone knows, his batting and fielding for the Gentlemen at Lord's gave him a higher place in English cricket than had ever been his before. His straight driving could almost have been described as the restoration of a lost art. Nothing quite so alarming has been seen since KL Hutchings was in his prime.' Hutchings, the Kent and England batsman was in his prime about 1909 and last played for Kent in 1912. He was killed in France in 1916.

*The Cricketer* selected twelve Cricketers of the Year, of which Carr was one. Whilst the *Wisden* plaudits did not mention Carr's leadership, *The Cricketer* commented: 'Carr is a splendid fieldsman in any position and an excellent captain, keen and determined, who gets the best out of the men under him.'

MCC decided to undertake two overseas tours in the close season of 1922/23. One, to South Africa, included five Test matches in its schedule. The other involved fifteen first-class matches and three 'unofficial' Tests against New Zealand, also including games in Australia. Only once before, in 1911/12, had MCC arranged two tours involving first-class cricket in an English winter.

The primary trip was clearly the visit to South Africa. Although English teams had toured South Africa since 1888/89 and the first South African side came to Britain in 1894, the self-governing colonies of Cape of Good Hope, Transvaal, Natal and Orange River Colony had not been united as the dominion of South Africa until 1910. MCC had last toured South Africa in 1913/14 when England won the five-match Test series by four to nil, due in the main to the bowling of SF Barnes (he took 104 wickets, sixty-four more than anyone else) and JB Hobbs' 1,489 runs, 662 more than the next best.

Kidson's *The History of Transvaal Cricket* gives a snapshot of South Africa at the time: 'The year of 1922 will best be remembered by old South Africans as the unhappy and tumultuous year of the great strike by miners on the Witwatersrand. Johannesburg, in particular, was the centre of upheaval and as the dreadfully cold winter drew to a close and the unrest settled down, the country was mightily relieved when some semblance of normality returned. Rifles, bombs and hand-grenades made way for bat and ball and the memories of hardship and unhappiness on the Reef were soon pushed into the background by the exciting prospect of a tour by the MCC.'

England had taken part in just two Test series since first-class cricket resumed in 1919; both against Australia, the first in 1920/21 which was lost 5-0; the second in 1921, which was lost 3-0. No Test-playing country visited England in 1922 and no major England cricket side had toured overseas the previous winter. The selectors therefore had no way to assess the present form of county players at Test level. Their best guides were thus the Gentlemen v Players match at Lord's in July (the preceding Oval match was unrepresentative and badly rain affected) and of the up-to-date first-class averages. The South African Cricket Association requested that the touring team should include six amateurs. FT Mann, the Middlesex captain, led the Gentlemen at Lord's and was chosen as the touring team's captain. Four other members of that Gentlemen's side were also selected: AW Carr (Nottinghamshire), PGH Fender (Surrey), AER Gilligan (Sussex) and GTS Stevens (Middlesex). Of the eight professionals to be chosen, six represented the Players at Lords: AS Kennedy (Hampshire), WH Livsey (Hampshire), GG Macaulay (Yorkshire), CP Mead (Hampshire), CAG Russell (Essex) and FE Woolley (Kent). VWC Jupp (Northamptonshire Secretary) filled the vacant amateur place, whilst A Sandham (Surrey) and G Brown (Hampshire) filled two remaining professional spots. JB Hobbs, JW Hearne and CH Parkin, the three of whom had been in the Players side, declined invitations. H Sutcliffe also declined.

In mid-September eleven of the selected team played in the Scarborough Festival against a strong CI Thornton's XI. Arthur Carr, batting at number four, made the most runs for the side, the only batsman to reach 50. The report comments, 'Although eight of the batsmen reached double figures, no one obtained a real mastery over the bowling except AW Carr.' He scored 73.

The third and final day of the game was washed out; there immediately followed the four-day showcase match of the summer, Champion County v The Rest at The Oval. Four of the South African tour party played for The Rest, among them Carr. He was dismissed by the amateur Rockley Wilson without scoring. Wilson, a master at Winchester, was a talented spinner, whose county cricket was generally confined to August – he had toured Australia with the 1920/21 side, but achieved little success.

Mead and Woolley were the only members of the present party who had taken part in the 1913/14 tour. Neither had been particularly productive. The only other member to have experience of South African conditions was Kennedy, who had acted as a coach there. The principal problem anticipated, especially for the batsmen, was the use of matting wickets. Aubrey Faulkner, the South African who had spent a season before the war in Nottingham club cricket, wrote a piece in the *Westminster Gazette* detailing the prospects for the tour and the individual players. In a long article, during which he underlines the difficulties of matting wickets, he comments: 'Of the hitters, I like AW Carr's chances the best. The others perhaps are just a little too uncertain to be really successful. I think that they will find that the ball pops too much.'

Faulkner was perhaps more familiar with Carr's batting than with the other 'dashers'. The team gathered together at Waterloo Station on 20 October in order to catch the boat-train to Southampton. As well as the players, Mann, Carr and Gilligan were accompanied by their wives, whilst Woolley brought his family. The team boarded the Union-Castle liner *Walmer Castle*. Carr doesn't mention the time spent on ship, either going or returning. He seems not to have been very successful during the numerous on-board games and competitions, though Ivy Carr did gain one prize, although she failed to win the odd horse racing game devised by Fender with the ladies as 'jockeys' – the one sport at which she ought to have excelled! However, despite Arthur's enthusiasm of everything related to horses, Ivy took little interest in either riding to hounds, or following racing.

Docking in Cape Town, the team went to stay at the Grand Hotel. It had been arranged that Frank Bond, Western Province Secretary, would act as the tour manager, he joined the team at their hotel and became acquainted with the individual players. A souvenir brochure was published by the Cape Times.

The author ID Difford provided pen-pictures of the tourists. In his piece on Carr he writes: 'Mr Carr is a dashing batsman and splendid field, especially in the country. He has increased in skill rapidly and during the past English season came right to the front rank, in fact he and Messrs Mann and Fender are the most dashing amateur batsmen in England and bigger hitters and faster scorers than Hobbs and Woolley.'

The first game took place in Cape Town and both this and the second match provided easy victories for the tourists. Carr played in both but did not shine. He reached 50 for the first time in the third match (at Port Elizabeth against Eastern Province). His runs came in eighty minutes including seven fours with some powerful driving and square cuts – the innings however was not without its flaws. Carr was destined to take part in all the twenty-two fixtures, as did the captain, Frank Mann.

It cannot be said that Carr's style of batting flourished through the rest of the tour. He played useful, at times vital, innings, but did not come off as had been expected. Without a doubt the captain included Carr in every match due to his unbounding enthusiasm and his willingness to undertake whatever role the captain required. In a minor match at Queenstown on 30 November, Livsey seriously damaged his hand. Carr volunteered to take over behind the stumps and performed well enough to be retained as keeper in the more important game at Kimberley against Griqualand West. However he cost the side 37 byes in the match and Brown, who had kept for Hampshire occasionally, was given the role until the wired-for replacement arrived from England. In his own notes regarding the tour, Carr does have one moan about a game in Johannesburg when, on a boiling hot day, he was asked to field on the long leg boundary at both ends, thereby involving a long dash the entire length of the ground at the end of each over .

In view of what would unfold a decade later, the comments on the Johannesburg match against Transvaal deserve
a mention: 'The match marked the introduction to South
Africa of what became known as "Leg Theory" bowling. The
MCC bowler to figure most prominently here was VWC Jupp,
who used the form of attack throughout his bowling spells.
All his deliveries were directed at the leg-stump with four and
sometimes five fielders close in on the leg side, two behind
the popping crease and three in front. It slowed down the rate
of scoring, preventing the batsmen from displaying their full
repertoire of strokes and creating a dull and uninteresting spectacle for spectators.'

In 1933 Jupp would be one of three people, Carr and Jardine being the other two, who voted against banning leg theory
bowling – although Jupp was not the captain at Northamptonshire, he attended the meeting as Secretary since the captain
was unavailable. Vallance Jupp had a most unusual cricket career, starting as a professional with Sussex in 1911. After war
service he turned amateur and won a Test cap for England in
1921. Offered the post of Northamptonshire CCC Secretary
in 1922, he missed Championship cricket for the two seasons
of 1922 and 1923, qualifying for his new county in 1924 and
was therefore in limbo during the 1922/23 tour. An outstanding all-rounder, he performed the 'double' ten times.

The first Test, also at Johannesburg, followed the Transvaal
game. South Africa won by 168 runs; no England batsman
reached fifty. In fact Carr's aggregate total of 54 (27 and 27)
was higher than any of his colleagues. Blanckenburg , whose
right-arm medium-pace deliveries were most suited to matting wickets, took a total of nine wickets and was the home
country's most successful bowler. He was to visit England in
1924 but found it much more difficult to baffle Test quality
batsmen on grass.

From Johannesburg the tourists made the long train journey back to Cape Town for the second Test. Here Carr continued his improvement as a batsman. His innings of 42, though it sounds not too impressive, was England's highest individual score in the first innings. Hall and Blanckenburg took nine of the ten wickets. England won the game by one wicket.

Carr's highest innings in the Test series came at Johannesburg in the fourth Test. *The Sportsman*'s comment was: 'Who could imagine an Old Sherbonian stopping in for 166 minutes on a batsman's wicket in England for 63?' Blanckenburg employed leg theory in an attempt to dislodge Carr and succeeded trapping him leg before. On the final day South Africa required 326 in 270 minutes. Despite a century from Taylor, they only reached 247 for four when time ran out. The fifth and final Test in Durban saw an England victory and they took the rubber two to one.

Carr rated Frank Mann a fine captain. He thought, however, that the hotels in which they stayed were poor and disliked the tedium of the long train journeys. Off the cricket field he found some consolation at the races, both horse and dog. He stated that 'the bookies were good to me', although he doubted if the Jockey Club and the National Greyhound Racing Club would have approved of some of the things that went on in South Africa. Carr received, as did the other amateurs, £100 from MCC to cover expenses, but he reckoned the tour cost him £600.

Carr put his foot in it during a speech he made at a dinner, stating that 'half the South African side would not get into the Nottinghamshire team'. Having said that he went on to bet anyone £50 that Nottinghamshire would beat South Africa the next time the team played at Trent Bridge. Fortunately Nottinghamshire did win – Carr didn't however mention whether anyone took up his bet.

Carr's best friend on the trip was Percy Fender, Surrey captain and all-rounder who, like Carr, had problems with matting pitches. In his autobiography, Carr noted that Percy Fender, whom he always referred to as 'Bill', had a brilliant cricket brain and was the finest captain who never skippered England. Carr was certainly not alone in that opinion. Richard Streeton interviewed Fender in the course of writing the cricketer's biography. Streeton wrote: 'Fender and Carr often practised at the nets together trying to work out their problems, Fender experimenting with different types of delivery and Carr trying to master the ball's steep rise. Fender long believed that Carr would be an even better batsman if he improved his cutting. "Arthur could drive like a team of runaway horses but he couldn't cut and I was always on to him to improve his cutting … Arthur's batting was better built to do this than mine, but he never did learn to cut properly, to my mind."'

Carr in 1923 –
the Notts captain forever on the fringes of the England team

# 8

# THIS YOUNG CAESAR

## 1923-1925

The MCC team sailed from Cape Town on 6 March 1923, arriving in Southampton on 26 March, thence by train to London. Carr had six weeks in which to relax before Nottinghamshire began their 1923 season with a Championship game at Aylestone Road, Leicester, on 6 May. He was just too late to indulge in any serious exercise on the hunting field since the season finished at the end of March. In April his sister Eileen married Jacob Wendell at St George's, Hanover Square. Carr's son, Angus, now nearly six, acted as page boy. The groom was born in New York. His father, also Jacob Wendell, had been a Harvard graduate who later appeared as an actor on Broadway. He died in April 1911. His widow emigrated to England with her four children, Jacob and his brother Reginald, also Katherine and sister Philippa. Eileen Carr had met Jacob Wendell the previous year, when Eileen was to be a bridesmaid at the wedding of Katherine Wendell to Lord Porchester – this wedding took place at St Margaret's, Westminster on 17 July 1922. Lord Porchester was the only son of the Earl and Countess of Carnarvon. As his father's heir, he would inherit the title Earl of Carnarvon in 1923 when his father died suddenly – supposedly the curse of Tutankhamun's tomb being opened was the cause since the Earl financed the exploration which was led by Howard Carter.

Katherine's sister, Philippa, was to marry the twelfth Earl of Galloway in October 1924, although it proved not to be the happiest of partnerships. They had two children, Antonia (b 1925) and Randolph Keith (b 1928), the latter succeeding as the thirteenth Earl in 1978.

Surprisingly it was not until 11 April that, at the Nottinghamshire Committee Meeting, it was agreed to write to Carr to invite him to captain the county side for the coming season. A week earlier, *The Cricketer*, writing on 'County Prospects', had ended its Nottinghamshire preview with, 'AW Carr enjoyed little success on the matting wickets in South Africa, but he is a dangerous batsman here, being a fine straight driver, and, moreover, is an excellent captain, who inspires his side with life and energy.'

The Nottinghamshire side began the summer with one change in the first XI. Garnet Lee had left the staff and would spend two seasons with Langwith Colliery in the Bassetlaw League before qualifying by residence for Derbyshire. The colliery was just over the Nottinghamshire border adjacent to Shirebrook. Lee's place as an opening partner to George Gunn had been taken over by Whysall and Willis Walker now competed for a batting place lower in the order.

The West Indies toured England in 1923 but the Caribbean side was yet to be raised to Test status and so no international games were staged – twenty of the matches they played were rated as first-class, eight others were mainly against minor county sides. In these circumstances the MCC decided to arrange two Test trials in order assess the progress of the best cricketers in preparation for the 1924 Test series against South Africa – MCC did not undertake a Test playing tour in the winter of 1923/24. Indeed, the only English trip of any note was to Canada by the Free Foresters with eight matches played during September 1923.

Carr was selected for both Test trials. In the first, at Old Trafford in June, he captained North against South. Carr made 77, the highest individual innings on either side – the pitch definitely favoured the bowlers. Scored in eighty-five minutes out of 117 runs, it was described as the finest innings of his career to date. In the second, at Lord's in mid-August, Carr captained The Rest against England. Carr scored 42 and 21, both typical innings, but in the first was dismissed by Tate, bowling the best ball of the match – described as floating back in the air from leg and breaking back at lightning speed. The highest team total in this game was only 206, so the bowlers were on top again. The other major game was Gentlemen v Players at Lord's, Carr was Nottinghamshire's sole representative. Batting first, the amateurs scored 451 for nine declared, with Stevens and Lyon hitting hundreds, but as the press commented not much could be read into this batting feast because the Players dropped at least twelve catches; Stevens being particularly lucky. Carr scored 25; Frank Mann captained the Gentlemen, as he did in the same fixtures at The Oval and Scarborough – Carr declined to play at The Oval since the dates clashed with Nottinghamshire playing the West Indies. The Players at Lord's were dismissed for 228; the follow-on was enforced, but the Players took no chances and only one second innings wicket was lost in the three hours play. At the end of the season Carr was not chosen for any matches in the Scarborough Festival.

For the second year Nottinghamshire ended the season as runner up to Yorkshire in the Championship. After the fuss that the press had made when Nottinghamshire were in second place the previous year and that the world would end if the points system was not altered (it wasn't), the editor of *Wisden* made no comment on the 1923 results. Sydney Pardon was considered *the* authority on most cricket matters, but it is worthy of note that his editorial remarks for 1923 contain the statement 'watching matches day after day at Lord's or The Oval, but nowhere else [in 1923]' which does rather suggest that the long-imagined bias in favour of metropolitan cricket and cricketers was not imagined after all!

The Nottinghamshire batting was very strong in 1923 with six of the regulars averaging over 30, four of them in the top thirty in the season's first-class averages – Carr just missed out. The surprise of the summer was the improvement in Frank Matthews' bowling. He topped the Championship bowling with 115 wickets at 15.30 each and came fifth in the overall bowling table. His reign at the top would be a brief one.

The most dramatic game of the year was at Headingley where Nottinghamshire beat Yorkshire by three runs. Yorkshire, with five wickets in hand, required 29 for victory, but the spinners Len Richmond and Sam Staples diddled out the lower order. It proved to be Yorkshire's only defeat, whereas Nottinghamshire lost, in all, three times. *The Observer* commented: 'Carr is AO Jones all over again – but with a dash of MacLaren's faith in himself. Surely Lord's will make note of this young Caesar – a man apparently fashioned by nature from his boyhood to lead English cricketers to victory; to attack the bowling of the antagonists of England; to stand on guard in the slips for England, even as MacLaren did, there to thrill us by his swift and lovely actions and to walk, at the over's end, across the wicket, eyes on the grass, thinking of new ways whereby to confound our enemies. We have no cricketer today that looks more moulded than Carr.'

The first Test trial, with Carr as one of the captains, took place eighteen days after this Yorkshire match. The return against Yorkshire, which might have had a crucial bearing on the title, was drawn due to rain.

Carr's highest innings of the season was 165 against Kent at Trent Bridge, during which he and Payton added 323 for the fourth wicket in just over four hours. Carr was dropped four times, but Payton never made a mistake. In contrast, Carr's 106 not out in the preceding home game against Northamptonshire was described as 'brilliant'. It was in this match that Matthews created a new Nottinghamshire record for the most wickets in a match, his figures were 30-6-89-17 – Northamptonshire were all out for 77 and 116. It should be admitted that Northamptonshire were dreadfully weak – even more so than usual.

During the 1923 summer Carr had the first of his rather too many road accidents, and there must have been many minor scrapes that went unnoticed by the press. This specific one meant that he missed a day's play. The team were playing Worcestershire at Stourbridge, the game having a Saturday start. On the first evening he was motoring to Malvern to spend the weekend with his sister-in-law at Upper Welland. He crashed the car at Wychbold. The damage was so serious that the vehicle was a write off and he missed Monday's play. Carr turned up on Tuesday morning with the Nottinghamshire total 119 for six, Payton 28 not out, Sam Staples' wicket having fallen with the last ball of Monday's action. Carr went straight in to bat, hit a six and a four, but was caught in the deep for 14. Nottinghamshire dismissed Worcester on the final afternoon in 42.4 overs and won the game by 191 runs. No mention of Carr's motoring accident appears in the Nottinghamshire CCC minutes, but one curious item regarding Carr is mentioned earlier in the season: 'It was decided that the sashes ordered by Mr Carr for the use of the team should be paid for by the Club.'

Carr's two hundreds at Trent Bridge against Kent and Northamptonshire were mirrored by his other two – against Kent at Dover and Northamptonshire at Northampton. Of the two, the Kent one was the finer with just one dropped catch.

From the end of the war, Carr and his family had shuttled between his father's Mayfair home and the Stevensons' home in Upper Welland. In 1924, a legacy enabled the Carrs to purchase a house of their own for the first time. Ivy's father, Charles Edward Borton, had died in Horley, Surrey, on 23 March 1924, leaving effects worth £15,417.3s.2d and Ivy was naturally among the beneficiaries. Carr, or more probably Ivy, chose 'Amberdene' – a pleasant Edwardian dwelling in the rural village of Walton-on-the-Hill adjacent to Walton Heath Golf Course in Surrey. The house cost £4,000. Charles Borton is recalled by the family today for one remark: 'Women and cows should never run!' This developed over the years into something of a family joke.

A hundred yards away from Carr's new home was the house built for Lloyd George when he was Chancellor of the Exchequer; in 1912 it was fire bombed by suffragettes. It is believed that one of the perpetrators was Emily Davison who, four months later, ran in front of the King's horse during the Derby at Epsom, some three miles from Walton. The Carrs bought the house from the family of Dr Haslip who, whilst at that address, had been Treasurer of the British Medical Association. It was not very far from Arthur Carr's birthplace at Mickleham.

After two successive no-Test-match summers, the South Africans toured England in 1924. Following his experience in South Africa, Carr was no doubt hopeful of selection for England. Indeed, with Frank Mann and Carr having been picked as captains of representative sides in 1923 and Mann being totally out of form in 1924 – his Championship batting average was little more than half Carr's – it would not seem beyond Carr's aspirations to be invited to succeed Mann as England's skipper in the forthcoming Test series against South Africa.

'Looker-on', in his prospects for Nottinghamshire 1924 season noted: 'The County will again have the services of AW Carr as captain and, on his form in the last two seasons, it is confidently expected that he will gain a place in the Test team.' Looker-on's optimism was soon to be dashed.

The Nottinghamshire programme began with two Championship matches and then a game against the tourists. In the first match, Saturday's play was reduced to thirty minutes, the wicket being unfit. On Monday Sussex were dismissed for 191 and Nottinghamshire reached 79 for five, Carr not out 43. Rain washed out the last day. The second match, against Warwickshire at Edgbaston, was totally washed out. The South Africans arrived at Trent Bridge on 14 May. This was Carr's opportunity to demonstrate his ability on grass wickets against the bowlers who had got the better of him on matting. He was dismissed without scoring in the first innings and made 15 in the second. John Gunn was the county's star batsman, scoring 89 not out in the second innings and giving Nottinghamshire a victory by three wickets; Carr may not have scored many runs, but he won that bet he had made whilst in South Africa.

A fortnight later the Test trial was staged at Trent Bridge. Carr was invited to captain The Rest against England. He was dismissed by 'Bill' Fender – the bowler against whom he'd spent hours practising in the nets in South Africa – for a single. Percy Chapman scored 64 not out for The Rest and was the only player in The Rest side who appeared in the England Test team for the initial match fifteen days later. In fact, by some selectorial quirk, the Test team had been chosen before the Test trial was staged! Chapman was not in the eleven picked, but Jack Hearne, who was, injured a finger in the trial and Chapman's innings won him the vacant spot. It was a place Carr could have had – he failed at the crucial moment.

Arthur Gilligan had already been picked as England's captain in the forthcoming Test and was therefore captain of England in the Test trial. Gilligan was also a year younger than Carr, but had only been appointed Sussex captain in 1922, so Carr had three years more experience as a county captain. Gilligan led England in four of the five Tests against South Africa (missing the fourth Test through injury) and went straight on to lead the touring side to Australia the following winter. For the fourth Test, when perhaps Carr hoped to fill Gilligan's place, the selectors played safe and back-tracked to Johnny Douglas, who had last led England in the second Test at Lord's in 1921. As for Chapman, he failed in the Test and was not chosen for any of the remaining four games.

Carr's final opportunity to prove his worth came in the Gentlemen v Players match at Lord's but he failed once more. By contrast, in county matches Carr flourished; in the overall first-class averages for the season, of those who scored 1,000 runs he came seventeenth, higher than any other Nottinghamshire player except for Whysall.

Carr's best century of the five he hit for Nottinghamshire in 1924 was possibly 112 not out against Surrey in the Whitsun match when 12,000 attended Monday's play. In Surrey's innings Abel began walking to the pavilion after being caught in the deep field, but Carr saw the fielder was over the boundary when the catch was taken and called Abel to return, a typical gesture. Carr's highest innings was also against one of the stronger counties, Middlesex (who were runners up to Yorkshire). He made 134, adding 196 for the third wicket with John Gunn, at which point Gunn had to retire with a strained leg. Nottinghamshire lost the game by 27 runs because their batting collapsed in the second innings, Gubby Allen taking six for 31. GOB Allen was in his first year in the Cambridge University side and had only made his Middlesex debut in 1921, it was not yet realised that he would become the power behind English cricket. For many years he was to live in one of the houses backing onto Lord's.

It was probably in this season and the two or three preceding ones that Carr made a habit, on the first and second evening of a home match, of calling on John Gunn after his evening meal. *The Trent Bridge Battery* (a biography of the Gunn family) tells the following tale: 'Arriving at Holme Road, he [Carr] would throw stones at the bedroom window where John and Grace had invariably retired to bed. "Not that bugger again", John would groan. Meanwhile Eric [John's son] would have been summoned by Carr to help him in with the cases of beer. Carr regularly selected the easy-going John as his late night drinking companion. So poor John would struggle into his clothes, mutter and curse his way downstairs, and keep Carr company until all the beer had been consumed, which often took until three o'clock in the morning.'

Holme Road, Gunn's residence, was less than half a mile from the Trent Bridge Ground, a useful stopping point since Carr would not move back to Nottinghamshire until the late 1920s. His usual residence when playing matches at Trent Bridge was the Victoria Station Hotel. Built at the turn of the century, it was the most modern hotel in the town. In the circumstances therefore it was hardly surprising that he liked to spend the evening in the company of cricketers, as he did for away matches. Most of the Nottinghamshire players lived, perhaps fortunately for them, in towns and villages outside Nottingham. John Gunn left Trent Bridge as a player at the close of the 1925 season – exactly thirty seasons after he played his first game for the county.

Nottinghamshire finished seventh in the 1924 Championship table, a great disappointment. The star of 1923, Matthews, failed to maintain his form and was dropped from the side. Towards the end of August, the leading bowler for Nottinghamshire Second XI in the Minor Counties competition was given his first outing for the senior side in the County Championship – a young collier named Harold Larwood. He took just one wicket but was quickly to become an integral part of Carr's side and Carr would evolve into being an integral part of the Larwood family life.

The prize for which the leading county cricketers craved in 1924 was not so much a place in the home series against South Africa, but a place on the MCC tour to Australia during the coming winter. Carr had been on the trip to South Africa in 1922/23, but in hindsight perhaps he would have been better off on the second 1922/23 tour to Australia? His rival for a vacant batting spot was Percy Chapman. Chapman's first-class batting record in 1924 was not as good as Carr's, but Chapman's admirers plugged the point that Chapman had had much batting success in Australia on mainly turf pitches, as against the matting ones of South Africa. Be that as it may, Chapman got the nod and Carr stayed at home. Chapman was to achieve little in the 1924/25 Test series, indeed so little that he was omitted for the final Test.

Nottinghamshire's sole representative during that trip was Whysall, whose Test average finished better than Chapman's. The captaincy went to Arthur Gilligan. Australia won four of the five Tests, all-rounder Gilligan failed both with bat (average 9.14) and ball (average 51.90). Gilligan had been hit over the heart whilst batting in the Gentlemen v Players game during the 1924 English summer and never really recovered his form after that accident. *Wisden*'s report credits him with being 'a popular captain'. Carr describes Gilligan's captaincy as of 'the easy-going smiling sort' in his book. MA Noble's *Gilligan's Men* puts the matter from an Australian's viewpoint: 'The importance of sending the right type of man in charge of a team, therefore, is tremendous. No doubt Gilligan's ability as a cricketer and his capacity for leadership were questioned at time – Australians would sooner lose a match than give up their prerogative as critics – but his natural qualifications socially, his tactful speeches, and the soundness of his administration won more adherents to the Empire's cause than the winning of a hundred test matches could have done.' If the MCC agreed with Noble's sentiments, Carr's chances of leading England to Australia, or any other Test playing country, would be remote indeed!

How Carr occupied his time during the winter of 1924/25 whilst England lost in Australia is not known. He must have played golf on the course bordering his new home and found a local hunt where he could get in some riding. He lived within easy distance of London, but as he commented in his autobiography, he had little interest in the theatre. There were a number of racecourses within striking distance and with his penchant for betting undoubtedly he would have frequented those.

In October 1924, the Nottinghamshire Committee approved the annual payment of talent money for individual players; the sums were proposed by Carr as captain then debated in Committee. The only adjustment the Committee made was to the sum for the wicketkeeper, Tom Oates, who received an extra £4. Whysall received the most with £29.10.0d – no one else was awarded more than £20. The Committee did state that the captain should be provided with a marks book. During AO Jones' captaincy, a points system for outstanding individual feats in each match had been used and the talent money reflected the total points obtained by each player at the season's close. The minute book does not explain how Carr arrived at the sums of money he judged should be given to each player.

Carr mentioned the question of talent money in his autobiography and explained: 'One of the most ticklish jobs that a county captain has to do, especially a captain situated as I was for Nottinghamshire, is to fix the payments of talent money for good performances. I had a system of "marks" kept in a private little book, each good mark representing five shillings. A good innings – not necessarily a century; sometimes a hard-to-get thirty or forty is more valuable to a team than an easy and

"cheap" hundred – a good bit of bowling – a catch was sometimes worth several marks, in my estimation.' It is impossible
to tell now whether the little book Carr kept was introduced
following the Committee meeting, or whether Carr did not
share his system with the Committee. Carr did not attend the
meeting – his attendance at these meetings was sporadic.

The first Championship match of 1925 was at Trent Bridge
against Hampshire on 6, 7 and 8 May. Carr attended the Committee meeting on 1 May when the thirteen players for that
match were chosen, with Carr to decide which two players to
omit. Neville Cardus in the *Manchester Guardian* of 11 April
1925 commented under the heading 'The Coming Season':
'There is no hiding the fact that something of a cloud hangs
over the coming season. Further evidence of our inferiority to
Australia having been afforded, it is impossible to feel happy
about English cricket.'

No Test-playing country toured England in 1925, the last
English season during which no major cricketing country
toured. The MCC had arranged for a tour to West Indies in
1925/26, but West Indies were not yet playing Tests and it was
not intended to send out England's premier team. The press
were already discussing the question of the England captaincy
for the 1926 series against Australia during the first months of
the 1925 season. In the course of the newspaper comments,
Lord Hawke made his infamous observation that a professional was 'constitutionally incapable of captaining a side in the
proper spirit'. The remark had been provoked by criticism of
the captaincy of England by both Frank Mann in South Africa
and Arthur Gilligan in Australia. Jack Hobbs was suggested in
some quarters as the best person to lead England.

The thought that Arthur Carr was the most suitable man to
lead England in the 1926 Ashes series gradually built up steam
through 1925 and his exceptional form with the bat could do
nothing but enhance his reputation. On 6 September 1925,

with the Championship competition complete, Cardus wrote: 'If we now try to balance up our prospective resources as compared with what they were in 1921, we shall certainly find a good deal to encourage us. In the first place, it seems eminently likely that in Mr Carr we shall find our captain readymade, a captain, moreover, worth his place as a batsman and a fielder alone, particular as his methods are pre-eminently adapted to three-day cricket and calculated to inspire his side with the doctrine that in combat the moral advantage lies with the offensive.'

After a rain-affected Nottinghamshire opening game against Hampshire producing the inevitable draw, the second Nottinghamshire Championship match was against Sussex at Trent Bridge. In Gilligan and Tate Sussex possessed two of England's Test bowlers and in general bowlers dominated the match. The highest innings by a batsman on either side was 39 (by George Gunn), save for Carr. *Wisden* reported: 'As usual Carr drove very hard and often jumped in to the pitch of the ball, a characteristic of his vigorous play that at last cost him his wicket.' Carr scored 104 in 110 minutes with ten fours and five sixes, one of which went over the secretary's office and landed somewhere near what today is the ticket office entrance adjacent to the Dixon gate – a very long hit from the Radcliffe Road End of the ground. Nottinghamshire won by an innings and 25 runs. Quite unusually, the Nottinghamshire Minute Book contained the note: 'Hearty congratulations were extended to Mr AW Carr upon his splendid innings of 104.'

Carr capped that innings with a score of 206, his personal best, against Leicestershire in early June – the innings won plaudits from all quarters, but with the opposition being not of the strongest, the match that really mattered was the next Championship fixture at Bramall Lane. Both Yorkshire and Nottinghamshire were unbeaten to date. The mere fact that 23,000 spectators attended should be enough to demonstrate the game's importance. The pitch was all in favour for the bowlers and by the close of the first day eighteen wickets had gone down, Carr's 29 being the highest score. On the second day Yorkshire gained a first innings lead of 18. Nottinghamshire made 165 in their second knock, Carr's 40 again the highest individual contribution. Yorkshire won on the second afternoon by five wickets – Carr did his best – three of the five wickets that fell were the result of slip catches by Carr!

The Yorkshire reverse was one of only three defeats during the summer; on the credit side the county claimed fifteen victories and ended the season in fourth place. Yorkshire took the title. In view of some misguided current thinking, it is worth quoting a line in the *Wisden* review of Yorkshire's season: 'In securing the Championship for the fourth year in succession Yorkshire equalled the record of Nottinghamshire, who gained that honour in the four seasons beginning 1883 and ending in 1886.'

The most promising development in the Nottinghamshire cricket during the summer was the emergence of Harold Larwood – from his single game in 1924, in 1925 he made twenty appearances, taking 73 wickets and overshadowing Frank Matthews as Fred Barratt's bowling partner – Barratt took 94 wickets, Matthews 37, at a much higher average than either Larwood or Barratt. John Gunn faded from the side, Willis Walker moving into his place as first wicket down. Larwood, born in November 1904, came from the mining village of Nuncargate, where he was a near neighbour of Joe Hardstaff. Hardstaff initially recommended him to Nottinghamshire, Iremonger was to realise his potential. There was a change of wicketkeeper as Tom Oates had finally retired; Lilley kept wicket in twenty-four of the twenty-five matches.

In all Carr hit seven Championship scores of 100 or more, but of perhaps more importance to his England prospects were his scores in representative matches. No Test trials were arranged, the major match was therefore Gentlemen v Players at Lord's. Carr was selected as captain of the amateurs and the match was drawn. GTS Stevens and Hobbs took the batting prizes for their innings, but Carr did his cause no harm with an innings of 82 hit in eighty-five minutes, 'He is the most determined and enterprising batsman, and absolutely declines to allow a bowler to bowl to him without a man in the country; even with Hendren stationed at long-on he drove Tate on several occasions to the ring and there has seldom been a more determined or attractive innings in this match,' so opined Pelham Warner. Carr hit a hundred in the Gentlemen v Players match at Scarborough to round of a summer in which he hit 2,338 runs, average 51.95 – of the amateurs who realised 1,000 runs, the next best was Perrin, averaging 37.88.

In the course of a summary of the season, the *Manchester Guardian* devoted more than 1,000 words to Carr, including: 'Arthur Carr has not only developed into one of the best captains in the country, but as a forcing bat he has no equal. Not even Gilbert Jessop drove with the precision and tremendous power which characterised the dazzling displays of the Nottinghamshire captain when thoroughly well set, and no cricketer of modern times has attacked the bowling with such hostility. Moreover the Nottinghamshire captain, time and again, has extricated his side from a position of some danger by his aggressive hitting and much of the team's success has been due to his indomitable pluck and enterprise ... it will indeed be a matter for surprise if he is not chosen to lead England against Australia next year. Who is there more fitted for the task?'

The winter of 1925/26 was a busy one for Nottinghamshire County Cricket Club. Two new concrete stands were in course of erection which, it was estimated, would increase the capacity by about 5,000 – 21,000 had attended the first day of the 1921 Australian Test. The main talking point in the national press continued to be the question of the England captaincy.

By January the three main contenders seemed to be Gilligan, Fender and Carr, though Gilligan's bowling had not been seen very often in 1925 and on doctor's orders he rested for a month in mid-season due to the injury he had received in 1924.

Fender was considered by the Australian press as the best man to lead his country, but the press in England appeared to prefer Carr: 'One can think of no quality required by a captain that Mr Carr does not possess. He has the personality which all may respect. He is young enough to have the grit to take risks – chances would perhaps be a better word – and to take his decisions quickly. The mantle of the late Mr AO Jones rests on his successor's shoulders. Mr Carr is fearless and has mastered the science of cricket. He is quick to weigh up a situation, to act and perhaps alter the whole course of a match. But beyond all these qualifications Mr Carr is a magnificent batsman – England's leading amateur batsman. A captain's influence is very much enhanced when he can take an indispensable place either in the batting list or the bowling forces. His worth is two-fold at least – leader and player. Mr Carr is also safe in the field and has his brilliant periods.'

A commemorative postcard for the third Ashes Test gives Carr
pride of place as captain – it was also Larwood's debut

# 9

# ENGLAND'S CAPTAIN

## 1926

The press seemed almost as interested in the selection of the Test selectors themselves as in the picking of the England XI in 1926. There was much newspaper talk before the five were chosen on 22 April: PF Warner (chairman), AER Gilligan, PA Perrin, W Rhodes and JB Hobbs. The last two were the most illustrious of the present-day professionals. Wilfred Rhodes, the Yorkshire all-rounder, had played for his county since 1898 and England since 1899. His career for both would end in 1930, by which time he acquired more first-class wickets than any player before or since. Jack Hobbs was England's premier batsman. He had played for Surrey since 1905 and with Herbert Sutcliffe of Yorkshire formed England's pair of opening batsmen. He retired from Test cricket in 1930 and first-class cricket in 1934, by which time he had compiled more first-class runs than any batsman before or since. Percy Perrin's county career with Essex spanned thirty-three seasons. He was a sound middle-order batsman, but the only one of the five selectors not to play in Test cricket – in 1939 he was to become the Chairman of Selectors. Pelham Warner was currently a well-known sports journalist, but had been captain of both Middlesex and England. He was later to become the Grand Old Man of English cricket.

The selectors were to be joined by the captain in due course. On 12 May, PF Warner announced that AW Carr had been appointed England captain. Another aspect of Carr's ability was related in the press on 23 May: 'Like all Nottinghamshire's captains he has never had much amateur help. Month after month he has travelled about with ten professionals and in doing so has come to understand the life of a professional cricketer as few men in England could. To see him lead Nottinghamshire into the field is to appreciate that here is a man who can identify himself with the feelings of the men whose living the game is, a man who is instinctively at his ease with them, friendly, almost, one might say, familiar, yet without surrendering for an instant the proper prestige of his position. It is no secret that last season several of the leading professionals openly said that, if picked this year for the Tests, they hoped to find themselves playing under Mr Carr.'

In early May, before the England captaincy question was resolved, the Nottinghamshire Committee carried a rather odd item to today's reader in the minutes of the meeting on 3 May: 'It was reported that Mr AW Carr had been invited to play for MCC against the Australians on May 15, 17 and 18. The Committee expressed the hope that he would accept.'

The match could hardly be called a precursor to the first Test as no fewer than eight amateurs were picked. The weather ruined the game; Carr scored 5 and 34, whilst the Australians made mincemeat of the MCC attack. The Nottinghamshire Committee held three meetings after Carr had been announced as England captain, but not until the third did any mention of this honour get a mention: 'The hearty congratulations of the Committee were accorded Mr AW Carr upon his appointment as Captain of England.'

Carr had an immediate response to Warner's letter inviting him to be captain. He went off and bought a brand new green car, crashing it into the back of a lorry on the way to Trent Bridge. Carr then tells that in August, when the Surrey match at The Oval ended, he drove the same vehicle, accompanied by Whysall, Barratt and Sam Staples, from London to Hastings, the venue where Nottinghamshire would meet Sussex the following day. He crashed into a telegraph pole as he 'mistook' the road. Later on that year, Carr wrote, the car then skidded and overturned! He wasn't very keen on the colour green.

The team chosen for Carr's first Test match to be staged on his home ground read: Hobbs, Sutcliffe, Woolley, Hearne, Hendren, Chapman, Kilner, Carr, Tate, Strudwick and Root. The twelfth man was Sandham and Holmes was pencilled in as a possible replacement for Sutcliffe, who was unfit when the side was selected. It was Worcestershire bowler Root's Test debut, all the others had previously represented England.

There is a general notion that detailed tactics are a post-war development, but Root in his autobiography *A Cricketer's Lot* discusses his Test debut and Carr's approach to him: 'The ordeal of the international is great. Apart altogether from cricket ability there is the psychological side to be considered. The scheming and tactics which are discussed before going on to the field are apt to have a very big bearing on the new-comer to Tests. All the strong points of opponents are emphasized, all the weaknesses pointed out. As the engineer's draughtsman supplies blue prints to the erector of machinery or bridges and such-like structures, so does the cricket intelligence department try to make Test cricketers familiar with their business by written and diagrammed plans to be studied before the match commences. Previous to playing my first Test game, AW Carr gave me pages of written instructions about our Australian opponents to go through. It proved to be remarkably accurate.'

Test matches in England were still of three-day duration and began on a Saturday. Trent Bridge was almost full (estimated crowd of 18,000) when Carr and Woodfull came out to toss. Carr won the call, the rain then came. Shortly before 12 o'clock the shower had passed and England went in to bat. The light was indifferent and, to accommodate more spectators, the ground was devoid of sight-screens; on the other hand the slippery turf did not help the bowlers. England reached 32 without loss off 17.2 overs in fifty minutes when a sudden downpour stopped Macartney in the middle of his over. At 5.45 the captains went out to inspect the conditions and were unable to agree whether or not play could restart. The umpires were asked and ruled the ground unfit. Rain on both Monday and Tuesday prevented any further progress (ironically Sunday was fine). The unsatisfactory conclusion to Carr's biggest game was surely the most disappointing episode in his life.

Nottinghamshire opposed Yorkshire at Headingley on the same dates as the first Test – in this vital match Nottinghamshire were captained by RHT Turner – and not a ball was bowled. Carr rejoined Nottinghamshire for the match at Northampton on a bowler's pitch. Not a single fifty was made and Sam Staples spun Nottinghamshire to victory. A Committee meeting prior to these two games contains one or two comments relating to the political situation, 'Owing to railway difficulties it was decided to engage a private bus for the whole of the tour'. A fortnight later, a minute read: 'A letter was read from R Clegg asking that a cricket match should be arranged in aid of miners' wives and children. The Committee very much regretted that they could not take the responsibility of organising the match.' The general strike had collapsed but the miners' strike was destined to drag on.

For the second Test at Lord's a fortnight later the selectors picked the same eleven as at Trent Bridge, save that Holmes took Hearne's place, but added Harold Larwood's name. Macaulay was listed as twelfth man. On the morning of the game, Holmes was omitted and therefore Larwood made his Test debut. Larwood had taken 43 wickets for Nottinghamshire at the time of his selection and was in brilliant form. The match, blessed by fine weather, was a high-scoring draw. There was some criticism of Carr's field placing on the first day, but the Nottingham press disagreed vehemently: 'Mr Carr's critic, Balaamlike, has blessed where he was expected to curse, and the captain fully deserves the supreme compliment involved in the misstatement of facts. Mr Carr not only placed his men wisely; he also set them an excellent example of diligent efficiency. It is a nice question whether he or Hendren, when their turn comes to bat, will go in credited with the larger number of runs saved.'

Australia were dismissed for 383. At lunch on the third day, England were 475 for three, Hobbs made 119, Hendren was not out 127. Carr then caused more groans from the London press by declaring. The Nottingham scribes would have none of it: 'At the luncheon interval Mr Carr declared the innings closed. He has now played twice for England without getting an innings himself. But his action was as wise as unselfish. By it he saved ten minutes possibly precious time.'

The match was also drawn. For the third Test, scheduled for Headingley starting on 10 July, the home selectors decided on a squad of fourteen players: Carr, Chapman, Hobbs, Woolley, Sutcliffe, Tate, Hendren, Root, Larwood, Strudwick, Kilner, Macaulay, Parker and Geary. Larwood, Parker and Root were omitted from the final eleven.

Carr won the toss and decided to put Australia in. The decision split the press. Approving of Carr's decision were Frank Mitchell, BJT Bosanquet, HDG Leveson Gower, 'The Adjutant' (*Daily Dispatch*), Philip Trevor and GA Faulkner. Against Carr were Frank Thorogood, Robin Bailey, HC Littleworth, GL Jessop and 'Throw In' (*Daily Express*). PF Warner and HJ

Henley hedged their bets. Added to the mix was the decision not to use the pitch lovingly prepared for the match, but switch to another strip. Carr inspected the original pitch accompanied by the groundsman, Leyland, and Sutcliffe; presumably he took their advice into account prior to his decision.

A controversial piece of captaincy should have been echoed by a sensational opening over. Tate opened and dismissed Bardsley first ball. With his fifth ball Macartney should have gone, but was dropped by Carr at second slip. Macartney went on to score 151 and Australia closed the day at 366 for three. After only three wickets on Saturday, fifteen fell on Monday. Australia's remaining seven added just 128 runs, and England ended the day 203 for eight. Carr was trapped leg before for 13. Despite a valiant ninth wicket stand of 108 by Macaulay and Geary, England were invited to follow on. Hobbs and Sutcliffe removed any danger of defeat with an opening partnership worth 156 and the match gently meandered to a draw.

On the day after the Leeds Test came Gentlemen v Players at Lord's. Carr naturally captained the Gentlemen. Judging by the press report at the start of this historic contest, the public were not evenly divided by Carr's decision at Headingley. The report on the first day begins: 'Mr Arthur Carr during the past week may occasionally have prayed to be delivered from his friends: sympathetic quotation of the familiar lines about the best laid schemes of mice and men are apt to pall. But he has some cause to be grateful to his enemies. The reception accorded to him when he went in to take his innings in Gentlemen v Players match at Lord's is only paralleled by that which greeted Mr Warner when he made his first appearance on that ground after winning a rubber of Test Matches in Australia. It was obviously a gesture of dissent from the unseemly and ill-informed attacks to which Mr Carr and the three original members of the selection committee had been subjected. The suggestion that Mr Warner, Mr Gilligan and Mr Perrin, when they invited Mr Carr to captain England, were actuated by any other motive than the desire to find the best man for the job is particularly outrageous.' The Lord's match was a run feast: Players 579, Gentlemen 542; centuries for Hobbs, Sutcliffe, Ernest Tyldesley and Chapman; Carr scored a brisk 45.

Two days prior to the fourth Test, Carr was stopped by the police for a motoring offence at Mitcham. The press report continued: 'When stopped by PC Williams, Mr Carr stated that he was hurrying to the Test match. His speed was estimated by the police at 22.5 miles per hour. "Mr Carr was a very busy cricketer then, and is to-day," remarked Mr Green, the Automobile Association's solicitor, who defended. Mr Carr was fined 40s, for exceeding the speed limit (10 mph) and 10s for failing to renew his licence which, it was stated, was a month out of date.'

There were changes in the England side for the Old Trafford Test, beginning on 24 July. Tyldesley, in view of his hundred for the Players, was chosen, also returning were Root and GTS Stevens. Chapman, Macaulay and Geary were omitted. The first day in Manchester was even worse than that in Nottingham. Australia decided to bat when play at last began at 2.45. Ten balls were bowled watched by 20,000 spectators, the rain then returned. Australia were 6 without loss.

There followed the usual Sunday break. On Monday morning England went out to continue fielding led by Jack Hobbs; Chapman was fielding in place of Carr. Ugly rumours were afloat. In *Background of Cricket* Sir Home Gordon writes: 'On the Sunday Arthur and his wife, as pretty as she is amusing, Percy Chapman and Colonel Gilbert Hamilton all dined with me. That night Arthur was seized with sharp illness and could take no further part in the match. Hints that he had unwisely exceeded were heard not only in the pavilion but suggested in some sections of the Press. Therefore I wrote a letter, inserted in the *Manchester Guardian* truthfully stating that all he had drunk as my guest was a single glass of champagne.'

Carr wrote in his autobiography that he woke on Monday morning with a temperature and unable to speak. This was reported to Percy Perrin, the Test selector, and it was decided that Hobbs, rather than the other amateur in the side, GTS Stevens, should take over the leadership. Carr was not very complimentary: 'Now I am quite sure that Jack did his best as an emergency captain, but I hope he will not mind my saying that captaincy was never one of his long suits. I have seen him in charge of a side several times and, if I may say so, I thought he was a rotten captain. But then, I am afraid, most pros are not much good at the job.'

Interestingly Hobbs, in *My Life Story*, rather repeats part of Carr's statement: 'Personally I prefer to see an amateur as captain and most professionals prefer it, especially in international cricket, chiefly because of its social side and because of the natural dislike of professionals to boss their own fellows.'

Hobbs continues in his autobiography to mention that after the fourth Test his next big match was a benefit game for him. In recognition of his years of service for Surrey, Hobbs was allowed to select the August bank holiday match against Nottinghamshire. Hobbs says that Carr had promised to play, and play he did, with his neck bandaged and still very hoarse – the illness he contracted in Manchester turned out to be tonsillitis. Surrey won by six wickets; Carr scored 0 and 33, Hobbs 24 and 60.

If the Headingley and the Old Trafford Tests were the cause of too much press gossip and speculation, the run-up to The Oval Test was to outdo both combined. From playing against Surrey at The Oval, Nottinghamshire travelled to Hastings and, as mentioned, Carr managed to crash his green car on the journey. Nottinghamshire won by 77 runs due some outstanding bowling from Larwood, who took six wickets in each innings.

The most remarkable batting however came from Arthur Gilligan (a rival to Carr for the England captaincy). He came in at number six and hit 107 out of 152 in eighty minutes.

It was back to Trent Bridge for the match against Derbyshire beginning on Saturday. Carr won the toss; Nottinghamshire hit 360 all out and by the close Derbyshire were in difficulties being 36 for three. On Saturday night Carr had to travel down to London in order to attend the Test selectors meeting arranged to choose the team for The Oval. Since all four Tests thus far had been drawn, it had been decided that the final game would be played to a definite finish. All six members – Warner (chairman), Carr, Perrin, Gilligan, Rhodes and Hobbs – were present. Unlike the previous match, a straight eleven were picked: Chapman (captain), Stevens, Rhodes, Hobbs, Woolley, Sutcliffe, Hendren, Tate, Geary, Larwood and Brown with Ernest Tyldesley as twelfth man.

Simultaneously with the publication of the team the selectors issued the following statement: 'Mr AW Carr, the England captain, who has not been in good health recently, generously offered to resign his place in the eleven, and after consideration this unselfish action on the part of Mr Carr was accepted by the Selection Committee with the greatest possible regret.'

In his autobiography Carr gives a different version. He wrote that Warner asked him to stand down 'for the sake of England', since he was not fit and not really in form. At least the first of those two reasons is scarcely credible because he'd just played through six days of county cricket and was due to return to Nottingham to play on Monday. In comparison with 1925 Carr's batting form was not as good, but he averaged 33 in Championship matches and could hardly be judged by his single innings of 13 in the Test series so far. Carr says he was 'very much taken aback' by Warner's remarks and withdrew from the meeting. He went on to say that Rhodes and Gilligan wanted him to continue, but the majority were for him to go. What seemingly amazed the press was that Chapman was chosen to replace Carr as captain. Chapman's experience of first-class county cricket amounted to fifteen games for Kent spread over three seasons. Chapman had had three seasons in the Cambridge University side but had not been appointed captain, so his leadership skills in top-class cricket were scarcely tested. It was pointed out in the press that Chapman was the youngest cricketer to captain England (though erroneously, MP Bowden in the England v South Africa match at Cape Town in 1888-89 was younger). The press effectively stated that Wilfred Rhodes had been returned to the England side to be Chapman's 'guide'.

Carr reprints in his book the letter Warner sent to him directly after the Selection Committee meeting: 'My Dear Arthur, I cannot say how deeply I feel for you in what I know is a great disappointment for you. I believe I feel it almost as much as you do; in fact, I can think of nothing else. You have been ill and are not now in your old form, naturally enough after being so seedy – and we were all only too anxious to do the best thing possible for England. It was a horrid and beastly job that we faced this afternoon, and we only tried to do the right thing. Don't take it too hard. Most of us have had great disappointments in cricket, and you giving up your place will give you an even greater hold, if such is possible, on the affections of the cricket world. What you said to me on the telephone about a wireless statement was no more to do with me than with you. You saw and approved of the statement that was issued by the Selection Committee and which will appear in all the newspapers to-morrow. There is no doubt whatever in my own mind that you are the best captain in England – you must know I think that – but you saw what we felt about the composition of the XI. Take it in the grand manner and don't be hurt and angry with me.' The whole episode vanished from the public's mind when Chapman's England proceeded to beat

Australia by 289 runs. Hobbs and Sutcliffe both hit hundreds, Chapman scored 49 and 19.

Chapman could not have foreseen what would happen at the end of the fourth Test four years later when Australia were next in England. That 1930 series was again unresolved, each country had won one and there were two draws, when the first four games had been completed. As the series had progressed there had been mounting criticism of Chapman (who had led England in all four matches) for his faulty field placing and bowling changes. On the other hand the press, as with Carr four years earlier, were divided on the issue as to whether Chapman should be removed for the fifth Test at The Oval – as in 1926, the 1930 final Test was arranged as timeless so a definite conclusion to the rubber could be made. With the press sensing a change prior to the England squad being announced, some papers suggested Carr should return: that would have been the ultimate irony. As it was Bob Wyatt took Chapman's place as leader – unlike Chapman, Wyatt at least captained of his county side, Warwickshire. Wyatt was not as fortunate as Chapman. Australia, aided by a double century from Don Bradman, won the match by an innings. Chapman never captained England again against Australia. He had, however, already been picked to lead the MCC side to South Africa in the winter of 1930/31. South Africa won the first Test and the other four were all drawn. Chapman captained the side for all five matches but had a batting average of 10, scoring just 75 runs in seven innings, and the selectors must have rued the day they chose Chapman for the tour. In 1931, Jardine's reign began.

At a superficial level, Carr and Chapman were similar characters – certainly they had the same muscular christianity schooling, though Chapman was at Uppingham rather than Sherborne and Chapman did survive three years at Cambridge whereas Carr seems to have just briefly visited Oxford. Both players were hard-hitting batsmen and both excellent fielders either close to or in the deep, at least in their younger days. The great difference was that Chapman's character, which would be his undoing, was of the 'hail fellow well met' variety, contrasting with Carr who didn't suffer fools gladly. Both were rather fond of a drink, sadly Chapman couldn't control his fondness and became an alcoholic. His post-war days were something not to be remembered. Seven years younger than Carr, he died two before the Nottinghamshire captain.

Returning to the county scene of 1926, the last game of the summer took place at Old Trafford. Dudley Carew, then a well-known essayist and a cricket watcher who supported Kent, attended the match and wrote a piece on it. This brief extract shows what Carr meant to the ordinary man in the street: 'Then AW Carr came in, and the moment he appeared at the pavilion door, a bare-headed, broad-shouldered, unsmiling figure, the crowd started to cheer him and they went on cheering him until he had reached the wicket and had taken guard ... the reception he got on that Saturday from a Lancashire crowd, madly keen on a Lancashire victory, must have made up for a very great deal. From the very beginning of his innings Carr hit. It does not matter what the state of the game may be, but whenever I see Carr bat I think of Browning's lines: "I was ever a fighter, so one fight more/ The best and the last." That is always it – "the best and the last". The man impresses you like that.'

Nottinghamshire finished fourth in the Championship table, the same position as the preceding summer. Thirteen matches ended in victory as against fifteen in 1925. The review of the county in *Wisden* has a revealing paragraph: 'Although RHT Turner and L Kirk did their best as emergency leaders, nothing on occasion could compensate for the want of Carr's inspiring influence and powers as a forcing batsman. In the field, too, the example of such a captain meant much. Lacking the help of a man capable of saving many runs and of holding any sort of catch, the team lost something of their usual confidence and dash.'

Lionel Kirk was a notable local club cricketer with Forest Amateurs and captained Nottinghamshire Second XI. He was a member of the County Cricket Club Committee from 1923 until his death in 1953. He played just fourteen matches for the county spread over ten seasons beginning in 1920. RHT Turner, who made his cricket reputation whilst at Repton, first played for Nottinghamshire as a schoolboy in 1906. His final game was not until 1927. He was looked upon as a possible Nottinghamshire captain in 1919, but as has been pointed out, could not afford the time for county cricket.

The county's batting line-up was changing very slowly – the first five in the 1926 Championship batting table had all played in pre-war days. Larwood headed the bowling table; Tich Richmond came second and took most wickets, with Sam Staples and Fred Barratt immediately behind. Matthews' star had almost faded away.

Off the cricket field, Arthur Carr's father, now at Hemingford Park, was steadily improving his racing stable, which in 1926 was being looked after by Basil Briscoe, one of the outstanding trainers of the inter-war period. In his reminiscences Briscoe tells how he had been invited over to Hemingford Park to see if he could tame one of Philip Carr's horses, Solanum. The horse had been discarded by a previous trainer who felt it to be a 'rogue'. Briscoe believed Solanum might become one of the best steeplechasers in the country and did indeed enter him in some races where he proved successful. As a result Briscoe took over the training of Philip Carr's horses and in the autumn of 1926 won two races on the same day – Philip Carr's Try, Try Again and Louise Carr's Honey Maker both at Newbury and both with long odds. Arthur, the dutiful son, placed money on both and won handsomely.

A sketch from 1927 when Carr was both former and future
captain of England

# 10

## BACK TO TRENT BRIDGE

### 1927-1928

At the Annual General Meeting of the County Cricket Club held at the Albert Hall Institute on 23 February 1927, the Duke of Portland, as chairman, made a presentation to Mr and Mrs Carr. In doing so, the Duke said that it was only sheer bad luck that prevented Mr Carr from leading the England team to victory, that sportsmen throughout the Empire believed that he did a very right and sportsmanlike thing in placing himself in the hands of the selection committee., his inspiring leadership in the previous matches was largely responsible for bringing about the victory for which they had been longing for so many years. The Chairman went on: 'We recall with pride his great performances in the season of 1925, when he scored more than 2,000 runs, played a three-figure innings on seven occasions, scored 206 against Leicestershire, and captained Nottingham-shire victoriously on six consecutive occasions. We trust he will long be spared to achieve not only many more centuries but to lead an English eleven to many victories. I hope Mr and Mrs Carr will long remember their innumerable friends in the city and county of Nottingham.'

Carr expressed the opinion that what he did for the county was very little. As a side they always went out to win. A captain if he had a chance of victory should be allowed to go out to win, because the policy was not only good from the point of view of match winning, but from the standpoint also of the public, who paid their shillings and deserved to see sport. The captain concluded: 'I have had three ambitions in life. One was to captain England in England; the second was to win a horse race – and as there were four starters and three fell, I have achieved that and the third is to captain the English side to Australia.'

The presentation from the members of the cricket club took the form of a silver bowl on which was inscribed: 'Presented to AW Carr, captain of England v Australia in Test matches 1926: Nottingham June 12th, 14th, 15th; Lord's June 26th, 28th, 29th; Leeds July 10th, 12th, 13th; Manchester July 24th, 26th, 27th, with hearty congratulations of the members of the Nottinghamshire County Cricket Club.'

A second presentation was made by Wilfred Payton, on behalf of the playing staff, of a silver salver and coffee set, Payton stated that Carr had earned the title of a real sport and was liked by every one of the professionals. Carr replied that it was through the professionals he was made captain of England. He knew nothing when he started and they had taught him everything he knew. A better lot of men one could not wish to meet. The salver was inscribed: 'To Mr and Mrs Carr, from the Nottinghamshire Professionals, as an expression of their esteem, 1926.' Mrs Carr was presented with a wrist watch by the members.

In Carr's autobiography he makes the following comment: 'In 1926 they wanted to chuck me out of the captaincy of Nottinghamshire cricket … because, so they said, I was not exactly teetotal and rather too fond of sitting up too late at night.' A search of the Nottinghamshire CCC Minute Book for 1926 failed to find any mention of Carr's drinking problem that year, there is the story printed in 1985 in the *Trent Bridge Battery* to which reference has already been made, but little other positive reports.

Carr's policy on fast bowlers and beer is set out clearly in his book: 'Now this matter of drinking and playing first-class cricket successfully is a ticklish one on which, as an authority in the matter, I shall have more to say presently, but of one thing I am pretty certain in my own mind: all really fast bowlers need beer to help them keep going. You cannot be a great fast bowler on a bottle of ginger-pop or a nice glass of cold water. Your fast bowler is in much the same case as your harvester and your navvy; he uses up an immense amount of physical strength in hard out of doors exercise and he must have something to give him a kick. Beer is best. A pint too much may make him slightly tiddly for a little while, but only a little while.'

The only extant detail which perhaps gives an indication of Carr's fondness for drink is a captain's petty cash expense book which covers the seasons 1929 to 1939. In the seasons 1936 to 1939 when Heane was sole captain, the principal item was 'laundry' with other sundries now and then including 'bar'. In Carr's case 'laundry' still came top, but 'bar' was a clear runner up, but there's no indication of course who actually consumed the liquid, it might not have been alcoholic!

The season of 1927 proved an unsatisfactory one for Carr and had a dramatic and sad finale for Nottinghamshire, which might have been in the county's favour had Carr been present. From a weather point of view the season was considered one of the worst ever in cricketing terms.

One match that escaped the worst of the weather was Len Richmond's benefit game on Julien Cahn's Ground at Loughborough Road, West Bridgford, less than a mile from Trent Bridge. There had been grand opening match the previous season for Cahn's new ground. A Nottinghamshire team had met

Cahn's team, but Carr was absent, playing in the Test trial, so his first appearance at Loughborough Road was to captain Nottinghamshire against Cahn's XV for Richmond's benefit. Larwood played for Nottinghamshire and took five wickets. Most amateurs who appeared for Nottinghamshire between the wars played quite frequently for Cahn's sides at some time, but Carr seems to have appeared on only three occasions – in 1929, 1930 and 1933.

Apart from cricket, Cahn's main sporting interest was fox hunting – it was estimated he spent at least £20,000 a year on cricket and another £20,000 on fox hunting. With their intense interest in these two sports it would seem logical that Cahn and Carr would be at least on the same plane, but though Cahn was the one who proposed Carr when the latter stood for the Nottinghamshire Committee in 1932, Carr rather cold-shouldered Cahn.

Countrywide, twenty-nine County Championship matches in 1927 were restricted by the weather to less than six hours play over the three scheduled days, plus five which were totally washed out. Nottinghamshire ended as runner up to Lancashire, who led the table until mid July, when Nottinghamshire replaced them. Lancashire then resumed the lead, but on 26 August lost to Sussex, allowing Nottinghamshire, who beat Glamorgan at Trent Bridge on the same day, to move ahead. Nottinghamshire had two matches still to play, Lancashire had one remaining. The table was still decided on a percentage basis, some counties played twenty-eight games, at the other extreme some played only twenty. Carr had appeared in every match, before he was taken ill during the Middlesex game at Trent Bridge on 20, 22 and 23 August. A paragraph from the Nottinghamshire Committee Meeting held on August 25 noted: 'Dr Dixon reported that he had been to the Victoria Hotel to see Mr Carr and that he would not be in a fit condition to play again this year owing to his present indisposition from which he had been suffering for some time past. The Secretary was instructed to send a letter expressing the sympathy of the Committee and thanks to him for his valuable services as Captain of the team during the past season especially for carrying on when he was so unwell.'

His ailment was in fact shingles. The press report simply noted that, 'Carr has been confined to his bed at the Victoria Station Hotel on the second day of the Middlesex match at Trent Bridge (August 22).'

As it happened there was no play on either the first or second days of this match. A token 150 minutes was played on the third day, during which Middlesex scored 164 for no wicket. On the next three days Nottinghamshire under Lionel Kirk beat, as noted, Glamorgan at Trent Bridge by 122 runs. There followed the final two matches, both away from home, with Nottinghamshire led by Kirk. Nottinghamshire beat Derbyshire at Ilkeston by nine wickets, and all that was now needed was to avoid defeat against Glamorgan at Swansea. Total disaster. Glamorgan won by an innings and the proposed Championship celebrations in Nottingham were hastily abandoned. It was not a day to be dealt upon by Nottinghamshire supporters.

Returning to the start of the summer, Carr's opening match could not have been worse. He was dismissed first ball in both innings, bowled Nichols and caught Nichols, bowled LC Eastman. Had his Achilles heel been circulated throughout the first-class counties during 1926? Bill Bowes in *Express Deliveries* explained: 'In my next match against Nottinghamshire I sustained my first bowling injury. How simply it happened! I was to deliver the first ball of the third day to Arthur Carr, the Nottinghamshire captain, and in his knowledgeable way Emmott Robinson said, "This chap always plays back at the first ball or two; he never comes forward – try and bowl him a long 'un." That meant I had to bowl a fast yorker, which, for the first ball of the morning, takes some doing as one is not sufficiently loosened up. Yet, had I gone and put the ball where I wanted it I could not have done better. The scorebook reads: "AW Carr, lbw, b Bowes 0." The effort of that first ball, however, caused me to pull my rib-muscles, and though I finished the day, I became stiff during the night and next morning had to see a London specialist.'

Nottinghamshire against Yorkshire at Bramall Lane on 11, 13 and 14 July was the game; a week later the return at Trent Bridge saw Bowes dismiss Carr for 6 and 24, though bowling medium pace, because Bowes was frightened he would again strain himself.

In 1927, Carr's sequence of low scores continued. Carr may not have been scoring many runs, but the Committee believed he was an absolute necessity as part of the eleven, a point proved by a Committee minute on 25 June: 'It was reported that as a member of the Selection Committee Mr Carr had been requested to be present at the Test trial at Sheffield to watch the match. It was carried that the following resolution be sent to him – "That it is the unanimous opinion of this Committee that Mr Carr should captain the Nottinghamshire team against Gloucestershire, rather than that he should accept the invitation of the Selection Committee to be present at the Test trial Match at Sheffield."'

Both Larwood and Lilley played in the Test trial, which was badly affected by rain, as was the Nottinghamshire v Gloucestershire match on the same dates. The latter does however possess some historical significance since it marked the debut (in Larwood's absence) of William Voce. In view of what would develop later and the effects it had on Arthur Carr's career, it is appropriate to take an extract from the report of the first day's play in this game: 'Since William Riley was killed in the war and John Gunn ceased to be a force in the attack, Nottinghamshire have prosecuted a vigilant search for a left-arm bowler and at last they seem to have discovered one, who promises to fill the long-felt want ... Not yet eighteen years of age, Voce who is tall, started his career as a cricketer with other lads from Annesley Colliery, where he went to work at the age of fourteen. For a couple of seasons he played for the Colliery second XI, showing excellent form, and joining the first team continued to improve. At that period he bowled a medium pace ball of the in-swinging type, but having last season been appointed to the Trent Bridge Ground Staff he has acquired the art of spinning the ball, and under the tuition of James Iremonger has made a rapid advancement.' Voce took five for 36 in Gloucestershire's first innings.

William Voce was born in Annesley Woodhouse on 8 August 1909, that village bordered on the south side of Harold Larwood's village of Nuncargate. Annesley Colliery had its own cricket ground, with the Colliery Welfare building acting as its pavilion. Nuncargate's ground was less than half a mile away. The Nuncargate crowd considered themselves superior to those in Annesley Woodhouse, the latter being almost entirely composed of colliery owned houses, whereas Nuncargate's houses were privately owned or rented.

Although Larwood and Voce would soon be permanently linked in the public mind and were to become very good friends, they were completely different characters. Bill Voce's family had a much harder upbringing than Larwood's. Voce's father died young and Bill Voce was at one stage the sole bread winner. What occurred when the Bodyline affair and its aftermath played out and in particular Arthur Carr's role in his managing of the two fast bowlers illustrates the different approaches each of the cricketers had to circumstances which were largely out of their hands.

When the final Nottinghamshire statistics for 1927 were published, Carr's figures are quite extraordinary. He scored 742 runs, average 19.02, which is pretty grim. Perhaps more to the point, though still batting at four, he finished eighth in the Nottinghamshire batting table. To place those figures in context, his average and position in the batting line-up during the previous five summers was:

| Season | Average | Place |
|--------|---------|-------|
| 1922 | 38.02 | 2 |
| 1923 | 33.47 | 5 |
| 1924 | 37.74 | 2 |
| 1925 | 56.12 | 1 |
| 1926 | 31.71 | 4 |
| 1927 | 19.02 | 8 |

In the following summer of 1928 and in 1929, his batting statistics were to resume the normal sequence of a mid-30s average. Something was seriously amiss. He must have borne the agony of shingles for a number of weeks before succumbing and being diagnosed by Dr Dixon. Carr stated in his autobiography: 'I am almost insensible to physical pain. True, I have never had a tooth taken out – perhaps I shall squeal loudly when I do – but I can honestly say that nothing hurts me much. I have had innumerable falls in the hunting-field; I have been knocked about and cut about in motoring smashes; I have had a thumb fractured and my nose broken, but never have I felt a lot of pain. I even had my broken nose reset without an anaesthetic and I hardly felt a thing.'

Carr and his wife, perhaps prompted by the illness, decided to move house and come to the Nottingham area, meaning Carr would no longer have to stay in Nottingham hotels for half the season. A vacant property at the time was Bulcote Manor House. In 1938, Arthur Mee describes Bulcote: 'Till the coming of the new road every traveller between Nottingham and Newark knew the sharp turn in this small place nestling under the hills. A stream wanders by the wayside facing the manor house and a row of ivied cottages, and the little church stands high on a wooden slope, catching lovely glimpses of the gleaming Trent. The church took the place of an ancient chapel.'

Bulcote has not grown too much since 1938 – the new road was built whilst Carr was in residence. The property which the Carrs bought has a large garden and a paddock suitable for a horse or two. In the 1980s the then owner, George Fish, converted the paddock into a cricket ground and Bulcote Cricket Club flourished. When he retired, Mr Fish converted Carr's stables into a comfortable dwelling. The Manor House parts of which were built in the seventeenth century, but very much altered and extended in the early nineteenth century, has currently eight bedrooms and eight bathrooms, as well as the usual accommodation downstairs. The Carrs moved in the winter of 1927/28 and Carr took the opportunity to join the South Nottinghamshire Hunt, which was based in the area.

The major tour undertaken by MCC in the winter of 1927/28 was to South Africa; the team was led by Capt RT Stanyforth, who had up to that time never appeared for a first-class county, most of his experience being with the Army team and sundry regimental sides. Stanyforth was a last-minute replacement for GR Jackson, the Derbyshire captain, who had to pull out of the side due to ill-health. Whether or not Carr was considered is not known – perhaps ill-health ruled him out of contention anyway – certainly the touring party was actually published on the same day that Carr's illness was made public. Sam Staples was the sole Nottinghamshire representative. The Test series was tied and in first-class games the team were nothing like as successful as the side of 1922/23 that had included Carr. On the earlier tour ten of fourteen first-class games were won; this time the visitors won seven of sixteen. The first-class games in South Africa at that time were, in general, matches against teams playing in South Africa's equivalent of the County Championship, the Currie Cup, plus the Test matches.

A lesser tour that winter was Lord Tennyson's team to Jamaica. The same side had toured Jamaica the previous winter, each time with no Nottinghamshire players in either party. Possibly Tennyson thought Nottinghamshire cricketers took the game too seriously! Although Carr and Tennyson were in some ways similar characters, they were never particularly close. Carr's enthusiasm of hunting possibly took preference over a minor overseas cricket tour. There is no mention of Carr in Lord Tennyson's *Sticky Wickets* and only passing references of Tennyson in Carr's memoirs. One larger than life character must have been sufficient for Tennyson's overseas trips.

On 17 January 1928, JA Dixon, in the absence of the President, Lord Belper, officially opened the new brick-built Practice Hall in the Hound Road and Fox Road corner of the Trent Bridge Ground. The guest of honour was Pelham Warner, who in the course of a lengthy speech took the opportunity to make the following remarks: 'The omission of Mr Carr from the English team in the memorable last Test at The Oval eighteen months ago, was due to his severe attack of tonsillitis. Rightly or wrongly the Selection Committee came to the conclusion that Carr was not quite fit and asked him to stand down. I have known Mr Carr since he was a boy and the action had hurt me bitterly. It was taken with great reluctance, and I hope it has not in any way hurt the feelings of so excellent and keen a cricketer and such an able captain as Mr Carr. The step had been taken in what was considered to be the best interest of English cricket at that moment.'

Julien Cahn paid half the cost of the construction and delivered a short speech, as did CW Wright and Dr Gauld. After the ceremony, George Gunn, Len Richmond and James Iremonger indulged in a brief practice session to demonstrate the value of the new matting wicket. There was no reference to Arthur Carr being present on the day and he did not receive any significant mention in the Nottingham press until 15

March, when it was announced that he would be captaining the county side for the coming season; the reference does not include any comment on his health.

Curiously, Carr's letter accepting the captaincy was noted in the following month's Committee minutes, unlike in previous years. Perhaps this is an indication that some members of the committee were not too happy with Carr's re-appointment? The cricketers were at practice on the Trent Bridge Ground on 25 April, when the *Nottingham Journal* photographer took a snap of Angus Carr taking a picture of his mother on the outfield.

The results of the 1928 season look very satisfactory, only three matches out of thirty-two were lost and third place secured in the Championship, but the six matches played in May caused supporters much concern, especially the Whitsun game against Surrey. On the Saturday Nottinghamshire scored 408 for eight; George Gunn, fast approaching his forty-ninth birthday, made what the press described as 'a display that was a perfect model of excellence, academic in style and polished in the highest sense of the term' and in the closing overs of the day Fred Barratt hit 96 in eighty-five minutes, 'he was cheered to the echo on returning to the pavilion.'

The innings closed at mid-day on Bank Holiday Monday, in front of an attendance of 22,000, for 457. Jack Hobbs hit a hundred for Surrey, but no one else did much. Surrey were all out for 288, a deficit of 169. Carr decided not to enforce the follow on. The light was poor and there was thirty minutes playing time remaining. At stumps Nottinghamshire were 15 for four. On the last day the home side simply continued their miserable exhibition, all out 50. Carr made 22 and was the only batsman to look confident until he played back to a ball from Fender that just grazed the stumps though not disturbing a bail, bounced off the wicketkeeper's pads and flew in the air. Brooks, the wicketkeeper, had time to catch it. Carr was not happy with the umpire's decision, but departed slowly. Surrey scored the 220 needed for victory, losing only three men. The national press went for Carr:

*The Times*: 'AW Carr could not have foreseen Nottinghamshire's utter collapse, and, to that extent, he is not responsible for their defeat, but the fact remains that his only chance of winning was to have put Surrey in again on Monday night …. For neglecting the first duty of every captain, the duty of following the course of action most likely to win the match, Carr was severely punished, but, nevertheless, there was poetic justice in the punishment. The match was a splendid one from beginning to end.'

*Daily Express*: 'The defeat of Nottinghamshire was due to the mistaken policy of AW Carr, who decided that Nottinghamshire should bat again. Disaster immediately followed, though Surrey's attack has been styled the worst in the Championship.'

*Manchester Guardian*: 'Arthur Carr committed an error of judgement in not compelling Surrey to follow on. The Nottinghamshire team gave a most feeble display for which no excuse could be offered.'

*Sporting Chronicle*: 'The moral effect of having to follow on, which Surrey would have had to do, if Carr had chosen to put them in again on Monday evening, was always great. That is why Nottinghamshire second innings collapse is all the more difficult to understand, as the home county was conscious of its advantage. The blame is not entirely Carr's of course, but he will get it just the same, because he declined what the gods offered.'

*The Sporting Life*: 'In these days of marl-dressed, carefully nurtured wickets, it is not often that a match between two of the giants in county cricket provides anything that even borders on the sensational. Yet Surrey, opposing Nottinghamshire at Trent Bridge, fought their way out of an apparently impossible position yesterday. Had Arthur Carr sent Surrey in again on Monday evening the whole history of the game might have been changed. As it was, PGH Fender and Peach in that short time delivered a blow from which their rivals never recovered.'

The following day Nottinghamshire were at the Bat and Ball Ground, Gravesend, where they scored 467 for five, George Gunn hitting another hundred. This time Carr made no mistake, Nottinghamshire went on to 555 for eight declared and Kent, making 164 *were* invited to follow on. Nottinghamshire won by an innings and 190 runs. It was Kent's first defeat, but they finished the summer one place above Nottinghamshire – as runner up. Kent's attack was far, far stronger than Surrey's!

Less than a fortnight later Carr scored 150 against Leicestershire at Aylestone Road, his first century since 19 August 1926 against Worcestershire at Trent Bridge. After the press drubbing in the Surrey match, the *Nottingham Guardian* noted: 'Nothing that has happened so far in the present season has given so much pleasure to Nottinghamshire cricket followers as Mr AW Carr's assertion of his old form at Leicester on Saturday.'

Carr's ambition, as stated in January 1927, was to captain England in Australia. He had missed out on the trip to South Africa, but that was never intended as a full-strength England side. West Indies were the 1928 tourists to England. A Test trial was staged at Lord's on 16, 18 and 19 June 1928, Carr was not in either team, though, in retrospect, the *Wisden* report of the game pointed out that five of those who later went to Australia were missing from the twenty-two cricketers on show, so Carr's hopes were not yet dashed. Larwood was the sole Nottinghamshire man at Lord's and he dominated affairs by taking six for 59, easily the best bowling performance.

The selectors chose the England team directly after the trial and matters dimmed for Carr as DR Jardine was given his Test debut and Chapman retained his place as captain. England won by an innings, Larwood again the only Nottinghamshire man. He bowled fifteen overs in West Indies first innings, but owing to a strain did not bowl in the second. This was West Indies' baptism on the Test arena and the series comprised just three matches. Chapman continued as captain for this second game, but retired hurt and JC White took over the reins; Jardine, run out for 83, compiled the highest individual innings of the match. White, generally referred to as 'Farmer' White, had taken over the Somerset captaincy the previous year. He had played for England occasionally since his Test debut in 1921, principally as a left-arm slow bowler, but he was also a fair batsman, scoring over 12,000 runs in his career. Chapman recovered for the third Test; White did not play.

Perhaps all was not quite lost. On the same day that the first Test began at Lord's, 23 June 1928, a journalist writing under the pen name 'Googly' contributed a long article for 'Our Cricket Page'; not, as might be expected, on one of the twenty-two players in the current Test match, but on Arthur Carr. The piece begins: 'A buzz goes round the ground when Arthur Carr strides out of the pavilion, padded and gloved to bat, a buzz of eager talk about what the mighty man of Nottinghamshire may do if he gets a proper sight of the bowling and starts to swing his bat truly against it ... Capless, smooth-haired, brown and brawny, Mr Carr is broad in the beam and big in the shoulders. He has a determined walk and a determined jaw, and a grand way of throwing himself back when he hits. He lies back to the bowler and lies into him ... Although he has occasionally fallen into errors of judgement in strategy, it is beyond question that Arthur Carr is one of the best captains playing. He is alert and masterful; he can frequently produce a captain's innings when it is wanted – one of those heroic knocks when things are going badly with the side that can turn the tide and restore shaken confidence and his example in the field is exemplary. He never spares himself; he will stand anywhere – I believe he has even put on the gloves in emergencies – and he will try to stop anything. He is tremendously keen and a great inspiration to his team, which generally consists of ten pros and himself.'

King George V and Queen Mary visited Tent Bridge to watch the Nottinghamshire game against the West Indies in early July. Carr marked the Saturday of the match with exactly a hundred made in 125 minutes including fourteen fours, though the talking point of the game, prior to the arrival of the royal party, was George Vernon Gunn's first-class debut – the first time in the twentieth century that a father and son had appeared in the same county eleven for Nottinghamshire. Sadly, George senior was dismissed without scoring and young George made only 6 in that innings. In the second innings with father doing better, Carr sent son in at the fall of the second wicket and the pair batted briefly together.

The team to represent England in Australia was announced on 30 July. The decision of picking Chapman as captain was not straightforward, as one press commentator noted: 'The wisdom of choosing APF Chapman as captain is one of the most debatable of the decisions, and for my part, I am doubtful if his form justifies his inclusion.' The press pointed out that the best alternatives to Chapman were JC White of Somerset or DR Jardine of Surrey. Both were in the party, with JC White appointed vice-captain. Carr doesn't seem to have been mentioned as a possible contender. When asked to comment on the side he said, 'I think the selected team are an excellent lot; certainly the best that could have been picked to go out there.' Nottinghamshire were represented by Larwood and Sam Staples.

Cardus, though, is of a different opinion and sets it out at the end of his report on the Nottinghamshire v Kent game played directly after the Australian party had been published; the game seemed to be heading for a draw at the close of the second day when Nottinghamshire still had two wickets to fall in their first innings: 'Carr captaining today was an inspiration to every man in the Nottinghamshire team. He visualised victory from the moment he reached the ground. If it is a fair question – would Lancashire or Yorkshire have closed an innings on the morning of the last day when in possession of a merely 111 lead? There is unfortunately nothing in the recent history of either county to suggest they would have attempted any such imaginative act. Carr's management of his attack was as thoughtful as MacLaren's. He invariably had on the very bowler most likely to search out a given batsman's weak spot. A fast bowler was in action whenever a Kent cricketer reached the wicket. Woolley who likes the ball to come through straight usually found himself confronted by Sam Staples, who bowled, spun and flighted the ball cleverly. Staples thoroughly deserved Woolley's wicket, for he angled after it perseveringly. Carr dominated his side all the time; you could see he was holding the reins, now pulling this one, now pulling that. The Australians would hail either Carr or Fender as captains by more or less divine right.'

It was in 1928 that Arthur Staples, younger brother of Sam, finally secured a permanent place in the first XI. He had made his debut in 1924 as an all-rounder, but vied with Billy Flint for the final slot. Flint played throughout 1927, but in 1928 made only five appearances – Arthur Staples appeared in thirty-one of the thirty-four first-class matches. Unlike his brother he was not destined to be capped for England, though he did play in a Test trial, staged in Cardiff in 1932.

Nottinghamshire, as previously noted, finished the season in third place and after a stuttering first month, they settled into the third or fourth slot through June, July and August, but never really threatened Lancashire who took the title for the third successive summer. Carr gained a modicum of recognition at the close of the summer, representing the Gentlemen v Players at Dean Park, Bournemouth. There were no less than seven county captains in the amateur side, with the 'home' captain, Hon LH Tennyson, leading the team of leaders. It was, however, Carr who enabled the amateurs to win. Carr scored 71 and 63, the highest aggregate on either side. The amateurs scraped home by one wicket. The two teams were then re-jigged to form North v South. The match was a typical Arthur Carr contest in which he captained the northern side. The South led by Tennyson hit an attractive 358 on the first day, with the North ending at 28 without loss. The North, due to Fender's spirited bowling (7.5-3-8-4), were brushed aside on Monday for 116 all out and the follow-on was enforced. The second innings was a different tale. By consistent application the total of 316 for seven was realised by the close, which was extended to 372 all out. And South required 131 to win. They achieved this by a margin of three wickets – if a catch or two had not gone to ground, the North would have caused a surprise.

On the tour of Australia that Carr might have led, England won the Test series by four to one. Chapman, as captain, was the hero of the hour, though his batting record was modest – in the first-class batting table he came tenth, the lowest of all the specialist batsmen. In fact he was omitted from the final Test, which was lost, being replaced by Leyland who scored 137 and 53* and vice-captain 'Farmer' White led England for the first time, though placed himself to bat at number ten, because England's batting was so strong. Carr's advice about saving Larwood for the Tests was ignored. He performed brilliantly in the first Test, but his effectiveness steadily declined on the bone hard pitches – he played in thirteen of the seventeen first-class matches (in 1932/33, under Jardine, Larwood played in ten out of twenty, in both tours he appeared in all five Tests). Sam Staples, Nottinghamshire' other representative, was struck down with rheumatism before the first game and was sent home during the second Test without having bowled a ball in anger.

With Carr, his wife and son happily back in Nottingham-shire, what of Carr's brother Gordon? He had been invalided out of the army before the war ended and taken up a post as a stockbroker with the family firm. In 1924 Gordon married an American lady, Cecilia Lucille Winslow, aged twenty-four. A boy, Philip Montague, was born in 1927; three years later Cecilia died and the boy went to live at Hemingford Park with his grandparents. He was to reside at their home until after the Second World War. Arthur Carr's sister, Eileen, lived with her husband in Hyde Park Gate, off the Bayswater Road. The couple had two children, Jac, born 1924 and June born 1927.

A commemorative postcard showing
the 1929 County Championship winners

# 11

## COUNTY CHAMPION

### 1929-1930

On 15 April 1929 Arthur Carr reported back to Trent Bridge to greet the Nottinghamshire pros. He had spent the winter hunting with the South Nottinghamshire and Belvoir Hounds, having himself several horses stabled at Bulcote. Young Angus came to the ground with his father. On 29 April, the Lord Mayor held a luncheon for 140 people to mark the return of Harold Larwood and Sam Staples and the retaining of the Ashes.

There were several changes in the regulations for county cricket in 1929; the most important being the increase in the width and height of the wickets both by one inch. This being in the first place an experiment, the enlarged wicket was to apply to County Championship matches only. The Championship programme itself was changed with all counties playing twenty-eight matches. Nottinghamshire had played thirty-two, i.e. every other county twice, in 1928. In 1929 the team arranged those twenty-eight matches, plus home and away with Essex in non-Championship three-day games which still ranked as first class. In 1928 some counties had only played twenty-four matches. The percentage system which had annoyed many journalists for years now disappeared; it had been in operation since 1896, although it reappeared in 1933 because the financially delicate counties couldn't afford to stage twenty-eight matches.

For some seasons the press had commented on the high average age of the Nottinghamshire batsmen. Despite these often derogatory remarks, the veterans had continued to produce the runs required. The expected line up for 1929, with the age of each player, read: George Gunn (50), WW Whysall (41), Willis Walker (36), AW Carr (36), Wilf Payton (47), Arthur Staples (30), Ben Lilley (35), Fred Barratt (35), Sam Staples (36), Harold Larwood (24) and Bill Voce (20). The average for the five specialist batsmen was forty-two. In 2016 the press consider it a miracle if a single member of the team is still active at that age! The general opinion as to the prospects of the county team was unaltered compared with that of the previous two or three years with the hope that the Championship title might return to Nottingham.

The South African tourists would play five Tests but Edgbaston was preferred to Trent Bridge as the initial game in the series. In Nottinghamshire's opening match, the friendly against Essex, Dennis Bland, the Shrewsbury School boy, was unexpectedly introduced when Sam Staples was declared not fit. Bland not only took three of the first four Essex wickets to fall, but broke a stump on bowling out Pope. The Committee ordered that the stump be suitably inscribed and presented to Bland.

In the early Championship games Nottinghamshire had moderate results. By 8 June, the county stood seventh in the table, however three successive victories at the end of June – against Worcestershire, Lancashire and Warwickshire – saw the team rise to the top for the first time. During the Worcestershire match at Trent Bridge, there was an extended tea interval while George Gunn, celebrating his fiftieth birthday, was presented with a mahogany clock from the Nottinghamshire Committee, a gold wrist watch from his fellow players and a silver cigarette box from Arthur Carr. Gunn scored 59 in the first innings, but his son Young George made the highest score, 73, in the whole game. Victory was expected against the modest Worcester team. More significant was the win over Lancashire at Old Trafford. In the final innings it was a battle between George Gunn and Ted McDonald – Gunn's 66 won the game for his county. From then onwards, Nottinghamshire did not lose a single match until they faced the Rest of England at The Oval in September.

Before that, however, Arthur Carr was to regain his reputation at a higher level. Nottinghamshire met the South Africans at Trent Bridge in a match beginning on Saturday 6 July. Some 10,000 spectators came to watch the day's play, seeing the county total 445 for seven. Carr won the toss and the scoreboard read a modest 35 for two as he strode to the crease. When he left the figure had risen to 360 for four. Carr made 194 with seven sixes and twenty fours, batting about 240 minutes – his only blemish was being dropped at long-off with 166 to his name. Carr was then invited to play for Gentlemen v Players at The Oval, the amateurs were captained by Lord Tennyson. Though Carr scored modestly, he had a better time in the second match at Lord's, where his 64 was the highest for the amateurs. An extract from HJ Henley's report noted: 'AW Carr found his long-driving game. He showed a particular affection for Freeman. A half volley from the little man from Kent was hit for six and, in addition, Carr treated Goddard as if he was a rustic bowler.'

JC White, who captained England in the first three Tests against South Africa, was captain of the Gentlemen in this Lord's game. Two days later the press were mystified when the England team for the fourth Test was announced. Carr was to replace White as England's leader. Interviewed by the *Nottingham Journal* Carr said, 'It was the greatest surprise of my life. I thought I was too old.'

*The Daily Express* commented 'The triumph of Woolley at Leeds came as a convincing justification of the drastic changes made in the team chosen for the third Test match and a further and no less sensational step in the same direction has been signalised by the appointment of AW Carr to captain England in the fourth match at Manchester next Saturday. Carr on his day is one of the fastest run getters in the country. He has returned this season to something approaching the wonderful form, which in 1925 raised him to a pinnacle as the best amateur batsman in England and he proved in the recent Gentlemen v Players match at Lord's that he has neither lost his ability to cope with good bowling nor to sprint in the field and between the wickets with an agility equal to that of youths fifteen years his junior. Carr has courage and force of character and every lover of vigorous and resourceful leadership will rejoice that he is once again in command.'

White, the vice-captain to Chapman in Australia, had been selected as England's 1929 Test captain because Chapman had taken an extended holiday in New Zealand and Canada after the Australian tour and had not come back to England until 16 July. His time in New Zealand was no doubt due to his engagement to the sister of the New Zealand captain.

Just prior to Carr taking charge of England, a row blew up between Nottinghamshire and Yorkshire over the match played between the two counties beginning 13 July. Later the *Wisden Almanack* began its summary of the game: 'A really appalling game was this return match, no more than 688 runs being registered in the course of three full days cricket and the average rate of scoring being only 40 an hour.'

On the first day Yorkshire reached 272 for six, Percy Homes being 167 not out made in six hours. On Monday Holmes took his score to 285 in nine and three-quarter hours, the all out Yorkshire total was 498. At the close Nottinghamshire were 56 without loss. George Gunn and Carr decided on the last day to give Yorkshire a taste of their own medicine. Gunn batted five hours and twenty minutes for 58; Carr two hours thirty minutes for 23.

The *Nottingham Guardian* report concludes: 'As it had long ceased to be a game of cricket, Nottinghamshire were justified in showing the world what an utter farce slow motion play is and they had the consolatory satisfaction of beating Yorkshire at their own game. Mr Carr's three runs in an hour and a quarter before tea will stand for long as a classic instance of what a Nottinghamshire hitter under the influence of Yorkshire's example can do.' This all led to some robust comments by Harold Larwood published in the *Sunday Chronicle* which caused more feathers to fly, but eventually calm was restored.

Carr moved from domestic to international cricket seamlessly. He won the toss for England at Old Trafford and the press noted, 'Nottinghamshire cricket enthusiasts will be disappointed that AW Carr failed [he made 10], but it should be remembered that he went in late, with the total over 350, and a hitting policy had to be carried out. Carr's handling of his team in the field will be closely watched, but he is not likely to fail there. He always said he "would come back", and we may see him again lead England against Australia.' England went on to beat South Africa by an innings and 32 runs.

Whilst Carr was preparing for England, Nottinghamshire met Somerset at Taunton on the three days prior, 24, 25 and 26 July, with Lionel Kirk as captain. JC White led the home side and hit 192 off the depleted Nottinghamshire attack (Larwood was absent injured). Though Nottinghamshire held out for a draw, the Nottingham press headlined their report 'Championship Chances Spoilt'. Nottinghamshire fell to fourth place, but just three points separated the first five counties.

With memories of the disastrous away game with Glamorgan two years before and with Kirk again in charge, there must have been some jangling nerves when Nottinghamshire travelled from Taunton to Pontypridd. Nottinghamshire already lacked Larwood (unfit) and Carr, but on the eve of the Test Nottinghamshire were further handicapped: Tate was declared unfit and Barratt was brought into the England XI, making his Test debut. Kirk fortunately won the toss and batted on an easy pitch. Whysall hit a century and most of the rest made useful contributions to a total at the close of Saturday of 398. Rain on Sunday changed the nature of the pitch. On Monday Sam Staples and Voce dismissed Glamorgan twice, victory being achieved by an innings and 121 runs. The Welsh bogey was laid. The fixture list delivered Nottinghamshire another minnow in the following game when Carr returned from the Test. Voce took fourteen Northamptonshire wickets; an innings victory placed Nottinghamshire at the top, four points ahead of Lancashire but also with two matches in hand.

To The Oval for the Bank Holiday game against Surrey – about 10,000 attended on the Saturday; Surrey were no longer the force they had been, so the crowds were not so large. Nottinghamshire batted all day for 409, Carr had the pleasure of hitting a hundred, as did Whysall. On Monday Surrey matched Nottinghamshire's total, then Tuesday was washed out. As had been the habit for some seasons, Nottinghamshire left The Oval to play Kent. The St Lawrence pitch at Canterbury was designed for the leg breaks of Tich Freeman. He had much the better of the Nottinghamshire batsman and the visitors were lucky to escape with a draw – Percy Chapman, back in England, played for Kent but scored only 1 and 9. Despite these successive draws, Nottinghamshire retained the Championship lead, but reduced to two points over Lancashire and now with one game in hand.

Derbyshire were Nottinghamshire's next opponents at Trent Bridge. About 12,500 came to the ground to view the battle of the neighbours. Harry Storer, the Burnley half-back; and the former Nottinghamshire cricketer, Garnet Lee, added 175 for the first wicket, when Derbyshire decided to bat. At the close the visitors' score was 354 for seven. On the second morning, poor out-cricket by Nottinghamshire allowed the Derbyshire eighth wicket to add 103; Hill-Wood gaining 70. In response Nottinghamshire were 136 for two when Carr joined George Gunn. Seven more runs were added. Carr drove the ball to mid-off and was heard to shout, as he rushed down the pitch, 'Come on George.' George didn't come on. Both batsmen were at the bowler's end when wicketkeeper Elliott had the ball in his hands. He did not immediately however remove the bails, but waited and George Gunn moved out of his crease. Then the bails were tipped off. Carr walked back to the pavilion and into the dressing room. Elliott then claimed Gunn ought to be the one to go and told both the Derbyshire captain and then the umpire. The umpire went to persuade Carr to return and after much delay the battle was re-engaged. The spectators occupied the rest of the day arguing. The *Daily Mirror* carried headlines 'Was George Gunn Out? Debatable Decision at Trent Bridge.' The *Nottingham Journal* ran the heading: 'An Extraordinary Run Out at Trent Bridge. Carr recalled from the Pavilion. George Gunn the Victim.' However the match was another draw and Nottinghamshire fell to third place, Lancashire and Gloucestershire tied with 126 points, Nottinghamshire with 123; Yorkshire were fourth with 119. On the same day as the run-out puzzle, Carr was appointed as captain for the fifth Test at The Oval.

Nottinghamshire went off to the scene of the 1928 batting record ground of Rover's at Coventry. In that game Nottinghamshire scored 656 for three declared; George Gunn, Whysall, Walker and Barratt all making hundreds. In reply the game ended with Warwickshire 371 for nine, EJ Smith and RES Wyatt also making hundreds. This time the nature of the pitch had changed, the press pointed out that if the Nottinghamshire v Derbyshire match at Trent Bridge had been played on a marble top, the one in Coventry was a cinder track. Due to Willis Walker, who produced the best innings of his career with 133 not out, Nottinghamshire reached 311. By the close of the first day Warwickshire were 42 for six, Sam Staples four for 21. The whole match was over by half past three on the second day, Nottinghamshire winning by an innings and 68 runs; Sam Staples took nine wickets, Voce ten, Voce also reached 100 wickets for the season. Nottinghamshire returned to the top of the table, five points ahead of both Gloucestershire and Lancashire.

With Carr away with England, the Committee minute regarding the team for the next game, against Lancashire, in the terminology of the day, read: 'It was reported that Mr Carr had accepted an invitation to play for England. It was resolved that the full side without Mr Carr be selected and that Gunn should be appointed captain. Harris was chosen to fill the eleventh place.' With Lancashire still hoping for the title, this was a crucial match. From the spectators point of view the game was to prove attritional. Lancashire reached 238 for eight on a first day when an hour or so was lost to the weather. On the second day, the last wickets survived twenty minutes. In contrast Nottinghamshire reached 352 for six, Wilf Payton not out 152. Gunn declared on the last day allowing himself four hours forty minutes to dismiss Lancashire, who were 222 in arrears. Lancashire were 174 for four when time was called. Perhaps Carr would have adopted different tactics?

Carr was at The Oval, frustrated by the weakness in the England attack. South Africa gained a first innings lead of 234 with just four hours playing time remaining. Sutcliffe and

Hammond hit hundreds and England lost just a single wicket in their second innings. The match ended as a draw.

The Championship table was as tight as could be with four counties entertaining some hope of the title. Nottinghamshire had 136 points, Yorkshire 132, Gloucestershire and Lancashire both had 129. The last Nottinghamshire home match was against Gloucestershire. Both Sam Staples and Payton were injured, Flint and Shipston came in as replacements. Neither were really required on the first day as Whysall hit 244 and the total reached 396. Larwood just had time to bowl an over and dismiss Sinfield. The fast bowler continued in the same vein on the second day, ending with five for 37, Gloucestershire 139 all out. Hammond was clean bowled with his off stump spinning some twelve yards, the England batsman had scored 4. Gloucestershire followed on at 3.15 and were 205 for eight when play ceased for the day. It took just fifteen minutes of the final morning to complete the rout. Nottinghamshire now led the table by seven points, all the top teams having three matches to play.

A holiday crowd of 7,000 were at the Saffrons Ground in Eastbourne for the first of Nottinghamshire's final trio of matches. The start, however, was delayed when Carr objected to the prepared wicket on the grounds it had been over-watered. An alternative was arranged but play was an hour late in starting. In the reduced playing time of the first day, Nottinghamshire, having chosen to bat, reached 245 for seven, with a cautious George Gunn on 101 not out. The final three wickets fell quickly on Monday, leaving the veteran still undefeated. If the Nottinghamshire scoring had been slow, Sussex literally crept – Jim Parks spent 165 minutes reaching his 50, but Duleepsinhji batted with more vigour and at number nine and Maurice Tate struck a fast 45 to bring Sussex a slender lead. The Championship race was really between Nottinghamshire and Yorkshire and an anonymous press report summed up the position of the two rivals at the end of the second day: 'Hats thrown in the air and a great clamouring by the biggest crowd which has ever attended a cricket match at Eastbourne marked the passing of the Nottinghamshire total by Sussex after a tremendous battle yesterday for first innings lead. The same exuberance manifested itself at The Oval where Surrey eclipse Yorkshire's first innings score.' Both counties had failed to capitalise on the failure of their rival. On the third day the rivals simply batted out time, so no change, Nottinghamshire remained seven points ahead with two games to be played.

In the penultimate matches both Nottinghamshire and Yorkshire met teams near the foot of the table. Nottinghamshire went to Northampton, Yorkshire to Worcester. It was hardly a surprise given fair weather that both Nottinghamshire and Yorkshire won, Nottinghamshire beat Northamptonshire by ten wickets. Larwood took eight for 84 and Ben Lilley hit a rare Championship hundred – 'wicketkeeper bats as never before'. Seven points therefore still separated the two clubs on 31 August when Yorkshire travelled to Hove and Nottinghamshire hopped across the border to Ilkeston. The notes in *Wisden* contained the comment: 'The visitors entered into the struggle in the position that, provided they escaped defeat, they carried off the Championship.' It was a very similar position to that in 1927 before the Glamorgan match.

In the event, rain allowed only ninety-five minutes on the Saturday, when Nottinghamshire scored 40 for one wicket. On Monday a full day's play did take place, but Nottinghamshire batted painfully to be dismissed for 175; Derbyshire found no terrors in either pitch or bowling and were 114 for one at the finish. Rain returned on Tuesday; no play was possible until 3 o'clock; Derbyshire proceeded to a first innings lead and on to 221 for three when rain finished an unsatisfactory final day. At Hove Yorkshire failed to obtain a first innings lead then, in a run chase on the final afternoon, lost by 78 runs.

The *Manchester Guardian* correspondent (not Cardus), writing on 1 September, condemned the Championship system which allowed points for first innings lead: 'One of the most eminent of England cricketers, now serving the Empire in a distant part of the world, made a perfectly correct forecast of the trend of play that would result from a first innings lead when the scheme for establishing the points principle first came under discussion. "You are making two matches in one," he said, "and the first will become the greater because the team winning the toss will concentrate upon first innings advantage." This has proved to be the fact among most county teams, though, happily not against all. There could be no better example of the evil effect of the first innings points system than was furnished in the Nottinghamshire and Lancashire match at Trent Bridge recently. When he had got the first innings lead the acting Nottinghamshire captain allowed a useless quantity of runs to accumulate, leaving his side with no chance of winning and his opponents with nothing practical to accomplish except "sitting on the splice".'

Arthur Carr, interviewed directly after the end of the Ilkeston match, commented: 'I feel one of the happiest men in England today. I think the Championship has been won by reason of the fact that all members of the team have been the best of pals. From a captain's point of view I could not have had a more loyal set of players to lead into battle. Nottinghamshire are one of those sides that can always go all out for a win, or can play the other game, because the eleven consists of batsmen capable either of forcing matters, or, when necessary, holding their end up. This, as every cricketer will realise, is a great asset. We had the best bowling side in the country particularly on fast wickets, of that I am convinced, and some of our performances, as facts and figures show, have been truly remarkable. Perhaps up to now the public have not realised the tremendous strain which has been thrown upon us all, especially during the last month. I can assure you we all feel extremely thankful that the season is now over. Next year I hope we shall win the Championship again. This season we have been over-anxious to secure a distinction which has not come our way since 1907, but another season we shall not feel quite the same anxiety. In conclusion, let me say that we have always tried to play the game, and that is the greatest satisfaction that any cricketer can feel.'

The *Nottingham Guardian* of 5 September commented: 'The Nottinghamshire cricketers are still blushing under the shower of congratulations which has descended upon them as representing the Champion County of 1929. It is particularly gratifying to note how unanimous are the experts in paying tribute to Mr AW Carr, whose captaincy has been an important factor in the success of Nottinghamshire. *The Times*, in a leading article, refers to his "genius for leadership" and emphasises that he has made a team of the men under him. This is more true than most people think. There is no captain in the country better able to get the best out of his men. Mr Carr made the English side which defeated Australia in 1926 and he would have led them to victory himself had he had a strong minded Selection Committee behind him. However, he has come back to batting form, and if he maintains it, he will certainly be the man to lead England against Australia in 1930.'

'Cricketer' of the *Manchester Guardian* hit the nail on the head when he said: 'Nottinghamshire this season was one of the few counties which could point to a real captain. Carr was the master; the others were the men – good workers, but all of them definitely under a leader who knew what he wanted, and, what is more, was not afraid to insist on getting it.'

On their return to Nottingham from Ilkeston, the Nottinghamshire players were invited to the Council House, in front of which had gathered a crowd of several hundred. Arthur Carr addressed the throng from the first floor balcony; the Lord Mayor proposed a toast to the team, with Carr responding.

Between the two World Wars the season's annual grand finale was the match staged at The Oval when the new Champion County opposed the Rest of England. It was unfortunate for Nottinghamshire that Bill Voce had to withdraw due to illness and Arthur Staples was absent owing to his professional football contract. GV Gunn and RDF Bland filled the vacancies created. *Wisden* described the Rest of England team as thoroughly representative.

The Rest won the toss and chose to bat, the crowd numbering some 12,000. The Rest were dismissed for 399 on the first day of the four-day game. Woolley's 106 was the highest score, whilst Larwood's three for 54 was the best bowling return. On the second day, the county gave a splendid response, scoring 364 all out. Whysall scored 97; Carr's score of 91 came mainly through his trademark off drives – 60 of his runs were the result of boundaries and he was at the crease a little over two hours. The third day saw The Rest dismissed for 282, Sam Staples taking four for 63 and at the close Nottinghamshire were 99 for one, requiring 219 for victory. The light was poor on the final day, but George Gunn batted four hours and twenty-five minutes for 96. When Bland, the last man, came in Nottinghamshire needed 20. Eleven were added when Robins dismissed Bland, leaving Sam Staples 18 not out – Nottinghamshire had lost by just eight runs. No Champion County had beaten The Rest since cricket resumed in 1919, but Nottinghamshire had come closest to success.

On 25 October, the Lord Mayor of Nottingham gave a banquet for over 200 guests at the Council House to celebrate the cricket team's triumph. The County Club had set up the Championship Shilling Fund, an appeal to the public which raised £888.1.6d. At the banquet each of the principal players, Gunn, Payton, Whysall, Walker, Barratt, S Staples, Lilley, Larwood, A Staples and Voce, was presented with a cheque for £80 and a travelling clock, given by Mrs Alice Roe. AW Carr was given a gold cigarette case from the club; silver cigarette cases were given to Kirk and RDF Bland. Players who appeared occasionally also received cheques, as did the scorer. Apart from the present players, a number of former players were invited to the banquet including Hallam and Wass of the 1907 Championship side.

The Lord Mayor proposed the toast of the evening to 'The Championship Team'. Carr, to loud applause, rose in reply: 'Nottinghamshire were a most remarkable side, one day they made 638 for the loss of three wickets, and the next were all out for 130. In other words it was like backing a hot favourite on a racecourse. One was told it was a certainty, and yet it was down the course. I would like to mention two people who were called veterans – George Gunn and Wilfred Payton. The Committee only gave them a contract for two years, but that idea would have to be altered to a contract for twenty-two years. Supporters had asked why do they field out in the country. The explanation was that George Gunn, one of the finest first slips in the kingdom, had a broken finger and was compelled to field there, and that Wilfred Payton, if he came close in, dropped all the catches. The great feature in the Championship win was that the whole of my professionals were Nottinghamshire born. I don't happen to be Nottinghamshire born. I was born in Surrey, but Mr Fender wouldn't have me! I think that next year it will be very hard to win the Championship because the Test matches are allowed four days and during those matches, I shall be very surprised if we don't have two or three members of the side playing for England.'

Carr continued his speech for some while longer, then came speeches from RH Lyttelton, WF Story, JA Dixon, JE Alcock, Sir Edwin Stockton, PF Warner, Lord Ebbisham and finally short responses from the Lord Mayor and Lady Mayoress.

Three Nottinghamshire cricketers travelled overseas with MCC teams during the winter, Fred Barratt went to New Zealand, George Gunn and Bill Voce to the West Indies. In addition Joe Hardstaff senior accompanied the West Indian party acting as umpire. Since Carr had captained England in the two final South African Tests of 1929 and the press had commented during the season that Carr ought to lead England v Australia in the 1930 summer, it worth noting that the captains of the two 1929/30 MCC sides were Arthur Gilligan to New Zealand and the Hon FS Gough-Calthorpe to West Indies. The latter was the current Warwickshire captain and had led the rather modest 1925/26 MCC side to West Indies. There was never a chance that Gough-Calthorpe would lead England in an Ashes series, though he was a very useful county all-rounder. Arthur Gilligan was forced to stand down before the New Zealand tour began and his brother AHH Gilligan was slotted into his place. Again there was no likelihood of him featuring in an Ashes Test. Both touring parties played four Tests – on two occasions England were playing two Tests on the same days!

In February Julien Cahn took his side to the Argentine, the side included two young Nottinghamshire amateurs, GFH Heane and SD Rhodes as well as the former professionals, John Gunn and Len Richmond. Carr spent his winter mainly on the hunting field.

The Trent Bridge ground had been transformed over the 1929/30 winter. The old secretary's office attached to the stand on the west side of the pavilion had been replaced by a two-storey building, the ground floor being for the Secretary and his assistant (Capt HA Brown and RM Poulton) and the first floor for the young players on the groundstaff. Ron Poulton joined the staff at Trent Bridge in 1929 at the age of twenty-one, he was to remain with Nottinghamshire until 1971, succeeding Brown as Secretary in 1959. A very useful club cricketer, Poulton played for Notts Forest CC and in one or two matches for Nottinghamshire Second XI. He died in 1979.

The west wing itself had an upper deck added, as did the Radcliffe Road Stand. Along the Fox Road side of the ground where the wooden stands for Notts County FC stood, a large single storey concrete stand was built. The cost of all this work was defrayed by Sir Julien Cahn. The whole work increased the capacity of the ground to 25,000.

The prospects for the county in the coming season were published in the *Nottingham Guardian* of 10 April: 'Fortunately for Nottinghamshire they still take the field under the captaincy of Mr AW Carr, one of the dominating figures in English cricket and a sportsman to his finger tips, who believes in going all out for victory and risking defeat, rather than sitting on the splice and thereby perhaps consolidating his county's position. While the old Sherborne boy leads the team, Nottinghamshire will never follow the "ca-canny" principle and though he will this coming season have to rely upon the same material that did duty in the last campaign, Mr Carr must in his own mind feel that Nottinghamshire hold a chance second to none of again winning the championship.'

Elsewhere Carr was still being spoken of as a definite prospect to lead England in the 1930 Ashes series. However during the first month of the season, Carr's name as a possible captain seemingly vanished from the national press. In the middle of May the selectors were looking at the two sides – England v The Rest – to appear in a Test trial at Lord's on 31 May. For this match Chapman led England, whilst White captained The Rest. Despite poor batting form, Chapman was retained as leader for the first Test. The announcement of the team was much delayed, but only one Nottinghamshire name was the frame, Larwood. It would not be until the fourth Test, at Old Trafford, that Chapman came in for severe criticism as to his captaincy ability – by then Carr had missed several county matches and Wyatt was the obvious choice to succeed Chapman.

On the county scene Nottinghamshire certainly began by raising hopes of another title. Rain prevented a definite finish to the opening match against Sussex, but the next two games, against Somerset and Kent, both provided innings victories. Carr's sequence of innings was 45, 24, 48 and 57. Then came the infamous match at Southampton. On the first day, the report notes, 'Nottinghamshire gave the impression of taking things much too light-heartedly at the start after winning the toss, and deciding to bat first, and by the time they realised the position had become acute, it was too late.'

The county were all out for 69; Hampshire fared almost as badly, all out 125, Nottinghamshire' second innings began tamely, three wickets being lost for 58, Carr was trapped leg before without a run to his name. On the second day, with Lilley not out on 51, Nottinghamshire did reach 226. Hampshire required 39 more runs in the final innings with five wickets in hand at half past six. Both captains agreed to play the extra half hour. The home county required one run to win when the thirty minutes were up. The umpires called time; Carr picked up the ball, put it in his pocket and walked off. The spectators, collecting round the pavilion to protest, were ignored. The following morning, play began on time. Carr, in a lounge suit and trilby hat, led the rest of the team, similarly dressed, save that Barratt and Voce wore overcoats. The two Hampshire batsmen were in cricket attire, the umpires wore their long white coats. Carr, still in his trilby, bowled two deliveries to Kennedy, who hit the second, an off-drive, to the boundary – no one chased after it. A large photograph of the scene hung for many years in the pavilion on the old Southampton ground.

To offset the reverse at the hands of Hampshire, Nottinghamshire followed with two comprehensive wins over Leicestershire at Aylestone Road and Glamorgan at Trent Bridge,

Voce's bowling being the main instrument in the successes – Carr scored 1 and 12 in the former match, the 12 being notably for a six into the car park, play being delayed whilst the ball was found. He did reach 42 in his single innings off the Glamorgan attack, but the report commented: 'It was not one of Carr's best innings, because he was frequently at fault in his efforts to time the bowling of Ryan and Mercer and required 100 minutes to gather 42, but even so he did not give an actual chance.'

Nottinghamshire then travelled to Old Trafford; Lancashire and Nottinghamshire seemed at this early stage to be the main rivals for the title. Carr won the toss and chose to bat, but George Gunn was dismissed in the second over without scoring, Walker also failed. Carr was due to come in at number four but promoted Arthur Staples, who with Whysall added 81 for the third wicket. The game coincided with the Test trial at Lord's and the Test selectors' deliberations. Mindful of this, did Carr hope that the pitch would ease and he would make an impressive score at the crucial moment? Pure speculation of course.

Carr batted very low down the order at number seven, batting an hour for 18, with the press criticising his uncharacteristic slow play. The match went to the inevitable draw; Nottinghamshire at least had the distinction of being the first side this summer to take first innings points off Lancashire. Carr hit his first hundred of the season off the Worcester attack at New Road: 'The amateur was a man of moods. He began with something approaching his old time nonchalance and reached 50 out of 93 in eighty-five minutes.' Nottinghamshire won the game by ten wickets inside two days. The Bank Holiday game against Surrey was drawn; over 20,000 watched the match on the Monday, filling the new stands to see Nottinghamshire unable to match Surrey's first innings total of 501. Despite this setback, Nottinghamshire were still chasing Lancashire. Both counties had five wins from nine matches with Lancashire at the top two points ahead of Nottinghamshire.

The first Test, staged at Trent Bridge, took place immediately after the Surrey game. Played over four days, Friday was the opening day. Larwood, as expected, was the only Nottinghamshire player in the final England XI, but the Nottinghamshire cricketer most frequently recalled when this match is discussed is Syd Copley, fielding substitute for Larwood (the England twelfth man, Duleepsinhji, was already fielding for the injured Sutcliffe.) Australia required 429 to win in the final innings at about the rate of a run a minute. The score had reached 152 for three when McCabe joined Bradman and the new pair seemed to have completely mastered the bowling. However, at 229, Copley took an unbelievable catch diving forward at mid-on to remove McCabe. This was the turning point which gave England victory.

Copley had never played in a first-class match even though he had been on the Nottinghamshire playing staff since 1924. He had been praised by Carr for his fielding as a substitute during the 1929 season. A letter from Carr to the Committee regarding bonuses given to players was noted in the Minute Book after the 1929 season: 'A letter from Mr Carr was read asking that some recognition should be made to Copley who had acted as twelfth man in many of the matches. It was resolved that a cheque for £5 should be presented to him together with a copy of the photograph and scorecard (Nottinghamshire v Rest match) and that he be called to the next meeting when these presentations should be made.' Copley duly came to the following meeting for his presentation.

Nottinghamshire went to Cardiff Arms Park during the Trent Bridge Test and won the game before lunch on the third day by an innings. The county were just two points behind Lancashire with a game in hand. Astonishingly the next twelve Nottinghamshire Championship matches were all draws – in addition Nottinghamshire met Oxford University and the Australians during this period and drew both those friendly first-class games too.

Although the weather did affect several of these drawn games, is it a coincidence that Carr was absent from three and most of a fourth? He was late arriving at Ilkeston on 28 June, the press reporting that this was due to traffic problems, but on 30 June, the Monday, George Gunn took over as acting captain and the newspapers reported that Mrs Carr was lying ill in a Nottingham nursing home and was to undergo an x-ray examination. Carr then missed the next three matches, his wife being reported as seriously ill.

Carr returned for the August Bank Holiday game at The Oval, but after a full day's play on the Saturday, Monday was completely washed out and the match was drawn. Nottinghamshire briefly rose to the top of the Championship: Nottinghamshire on 110 points, Lancashire and Yorkshire both on 109 points but with a game in hand. Canterbury saw another Nottinghamshire draw before victory at last, against Leicestershire – Carr hit the winning run, a dropped catch which went over the boundary for four. Lancashire, Nottinghamshire and Yorkshire had all played twenty-three matches, the Red Roses were two points clear of Nottinghamshire and Yorkshire, who were tied at 121.

Douglas Jardine and Bill Woodfull toss a coin in the
1932/33 Ashes – but how much did Carr influence Jardine's
controversial tactics?

# 12

# THE GRILL ROOM CONSPIRACY

## 1930-1932

With three matches to play in the 1930 season, Lancashire came to Trent Bridge. Nottinghamshire really needed to win and, in retrospect, a win would have given them the title. Carr had been to The Oval to watch the final Test immediately before the Lancashire game and a rumour was floated that he intended to retire as county captain. RWV Robins, who was employed by Julien Cahn and played for his team, would, it was suggested, succeed Carr. It's difficult to know the original source of the Robins rumour. Robins made his Test debut in 1929 and played county cricket for Middlesex. There is no mention of the rumour in the recent biography of Robins by Brian Rendell.

Interviewed by the *Nottingham Journal*, Carr dealt summarily with the rumour. 'It's all bosh, I have no intention of giving up the captaincy,' was his immediate response. The Saturday of the Lancashire match was rained off, but on Monday Lancashire were not taking chances. The Nottingham press began their report of the day's play, 'Six hours' loitering at Trent Bridge carried Lancashire a step nearer the County

Championship. It was the type of cricket inseparable from the championship system.' Lancashire scored 254 for six. If that was not enough, Lancashire batted a further eighty minutes on the third day. Carr was so disgusted that he put George Gunn and Whysall on to bowl, the latter bowled two overs for five runs! Nottinghamshire were given 255 minutes, including the extra half hour to score 319, for first innings points. George Gunn managed to run himself out off a no-ball and young Joe Hardstaff on his county debut made an unbeaten 53.

The final two matches of the damp summer both ended in victories, but Carr was absent from both games. The press give no reason for his absence. In mid-November Carr was reported to be ill in a London nursing home, but his illness was described as 'not serious'.

In the final Championship table only six points separated the first four counties – Lancashire 155, Gloucestershire 152, Yorkshire 150, Nottinghamshire 149. Close though the battle appeared, Nottinghamshire's victories were all gained at the expense of the weaker counties.

Reading the reviews of the Nottinghamshire performance in 1930, both Nottingham morning newspapers suggest that the county failed to retain the Championship title because Harold Larwood was missing from many matches due to Test selection. This absence was made worse because Fred Barratt had a very moderate season with the ball. There is scarcely a mention of Carr in either review. Similarly the review which appeared in *Wisden* hardly mentions Carr. *The Cricketer* commented: 'Arthur Carr has proved but a pale reflex of his inspiring self, falling lower in the batting averages than ever before, whilst in the latter half of the season his captaincy has only been periodical.'

The question of Carr remaining as Nottinghamshire captain resurfaced near the end of December:

A bombshell has been dropped on county cricket by the announcement on Saturday – as yet unofficial – that Mr Arthur W Carr, captain of Nottinghamshire, has been asked to resign. This cricket sensation of the year was disclosed by PGH Fender, but no authoritative statement can be obtained from the club as Dr GO Gauld, the Hon Secretary, is in Kent and Ald JE Alcock of Mansfield, chairman of the committee, declined to make any reference to the matter when approached by a representative of the *Nottingham Journal*. Mr HA Brown, the secretary, when asked if he was prepared to make an authoritative statement, said, 'I have nothing to say on the matter.' Asked whether the committee were likely to make a statement, Mr Brown replied, 'I have not the slightest idea.' Lord Belper, the President of the club, when approached on the subject, emphatically declared that nothing at all had been settled, 'I am very sorry any statement has been made,' said Lord Belper, adding, 'and I shall issue no statement at present.'

Mr Shelton (a member of the committee) said to the *Journal*: 'It is not a matter in respect to which I am in a position to say anything. Most of this pitiable business, I think, has been brought about by people being too free in their methods of speech. In a matter of this kind, which comes up unexpectedly, I must be loyal to the committee and also to such a sterling cricketer as Mr Carr.'

Naturally, Mr Carr is very reticent concerning the whole matter and would prefer to remain silent. Sufficient to say that he is mystified concerning the action of the committee, and when interviewed by a representative of the *Nottingham Journal* on Saturday, expressed pain and surprise at the fact that the committee, following his illness, should have urged his retirement from the captaincy.

It can be stated that a sub-committee of the Nottinghamshire County Committee has definitely asked for Mr Carr's resignation, and that he has just as definitely refused. 'I have given my answer,' he said. 'I have told them I am not going to resign. If they do not want me then they must say so. I am not ill and shall be ready for play next season. Most likely the whole matter will be discussed by the full committee in January. Candidly I cannot understand the reason. I know of no other amateur who will sacrifice the time to play. Anyhow I have asked the committee for a quick decision because I want to prepare other plans if I am not re-elected. Naturally they have the right to get rid of me, but I am not going out with the excuse that I am ill.'

Incidentally, the first whispers that a change was contemplated came to the captain through an indirect channel, and he was somewhat nonplussed at the fact that he had not been approached personally, particularly in view of the increasing number of rumours circulated concerning him. On one occasion, it is said, someone actually rang him up and asked, 'Who's the new captain?' His position to say the least of it was an unfortunate and ambiguous one and all true sportsmen will sympathise with him in his present dilemma ... Asked if he would carry on as a member of the team if a change of captaincy was made, Mr Carr replied, 'Rather I would.'

Then he repeated his assertion that he was not going to resign the captaincy. 'What would the public think of me if I resigned the captaincy at this stage, when Nottinghamshire have lost Whysall and other members of the team? Why, they would regard me as a deserter of a sinking ship, No, I cannot see myself doing that sort of thing.'

Mr Carr emphasised that what annoyed him so much was 'all this had been going on behind his back. If the Committee had come to me in a straightforward way and stated their views I would have probably fallen in right away with their desires were it in the interest of the county cricket club.' He added that if Nottinghamshire did not want him as a member of the team he would be ready to play for anyone who might desire his services.

The reference to Whysall regarded the tragic death of that cricketer following an accident on a dance floor in Mansfield. Whysall died of septicaemia in Nottingham General Hospital on 11 November; Carr, owing to his illness, was unable to go to the player's funeral and was represented by his wife.

If the letter pages of the press are a guide, the Nottingham public were aghast that Carr might be replaced, a typical letter from EG Coghill of Holy Trinity Vicarage, Southwell, was written on 30 December 1930: 'I was pleased to see in today's *Nottingham Guardian* two letters concerning the captaincy of the Nottinghamshire Cricket XI, and I should like to say that I am in complete agreement with both correspondents. I was amazed when I first heard of the suggestion that Mr Carr should resign, and I do sincerely hope that this drastic step will not be taken by the Committee. The team will be weak enough through the death of Whysall and the retirement of G Gunn and Payton, and I am sure that all Nottinghamshire cricket lovers will agree with me that Mr Carr must remain captain. I have always admired his splendid leadership, his hard hitting, and his fine fielding; and his sporting declarations and management of the side in a crisis have been magnificent. I sincerely hope to see him as leader again this coming season, and that his magnetic personality will not be lost to Nottinghamshire. He could never be fitly replaced. I hope all other members of the Club will express the same view.'

The newspaper repercussions of Carr's captaincy brouhaha continued in the *Nottingham Journal* of 5 January, but added little to the previous catalogue of confusion. With notices for the AGM being dispatched to members at the beginning of February 1931, the club were clearly keen to resolve the captaincy problem before the membership had a chance to air their views. At a General Committee Meeting held on 27 January 1931, the main item on the agenda was headed 'The Captaincy' and ran as follows: 'The Sub-Committee appointed to meet Mr Carr reported that Mr Carr had met them and that the position had been fully explained to him and that he expressed himself to be in full agreement with the wishes of the Committee. The Sub-Committee therefore recommended that Mr Carr be invited to Captain the County XI for the coming season. It was unanimously resolved that this invitation be conveyed to Mr Carr by the Hon Secretary and that upon receiving Mr Carr's acceptance, the Hon Secretary should make a short statement to the press to the effect that the Committee had invited Mr Carr to become captain for next season and that he had accepted the invitation. The Committee expressed sincere thanks to the subcommittee for the satisfactory way in which they had carried out their duties.'

The Sub-Committee had consisted of Lord Belper, PA Birkin and Dr Gauld, the Honorary Secretary. When the press statement was issued by the club, Arthur Carr was in a nursing home in Regent Street, Nottingham, due to injuries sustained in a fall whilst hunting with the Quorn on 26 January. The statement was succinct: 'The Committee of Nottinghamshire County Cricket Club has offered the captaincy of the County XI for 1931 to Mr AW Carr, and it has been accepted by him.'

In his autobiography, Carr speculates that this whole episode was due to the fact that some of the Committee objected to him drinking rather heavily after a day's play, especially during away matches, and that he was setting a bad example to the younger members of the Nottinghamshire team.

Whilst the arguments over Carr and the Nottinghamshire captaincy occupied the cricket press and the members of the county cricket club, the controversial captain's father was busily engaged in horse racing from his home in Hemingford Abbots. Philip Carr had switched his successful horse, Solanum, from Harvey Leader's stables to those of Basil Briscoe. Briscoe had worked miracles on the horse and Carr promised to let Briscoe train other horses for him. The first of these appears to have been a difficult but most promising three-year-old, Golden Miller. His first race under Carr's colours was at Newbury on 29 November 1930. Golden Miller finished third. In his second race, at Leicester, Golden Miller won by five lengths. Six days later at Nottingham, Golden Miller won again by the same margin. Both races were over hurdles, but it was clear that the horse was really made for steeplechasing. Briscoe had the horse schooled over fences at his stables at Longstowe in Cambridgeshire, not too far from Philip Carr's home. He was entered for the Juvenile Chase at Cheltenham, but with a new jockey, Gerry Wilson. Golden Miller lost by a head.

Golden Miller and a second horse owned by Philip Carr, both being with Briscoe at Longstowe, came straight to Briscoe's mind in June 1931 when he had a telephone call from a Miss Dorothy Paget. Philip Carr had unexpectedly asked Briscoe to see all of his horses. Miss Paget had heard rumours about Carr selling up and Briscoe responded to the call with the declaration, 'I knew of the best steeplechase horse in the world, and also the best hurdleracer in the country.'

Miss Paget, a very rich and exceedingly eccentric lady, seemingly went up to Hemingford Abbots and agreed a price for both Golden Miller and Insurance – the amount published in sources varies, but the sum of £12,000 for the pair is the most frequently quoted. It is said that Philip Carr considered Miss Paget so 'odd' that he did not allow her in the house, but met at the lodge. Golden Miller won the Cheltenham Gold Cup five times for Miss Paget and the Grand National in 1934 – the horse is the only one to win both the National and the Gold Cup in the same year. A statue of the horse still stands at Cheltenham. Insurance also had a successful racing record. One can only speculate as to what might have happened if Golden Miller had come into the ownership of Arthur Carr.

The Nottinghamshire players reported for training on 13 April 1931; unusually Carr also came and joined the team for practice in the afternoon – in the past, as an amateur, Carr had not been at Trent Bridge so early in the summer. Apart from Whysall, Wilf Payton was also absent; he had accepted a post as a coach at Eton, a post obtained for him through the offices of Lord Belper, whose son was currently at the school. George Gunn had officially retired but turned out on the initial practice session to 'observe' the proceedings. When interviewed, Carr commented: 'We can hardly hope to do as well as we have done, but it will not be as bad as many people suppose. Naturally we shall be weakened, but it may only be temporarily and I don't see why we shouldn't make a good show after the team has settled down.'

For the third and what proved to be the last time the Nottinghamshire Committee arranged no less than thirty-four first-class fixtures – the now standard twenty-eight Championship games plus six friendlies. With three of the 1930 leading first XI batsmen absent (Whysall, George Gunn and Payton), and Carr supposedly not 100% fit according to several officials, the youngsters on the ground staff were certainly going to be thoroughly tested.

There was one Test match arranged against New Zealand, but of only three days duration. In 1927, during New Zealand's last visit, no Test matches were in the schedule, this time New Zealand performed so well in the one Test that two county fixtures were scrubbed and extra Tests added.

Voce had been Nottinghamshire's sole representative on the winter trip to South Africa and he had been highly successful, taking most wickets in the Test series and in all first-class matches while bowling more overs than anyone else. In retrospect had Chapman, who was the captain again, committed the same crime as in Australia in 1928/29, when he overbowled Larwood? It would seem, judging by the single Test Voce was to play in 1931, that Chapman now overused Voce.

Nottinghamshire began their campaign with two friendly inter-county games against Sussex and Glamorgan. On the eve of the first match, the press headline read 'Carr's Opening Pair Secret' and the *Nottingham Evening News* commented: 'Who will open the innings is a secret known only to Mr AW Carr. When I asked him to enlighten me as to his probable batting order he would only say: "I have made up my mind, who will open the innings, but I am not prepared to divulge who they are until the day of the match."' The journalist guessed GV Gunn and Willis Walker (Walter Keeton, another young player, was not available since he was still playing football for

Sunderland). On the day the answer was Arthur Staples and wicketkeeper Ben Lilley. The latter was dismissed without scoring and Nottinghamshire struggled to 131 for nine. Voce then joined Larwood and the last wicket doubled the total! Nottinghamshire ended on 269, Larwood hitting 102 and Voce 47. In Nottinghamshire's second innings, the experimental opening pair added 104 before the first wicket fell and, much to the delight of everyone, young Joe Hardstaff hit his first century; this tickled the statisticians since his father's last century at Trent Bridge had been against Sussex (in 1922). The match against Sussex was drawn; Nottinghamshire had an easy win in the friendly against Glamorgan.

The Championship matches started with a visit to Bristol. Arthur Staples and Lilley were retained as openers, but Carr dropped himself to number eight and remained there for the second game. The press were baffled. The third game, against Northamptonshire, saw Carr back at number four. The *Nottingham Evening News* noted: 'Carr's innings – it was his thirty-sixth hundred for Nottinghamshire – was reminiscent of his heyday as England's captain. All too long he has been dogged with ill-luck, but yesterday he laid the bogey by the heels, resurrecting that powerful drive to such perfection that in all his two hours fifteen minutes in scoring 100 not out, there was no trace of mistiming or recklessness. Carr's vigour brought him no fewer than ten fours in addition to his six sixes.'

The Staples-Lilley trial was cast aside for the seventh Championship match against Hampshire, being replaced by the return of fifty-one-year-old George Gunn and Walter Keeton. The team hit a winning streak. After ten matches Nottinghamshire were in second place behind Kent with just one point separating the two counties. Carr had been instrumental in victory against Middlesex at Lord's with another century. The next Nottinghamshire Championship game, as chance would have it, was against Kent. By obtaining victory with a 306-run margin, Nottinghamshire moved to the head of the Championship – fourteen points above Kent and twenty-one above Gloucestershire in third – but had played an additional match.

The Test team for the match at Lord's had been chosen and included both Larwood and Voce. The captain, who had been chosen a few days earlier, was to be DR Jardine. He had not led England before and was not even his county's captain, the latter being Fender. When the editor of *Wisden* wrote his notes on the 1931 season, it was clear that he still favoured Chapman returning as England captain for 1932 and presumably the 1932/33 tour to Australia, provided he scored a reasonable amount of runs in the coming summer (Chapman had a terrible summer with the bat in 1931).

On the Sunday of the Kent match, Arthur Carr went to Mansfield where he unveiled a memorial to Whysall and gave a moving speech, ending with, 'This is certainly the saddest duty I have ever had to discharge in my life – but it is also a great privilege.' The rest of the Nottinghamshire team were also present, as were the Kent cricketers and most of the Nottinghamshire Committee. In all about 10,000 crowded the cemetery.

Middlesex came to Trent Bridge for the return fixture. Nottinghamshire were without Voce and Larwood; Voce was at the Test match, Larwood should have been but cried off due to an ankle injury. Middlesex also lacked two principal bowlers – Allen and Peebles, also Robins – so no surprises, the game was a very high-scoring draw.

Carr became the first Nottinghamshire batsman to reach 1,000 runs and also headed the Nottinghamshire batting averages. His form was recognised when he was picked for the Gentlemen v Players game at Lord's. The draw against Middlesex was followed by a second against Leicester, which meant that though Nottinghamshire still led the Championship table, they were only six points ahead of Yorkshire. Gloucestershire occupied the third place, whilst Kent had fallen to fifth.

For the second time within a few weeks, the top of the table was pitched against second; Nottinghamshire v Yorkshire, as opposed to Nottinghamshire v Kent. Could Nottinghamshire win again? The unforeseen occurred as the team returned from the Aylestone Road Ground at the end of their match with Leicestershire. Driving down Loughborough Road in West Bridgford, it appears that the lorry carrying the team's bags, with GV Gunn at the wheel, attempted to race against Larwood's car, driven by Larwood with Sam Staples and Ben Lilley as passengers. The two vehicles collided and then overturned. The injured were taken to hospital and Carr, as soon as he learnt of the accident, went directly there. According to the press report, Carr was standing by Sam Staples' bed when the latter regained consciousness. Seeing his captain, Staples gasped, 'I'm all right, I shall be playing at Sheffield tomorrow.' Staples then lost consciousness again. Larwood, who had a badly damaged arm, also assured his captain he would be fit to play against Yorkshire. In fact Larwood, Staples and Gunn were not fit to play, but Lilley did turn out.

Arthur Staples with 131 and Willis Walker with 92 enabled Nottinghamshire to score 288 all out on the first day at Bramall Lane – some 19,000 spectators turned out, which indicated the importance of the game. Monday was badly affected by rain and the game ended in another draw, meaning that Nottinghamshire were still in front by four points. Due to the road accident, Carr contacted Lord's and explained that he would be unavailable for the Gentlemen v Players game which clashed with Nottinghamshire' next fixture against Gloucestershire. Jardine, rather than Carr, had been chosen as the captain of the Gentlemen's team and his innings of 49 was the highest in a rain-affected match.

Nottinghamshire managed points for a first-innings lead in what proved to be the county's fourth successive draw with Gloucestershire refusing to make a sporting declaration on the last day. Yorkshire won their game, taking them six points ahead of Nottinghamshire before the two counties met for their return at Trent Bridge. Nottinghamshire's attack was seriously weakened, not only were Larwood and Sam Staples still on the injured list but Voce strained a leg muscle bowling against Gloucester and was also absent. However it was the Nottinghamshire batting that let the team down. Carr's *bête noire*, Bowes, dismissed him twice for low scores. Only Walker played a decent innings. With the bowling so thin, Carr decided to open the attack himself.

'Corney', the *Nottingham Journal* reporter, certainly got excited: 'Carr opened the bowling. In his first over, when the umpire disallowed an appeal for leg-before, I am pretty sure he nearly lost his temper. The crowd cheered him on. In his third over there was no doubt about it. Sutcliffe was bowled. An off-break rattled the middle stump and disturbed the other two. For a moment or two Trent Bridge went mad. No wonder!'

For this game Nottinghamshire brought back Wilf Payton from his job as Eton's coach; gave a first-class debut to Archer Oates, nephew of the former Nottinghamshire wicketkeeper; and brought in Charlie Harris, who had not played since 1929. Yorkshire won by nine wickets and Nottinghamshire found themselves overtaken by Gloucestershire as well as Yorkshire.

An amusing aside resulted from Carr's dismissal of Sutcliffe. The next day Carr received the following telegram: 'In view of your astonishing success, please hold yourself in readiness for The Oval. Signed Selection Committee.' The sender of the message was Nigel Haig, the Middlesex captain; The Oval was the venue of the next Test match.

The game against Warwickshire at Edgbaston brought little comfort to the depleted Nottinghamshire team. Warwickshire made 394 for three on the opening day, Carr again opening the bowling. To Carr's fury Warwickshire did not declare overnight but continued on the second day. Carr showed his frustration by bowling under-arm lobs, his five overs costing 31 runs. The report noted, 'If Carr could have infused some of the wizardry of those old hands (i.e. Simpson-Hayward, Jephson etc) into his deliveries, Warwickshire's fourth-wicket stand might never have realised as it did 164 runs in less than two hours. There was no guile however about the amateur's lobs. They were fairly straight and normally low, but once the batsmen had recovered from the initial shock of the departure from the modern canons of the game, Carr ceased to worry them.'

Carr instructed the Nottinghamshire batsmen to play Warwickshire at their own game and Nottinghamshire batted through to 521 for seven, gaining a first innings lead of 10. The game did produce a second talking point – George Gunn and his son both scored hundreds, a new Championship record.

According to EW Swanton's biography of Gubby Allen, Carr left Edgbaston on the last afternoon of this game and travelled to Worcester, where Middlesex were playing the home side. Allen had taken six for 38 and had been picked for the England team to face New Zealand in place of Larwood who was not available due to his road accident. Carr supposedly went into the Middlesex dressing room and had a blazing row with Allen – Carr had previously written that he did not believe Allen worthy of a Test place. Did this incident actually occur? The press report of the last day's play at Edgbaston stated that Arthur Carr requested the extra half hour at 6 o'clock in order that Nottinghamshire could take the first innings lead!

Carr opened the bowling in the match against Lancashire at Old Trafford. He took the wicket of opening batsman, Charlie Hallows, who had scored 10. Carr conceded only 30 runs off fourteen overs but, at the close of play on the first day, he received a message that his father was gravely ill at his home at Hemingford Park. Carr therefore left Manchester and George Gunn assuming the captaincy. Philip William Carr died nine days later on 7 August. Philip had realised several months earlier that his illness was incurable, hence the sale of his racehorses. His funeral was held in St Margaret's Parish Church, Hemingford Abbotts followed by burial in the churchyard. His widow, Louisa, had been brought up in a Presbyterian household, but in her forties she had been confirmed into the Church of England. Like similarly situated families in villages all over England, the Carr family attended Holy Communion and Sunday services on a regular basis. After Philip died, Louisa went to his grave each Sunday to pay her respects and to furnish fresh flowers when necessary. It cannot be said that either Arthur or his brother was a regular churchgoer.

Carr did not return to the side until 12 August. He missed four matches excluding the Old Trafford game. After the completion of his return game (against Leicestershire), Nottinghamshire still stood second to Yorkshire in the Championship table – unfortunately that county had an unassailable lead of 72 points with four matches remaining.

Carr broke his thumb in two places whilst catching Crabtree off Voce's bowling at Southend on 20 August, an injury which ended his season, there were two Championship matches and a friendly against Glamorgan still to be played. Carr watched those games with his arm in a sling and a large bandage on his thumb.

Nottinghamshire finished the season in fifth place, perhaps a little lower than might have been hoped a few weeks previously, but higher than many had predicted at the season's start. Yorkshire were the runaway winners and there was little separating the next four in the table; only Yorkshire lost fewer matches than Nottinghamshire. Aside from the retirement of Payton and the death of Whysall, the county suffered more injuries than usual. Both Larwood and Voce missed several matches when Nottinghamshire were topping the table and then Carr had the double misfortune of his father's death followed by his own broken left thumb. The road collision in West Bridgford had not helped the county's cause either.

The *Nottingham Guardian* review noted: 'It is safe to say that no county in the country had a better captain than AW Carr showed himself to be. On the field he was both an example and an inspiration to his team and in scoring 1,285 runs in all matches he batted not in his old carefree style but with a solidarity and purpose, which saved the side at many a critical juncture. His slip fielding too was brilliant and when Nottinghamshire were in such a tangle that they scarcely knew which way to turn for bowlers, the captain took the ball himself.'

*The Cricketer's* review of the county summer made an interesting comment: 'The county started to play the brightest cricket, and in the hearing of the present writer, AW Carr told his men he wanted them to hit two hundred sixes in the season. That they only hit one hundred and five was due to the adverse pressure of circumstances.' It is believed that the writer was in fact Home Gordon, who attended the initial game against Sussex at Trent Bridge and was a particular friend of Carr's!

At the end of September probate of Philip William Carr's will was granted; he left £176,853.16s.7d. The executors were two of the stockbrokers who worked with the firm of WI Carr and Sons, LJ Bell and EGD Fawcett, plus his son Philip Gordon and his son-in-law Jacob Wendell. After substantial bequests to his widow, Louise Yates Carr, and generous bequests to his staff at both Hemingford Park and in his office, in broad terms the remainder was split three ways: a third to his son Philip Gordon and a third to his daughter Eileen Victoria Wendell both absolute, then the remaining third split in two and given in trust to his son Arthur William and Arthur's wife, Ivy. It was quite clear that Philip William Carr saw his son Arthur as someone incapable of managing large sums of money! This will and the subsequent will of Arthur's mother, who was to die in 1946, was the cause of much ill feeling in the family. The sum in the trusts for Arthur and Ivy amounted to £16,262, they received the income from that capital.

TS Pearson-Gregory, who had played county cricket for Middlesex from 1878 to 1885, moved to Harlaxton Manor, on the Nottinghamshire-Lincolnshire border, in the 1880s. He had been President of Nottinghamshire CCC in 1902 then a Committee member from 1904. His son was thought of as a possible Nottinghamshire captain directly after the war. Now aged eighty, father decided the time had come to retire.

At the AGM on 10 March 1932, on a proposal from Sir Julien Cahn, Arthur Carr was elected to fill the vacancy. It was pointed out during the meeting that in several counties the captain was an ex-officio member of the Committee, but although Carr was invited to attend meetings when appropriate he was not entitled to attend by right. Four days after the AGM the chairman therefore welcomed Carr to his first 'official' committee meeting. The next item in the minute book was that electing Carr as captain for the coming season.

Carr's only intervention during the early season Committee meetings was in the matter of hours of play – MCC had written to counties to canvas their opinions and try to standardise the hours for Championship matches. Carr stated that it was not desirable that periods of play should extend beyond two hours and the Committee agreed to put forward the following suggestion: 12 to 2, 2.45 to 4.45 and 5 to 7.

The Nottinghamshire playing staff reported for their first practice on 10 April. The only major player who had left the club was Fred Barratt, but George Gunn had yet to sign a contract and it was believed that he probably would only be called upon in emergency. The press report covering in detail the arrival of the players, using ample photographs to illustrate the piece, added 'AW Carr (capt) will be down later in the week'. A later illustration of players in the nets showed Carr, an overcoat draped over his blazer, and commented, 'Like a thoughtful general preparing to dispose his forces for the coming fray, AW Carr, Nottinghamshire captain, watched his men in the nets yesterday.'

George Gunn, though reportedly only playing in emergency, in fact opened the innings with Keeton in the first match. The match report commented: 'George Gunn, who will be fifty-three next month was reported to have had less than half an hour's practice prior to the match, but to have stated that if he could survive the first three overs he would be quite all right. The chance to substantiate his claim came straightaway, for AW Carr won the toss and sent the veteran in to open with Keeton. With the first delivery sent down, a poor delivery from Tate just off the off-stump, Gunn was as much at home again as if he had been batting for weeks. The four which rewarded a characteristic pull brought all the confidence needed and during the next hour and forty minutes .... "the man who never grows old" gathered 67 of the 132 runs produced in a wonderful first wicket stand.'

The match was drawn with rain interfering, but the following day a practice game was started in which George Gunn captained one side that also included son GV Gunn and his other son, Jack, described as a promising leg-break bowler. Jack's cricketing career did not even extend to Nottinghamshire Second XI and he never joined the Nottinghamshire groundstaff. He later abandoned his cricketing aspirations, becoming a successful businessman.

Matters took a turn for the worse when Nottinghamshire began their second game, the Whitsun fixture versus Surrey, and another draw. After Surrey had been dismissed for 108, Gunn, opening with Keeton, was struck on the temple by the first ball, a fast delivery from Gover. Gunn was felled and stretchered off the field, accompanied by Dr Gauld. Gover, in his autobiography, stated that the ball slipped out of his hand, resulting in a beamer. He went to see Gunn that evening in hospital to apologise, but Gunn said it was not Gover's fault, he had just lost sight of the ball. Hobbs, who was not playing in the match, stated in the following week's *Sunday Dispatch* that Trent Bridge, which had no sightscreen at the pavilion end and only a token one at the Radcliffe Road End, was unsafe for batsmen – ironically, Hobbs had discussed the sightscreen question with George some years back when Gunn's response was, 'One fine day someone will be killed.' Carr responded to Hobbs' criticism, saying that Hobbs was simply afraid to face Larwood at Trent Bridge – it had nothing to do with sightscreens. The injury to Gunn was the result of a full toss and could have happened on any ground. Larwood himself said that there was no justification whatsoever for Hobbs' criticism.

Gover, in his book, also tells the story of an incident involving Carr at The Oval. The tall, amateur fast bowler Maurice Allom bowled a bouncer to Carr, who fell backwards landing on his posterior and his bat flew into the slips. He shouted at the Surrey captain, Fender, 'Percy this is no way to play cricket,' to which Fender responded, 'Come on, get up Arthur and take the bouncer like a man!' This infuriated Carr, who started to thrash at every ball and was soon caught out. Hobbs watched Carr depart and commented to Fender, 'You talked him out, skipper.' With both Larwood and Voce playing and Carr leading them, it was the Nottinghamshire side that usually bounced out the opposition.

Although George Gunn recovered sufficiently to play in one or two later games during the summer, the injury effectively ended his career. If George Gunn had continued to play for two more summers, would the dramas that then played out have not occurred? Carr, whilst he praises George Gunn's ability both as batsman and fielder in his book, does not single him out as a man from whom he could ask advice but, by 1932, George Gunn was (aside from Walker who only played briefly prior to the war) the last of the great pre-war team on whom Carr had most certainly relied in his first term as captain in 1919.

India toured England in 1932 and played Test cricket in England for the first time, however there was only a single Test match, staged at Lord's. Interest beyond the Championship therefore centred on the selection of players for the forthcoming tour to Australia in the 1932/33 winter. Two Test trials were arranged. The first, at Old Trafford, included Larwood, Voce and Keeton. Larwood failed to take a wicket, but Voce returned the best innings analysis with five for 108. Keeton was forced to retire hurt in his second innings, having an injured knee. In the Nottinghamshire Championship game immediately following the trial, Larwood and Voce bowled unchanged through both Leicestershire innings; Larwood took ten for 88, Voce ten for 35.

The *Nottingham Journal* commented: 'Jointly their performance was remarkable, for under the astute guidance of Carr, it proved to my mind that properly used, Larwood and Voce are the most dangerous and formidable combination of fast bowlers in county cricket today on a hard wicket. Larwood's answer to the Test selectors is conclusive: the theory of him being unfit is exploded, and, his latest performance, even taking into account the puerile batting of the opposition, may go a long way towards restoring him to favour.' Larwood had been omitted, in favour of Bowes, for the single Test in India.

As a result of the victory over Leicestershire, Nottinghamshire now stood second in the Championship table, ten points behind Yorkshire, but with a match in hand. Larwood had taken 50 wickets at 9.80 and Voce 62 at 11.96. England beat India in the Test, Voce took five for 51, Bowes six for 79. Jardine captained the England side, continuing his leadership from the previous summer. He was, in addition, easily the most successful home batsman with scores of 79 and 85 not out. The following week it was announced that Jardine would captain the

MCC team to Australia, being supported by PF Warner and RNC Palairet as joint managers. After the easy hail-fellow-well-met leadership of Arthur Gilligan and Chapman, the selectors had changed tack, but appeared wary of what they thought was Jardine's ruthless streak. It was unfortunate for Carr that his batting was now unreliable and he couldn't stand comparison with Jardine, who had the added advantage of being seven years his junior. Jardine had also taken over as Surrey's captain, replacing Fender at the start of the 1932 season.

The vital Championship match began at Headingley on 9 July; Nottinghamshire attained a first-innings lead when Sellers declared with nine wickets down, 71 runs in arrears. Then came the most incredible bowling analysis in Championship history: Hedley Verity took all ten Nottinghamshire wickets at a cost of just ten runs. Chris Waters' *Ten For Ten* relates the terrible story of Nottinghamshire' abysmal innings in minute detail. Carr failed to score a run in either innings. If that wasn't embarrassing enough for Nottinghamshire, Yorkshire, requiring 139 to win in their second innings, knocked off the runs without losing a single wicket.

Carr's star, however, waxed against Essex at Trent Bridge, as the *Nottingham Guardian* reported: 'What bit of good fortune the Nottinghamshire captain enjoyed, for nothing seemed to have gone right with him since the season commenced. There may be ground for the opinion that Carr has spoilt himself by cramping his old care-free style and seeking to wear the mantle of the cautious batsman, which fits him where it touches. His display yesterday would certainly support that conclusion for a return to the methods of old revealed more of the real Carr in the space of the eighty minutes that elapsed before Nottinghamshire declared at a total of 306, than anyone had seen since days long gone by ….. With a hook for 6 off Smith to give him confidence, the ball striking a motor car in the car park, the amateur set about the attack with joyous enthusiasm driving superbly in front of the wicket to put boundary after boundary on the scorers' books.'

Carr hit 132 not out. This moved Nottinghamshire to 21 points behind Yorkshire, still with two games in hand. On the same day as Nottinghamshire beat Essex, the Test selectors announced the names of five players – Duleepsinhji, Hammond, Sutcliffe, Ames and Duckworth – to join Jardine on the trip to Australia.

A second Test trial was then arranged, England v The Rest at Cardiff Arms Park. Voce was in the England XI, Larwood, Keeton and Arthur Staples in The Rest XI. Before this trial was played the four Nottinghamshire trialists were available for the return with Yorkshire at Trent Bridge. The position at the top of the table had altered but was very tight: Kent were first with 163 points from nineteen matches, Yorkshire were second with 160 from seventeen, Sussex were third with 158 from fifteen, Nottinghamshire were fourth with 157 from seventeen.

The rain returned and more than half the playing time was lost; Yorkshire just managed a first innings lead. The next Nottinghamshire game, at Worksop, was another washout; as was the coinciding Test trial. The Surrey v Nottinghamshire Bank Holiday match at The Oval was yet another rain-ruined event. The match began on Saturday 30 July. Jardine won the toss and put Nottinghamshire in to bat; the sun was shining after overnight rain had produced a moist pitch, identical to the one on which Verity had caused chaos. This time Nottinghamshire did much better, Carr batted 150 minutes for 65, though Jardine dropped him in the slips when the Nottinghamshire captain had reached 50. Nottinghamshire's total was 267. Surrey fell to 43 for four with Voce, exploiting his leg theory, dismissing Hobbs for 2 and Sandham for 16. Bad light ended play early. On the same day it was announced that seven more players had been added to the six already chosen for Australia – Robins, Wyatt, Allen and Brown, all amateurs, plus Larwood and Voce.

There have been numerous books on the 1932/33 tour to Australia and many of them mention the meeting in the Piccadilly Hotel grill room of Carr, Jardine, Larwood and Voce. Indeed, this meeting is a major feature in the recent play on the tour, but no one seems to be able to pin down the day on which the meeting took place. Sunday 31 July is, I suppose, the most likely, but any of the other days from Friday to Tuesday are possible. The most detailed description of what happened springs from an article written after the Second World War by Walter Hammond, who was not present and doesn't seem to have been a particular friend of any of the four who attended.

For any reader unfamiliar with the grill room meeting, the conversation mainly involved the tactics required to dismiss Bradman, particularly by employing leg theory. Arthur Carr did not go into any specifics in his autobiography. He wrote: 'We all went to the grill room at the Piccadilly Hotel and although it took some time to warm up Larwood and Voce to talk in the company of their not exactly hail-fellow-well-met captain-to-be in Australia, they did eventually get going. What was discussed between us four that evening over dinner was subsequently developed on the ship on the journey out by Jardine and Larwood.'

Bank Holiday Monday saw Surrey score 87 more runs for the loss of four more batsmen. A thunderstorm ended play twenty minutes after lunch with 10,240 spectators present. On the final day the soaked ground made play impossible until half-past three – little interest could be engendered, few of the paying public turned out and Nottinghamshire were satisfied with first innings points. The county were twenty-five points behind Yorkshire and still in fourth place. Leyton was the next port of call for the Nottinghamshire cricketers. Rain prevented play before lunch on the first day against Essex, which left Nottinghamshire 230 for four and Arthur Staples unbeaten on 94. Nottinghamshire were all out for 290 on the second morning, then watched as Cutmore and Wilcox laid into the Nottinghamshire attack – 99 added for the second wicket in seventy minutes with the total reaching 144 for two. Despite having six fielders in the leg trap, Larwood and Voce made no progress until Cutmore was dismissed. Larwood hit the incoming batsman, O'Connor, in the groin causing him to retire and the rest of the batting simply folded, providing Nottinghamshire with a 94 run lead. A sporting declaration by Carr on the last day ought to have brought success, but Nottinghamshire ruined their chances by dropping crucial catches.

A report in the *Nottingham Guardian* of 6 August stated that Arthur Carr had agreed with the Western Province Cricket Association to take a combined team of Nottinghamshire and Yorkshire cricketers on a tour of South Africa in the coming winter, provided that the tour was sanctioned by MCC and did not include Tests. No further mention of this proposal appeared in the press and it received no mention in Carr's book.

Following the Essex match, Nottinghamshire had seven matches to play – the results were four wins, two draws and one loss. Quite a respectable return, but Yorkshire demonstrated their superiority, winning every one of their last seven games. Nottinghamshire ended in fourth place. Larwood took 149 wickets at 11.49 runs each, Voce 123 at 15.95. The *Nottingham Guardian* review of the season noted: 'A special tribute must be paid to the excellent captaincy of AW Carr. The amateur did not enjoy a particularly profitable season in the batting sense, although managing to complete a thousand runs, but his leadership was exemplary and marked by good judgment and keenness ..... Carr fielded splendidly and the way in which he handled his attack was beyond reproach. His troubles were many, for in the second match of the season, George Gunn senior was badly injured by a blow on the head from Gover, the Surrey fast bowler, and the old first-wicket problem loomed up again, large and ugly.'

Hemingford Park,

St Ives,

Huntingdon.

Thursday 25th May.1933.

Dear Brown,

Enclosed receipt for money received.

This is the most awful team I have ever had, the batting is awful and the bowling,my God. I have not got a bowler. Voce can hardly move and you know what the rest are like. We shall not win a match until Larwood is right. Its most disheartening and I am feeling it very very much. If anyone would like to take on my job they can have it. I wired Hogarth suggesting Larwood should see a specialist in London,,he replies nothing can be done without the sanction of the M.C.C. I will see Findlay. He must be operated on at once or he will never bowl again. Will you arrange for a Selection Meeting next Thursday? I shall have a lot to say. I hope it rains for the rest of the season.

Yours,

(Signed) Arthur Carr.

"I hope it rains for the rest of the season" –
Carr does not look forward to cricket after Bodyline

# 13

## BODYLINE FALLOUT

### 1932-1933

On 16 September 1932, Larwood and Voce caught the 3.00 pm train from Nottingham LMS Station bound for London St Pancras. There was a large crowd of well-wishers, some county players and family. Arthur Carr was absent on holiday. The two Nottinghamshire players went from St Pancras to Lord's where a banquet was held for the touring party. The details of the voyage out to Australia and the match series have been the subject of much writing (*Bodyline Autopsy* written by David Frith provides as good a description of the tour as can be found) so it would be repetitious to go into detail on the tour, but England won the five-match Ashes series by four to one. Eighty years later it remains the most talked about Test series of all time.

The press in both England and Australia perhaps made more of the controversy created by leg theory than it warranted. Politicians became involved and Harold Larwood suddenly became a name with which every man in the street, cricket fan or not, was familiar. By extension Arthur Carr, as Larwood's captain and mentor, was becoming known outside the circle of cricket enthusiasts. This explains the excitement which would unfold in Carr's life through the several years which followed the 1932/33 tour.

The popular weekly magazine *John Bull* carried a long article in its edition of 17 September 1932 which, though it doesn't mention Carr, compares Jardine to the two preceding touring captains to Australia: 'There are some players who criticise him [Jardine] as belonging to the old school of cricket and regard him as a reactionary who will destroy much of the happy family spirit that prevailed in All-England teams serving under Percy Chapman – the best-loved captain England ever had, with both teams and spectators – and "dear old Gilligan". Chapman and Gilligan never really succeeded in stamping out that over-generous hospitality of the Australian crowd and that indifference of many players to the rigorous training that is essential if they are to leave Australia as fit as they entered it.'

Carr's direct involvement in the Bodyline fallout did not begin until after the final Test in Sydney, which finished on 28 February 1933. Any correspondence that Carr might possibly have had with the England party in Australia – if any such correspondence ever existed – is, as far as can be gauged, no longer extant. Even before the final Test had ended the Nottingham newspapers launched a 'Shilling Fund' for Larwood and Voce, but it was not until 15 March that the newspapers interviewed Arthur Carr for his opinions. The *Daily Express* cricket correspondent, William Pollock, quoted Carr on leg theory bowling, with Carr stating that he would use it when the ground was suitable and that it was not against the Laws of the game.

The following week Carr went to see Mrs Larwood and surprised her by saying he was off to Port Said to meet Larwood when the *Otranto*, on which Larwood and the Nawab of Pataudi had travelled from Australia, would call there. Mrs Larwood gave Carr a letter for her husband. The English press must have been aware that the most promising source for any stories directly from Larwood was Arthur Carr. The *Daily Sketch* took the initiative by paying Carr to go to Egypt to obtain some exclusive interviews with the most famous England bowler of the moment. Carr sent a Marconigram to Larwood from London on 21 March which read: 'Meeting you Suez Don't talk to anyone until I see you. AW Carr.' Carr then sent a second message on 25 March: 'Important Meet Alone Suez. Please come ashore and rejoin boat Port Said. Letter wife. Carr.' A third message was sent when Carr arrived in Cairo: 'Travelling with you from Suez. Mystery Wifes Letter. Crowds journalists boarding Otranto. See me first. Carr.' These Marconigrams were preserved by Harold Larwood and the originals are now to be found in the Bradman Museum in Bowral, New South Wales. If Carr himself was the recipient of any written material either from Larwood or from journalists in these early months of 1933, it is most likely that the material was thrown away when Carr's marriage collapsed.

The comment made by Carr to the *Daily Express* on the use of leg theory in the coming season led to an item in the 4 April meeting of the Nottinghamshire CCC Committee (at the previous month's meeting Carr had been reappointed captain for 1933): 'The question of the use of leg theory by certain members of the team during the coming season was considered and it was resolved to refer the matter to the Selection Committee to see Mr Carr and to report. The attention of the Committee was drawn to a statement in the press made by Mr Carr to the effect that he intended to employ what was known as Bodyline Bowling this season in county matches. It was resolved that a letter be sent to Mr Carr expressing regret that he should have made his statement, considering that this matter is in abeyance at present until it has been considered by MCC and asking him to refrain from any further statement of this nature.'

It was all very cloak and dagger. Initial rumours in the press stated that Carr was on his way to see Larwood with messages from Nottinghamshire CCC and MCC. Both bodies when approached denied any knowledge of these 'messages'.

Mrs Carr was interviewed and stated: 'With regard to the unfounded rumour published today. Mr Carr has not made any hurried departure from England, but has gone on a short trip to Egypt. He may see Larwood if he arrives in time, but has not gone in anyway in connexion with Nottinghamshire County Cricket Club and does not bear any message from them.'

A member of the County Cricket Club Committee stated: 'I did not even know that Mr Carr had gone abroad, but if he has done so, it is entirely for personal reasons. The subject of Larwood's leg-theory has not been discussed by members of the Committee and the suggestion that Mr Carr has gone out at the request of the Committee to see Larwood is absolute nonsense.'

Whilst Carr was on his Egyptian trip his wife, Ivy, had asked her son, Angus – then aged fifteen – to drive her to Loughborough. The car was stopped by a PC Jesson. Angus was charged with driving whilst under the age of seventeen and the case was heard by the Loughborough magistrates. Ivy Carr was fined three guineas for permitting Angus to drive. Two mitigating circumstances were offered, that Carr was in Cairo meeting Larwood and that Mrs Carr did not expect to meet a policeman on the road!

Despite instructions from Carr not to talk to anyone, LV Manning of the *Daily Sketch* managed an interview with Larwood at Suez on 2 April. Larwood is quoted as saying: 'I just can't say one word, but that does not mean I am not going to.' He went on to tell Manning that he had come home before the rest of the team because he was anxious to get his troublesome leg attended to before the English season opened. LV Manning had begun his career as a sports journalist in 1919 and was known for his coverage of controversial stories, though more in football than cricket. His son Jim Manning followed the same career and was better known in cricketing circles.

The *Daily Sketch* of 7 April reported that Manning was travelling with Carr and Larwood across the Mediterranean and then via the Blue Train from Toulon to Victoria Station. Using a radio link, Manning reported Carr's comments: 'Nothing short of a legislative move by MCC would prevent Nottinghamshire using leg theory.' Manning asked if Carr was afraid of retaliation, to which Carr replied, 'No, anyway, who is going to bowl it? There is no one in first-class cricket with Larwood's accuracy, let alone pace. Bowes can bump, but that is not the Larwood ball, and I can see a lot of cheap runs for my batsmen if this ball is not bowled with Larwood's amazing accuracy.' When asked if leg theory tactics would ruin English cricket as a spectacle, Carr replied, 'Rubbish, we are going to make it more exciting. An army of critics won't deny that. Long innings and big totals can be a bore. It may restrict scoring strokes on the off, but it may also produce some brand new ones. Anyway, it's up to the batsmen. Bowlers have not had much encouragement in the last few years. My actual plans for using fast leg theory I shall have an opportunity to discuss in the *Daily Sketch*. Suffice it now to say that my talk with Larwood left me with higher admiration than ever for a game boy, who, I can tell you, is just dying to get into flannels again in spite of all he has been through – and the mental strain has been greater than the physical. You have no idea how the boy has been pestered, worried and maligned. My county never had a bigger hearted player, and it won't be his fault if Nottinghamshire don't win the Championship this summer.'

When Larwood and Carr arrived at Victoria Station, they were met by Lionel Kirk, representing the Nottinghamshire Committee, and the Nottinghamshire Secretary, HA Brown, as well as Mrs Larwood. The five took a taxi to St Pancras where the Secretary of MCC, W Findlay, spoke to Larwood emphasising the fact that his contract forbade him talking to the press on matters relating to the Australian tour.

The *Nottingham Evening News* of 25 April published a long article supporting leg theory. It includes the following comments: 'Leg theory won the Ashes in Australia, and as it is a Nottinghamshire product, quite naturally many people are wondering whether it will have the same controversial effect in the county cricket. Frankly I don't think so. There are three people in England who know more about leg theory than anyone else. One is AW Carr, the Nottinghamshire captain. The other two are Larwood and Voce. If there is to be competition in leg theory methods, Nottinghamshire, then, will start with a big advantage. To impose scaremongering legislation against it would be like putting all left-hand bowlers in handcuffs and turning Larwoods into lob bowlers. It is no use disguising facts. Some cricket administrators even in Nottinghamshire are on tenterhooks about this leg-theory problem. Private talks have been going on at Lord's, but until MCC issue a definite ruling on the subject it is difficult to say what will happen. I find that those who are ready to condemn leg theory do not know what leg theory really is and for that reason the first authoritative statement given last week by AW Carr in a newspaper article was welcomed. In that article Carr gave quite plainly the reasons for leg theory ... Carr knows and Larwood and Voce also know, that whether it is leg theory or any old theory, the Woolleys, the Sutcliffes and the Hammonds will always get hundreds against it. So why tamper with the rules? The English way out is to train batsmen how to play it. Perhaps some of them already know.'

The Nottinghamshire players reported for pre-season practice on 18 April. Carr was present but did not take part. Larwood was absent, being in London at a West End store, where he gave bowling demonstrations. The first Nottinghamshire match was arranged for Trent Bridge against Worcestershire on

3 May. Despite much newspaper discussion on the fitness of Larwood and in particular his damaged foot, he was among the Nottinghamshire eleven who took the field. Rain seriously interfered with play, only 330 minutes spread over the three days, not even first innings points being decided. Larwood bowled two overs but did not bat. Voce was absent, still travelling home with the MCC team. On the first morning of the match, the new gates dedicated to JA Dixon were formally opened by Sir Stanley Jackson, the former Yorkshire and England cricketer. Among those present were the Lord Mayor and Lady Mayoress of Nottingham, Councillor H Seely Whitby and Mrs Whitby. The former was soon to play a large part in Carr's final days as a county cricketer; the booklet *Oh! Those Ashes* was dedicated to the Lord Mayor and almost certainly funded by him.

Three days later Larwood spoke for the first time about the tour – the details were published in the *Sunday Express* of 7 May, the interview and subsequent article being by the paper's sports editor, Charles Eade. The article was accompanied by a handwritten letter from Larwood to Eade, pointing two small changes and thanking Eade for the cheque. 7 May was the date on which the main touring party finally arrived home, and were greeted by a crowd of pressmen, but as a body the tourists would not talk to the media.

The following day, in the course of a Nottinghamshire CCC Committee meeting, the article was discussed and the following minute written: 'It was resolved that the following resolution be sent to Larwood: "That the Committee depreciate the action Larwood has taken in signing the article which appeared in the *Sunday Express* on 7 May and that his attention be drawn to the terms of his agreement." It was resolved that this resolution be conveyed to him by letter.' Back in March, the *Daily Express* had written to the Committee to ask permission for Larwood to write articles for the paper. It was resolved that permission cannot be granted.

Directly after the Worcester game came a second home match against Glamorgan. Carr made a sporting declaration on the third day, but so much time was lost through the weather that another draw was recorded – as Worcester and Glamorgan were two Championship minnows, both ought to have provided Nottinghamshire victories which would have given the county an encouraging start. Larwood again played. He took Glamorgan's first wicket, that of Arnold Dyson, the opener, caught at backward point, but the ground was so wet that Larwood struggled to keep his footing and bowled just five overs for 10 runs. The off breaks of Sam Staples proved the most successful. The principal press interest centred on the appearance of Bill Voce on the second day – he attracted many handshakes from spectators and a crowd of autograph hunters.

The day after the Glamorgan game ended, a dinner was held at the East Kirkby Miners' Welfare Institute at which Larwood and Voce were both presented with various gifts, tokens of the appreciation felt by the people of Kirkby and district. The presentations were made by FJ Aspinall, manager of Bentinck Colliery, where both players had at one time been employed. AW Carr was unable to attend due to a chill and the County Cricket Club was represented by HA Brown.

There followed no less than five successive away games. The first of these was at Aylestone Road. Larwood had been down to play but complained on the eve of the game that his fractured foot was giving trouble. Carr commented: 'I'm expecting Larwood to see Mr Hogarth today. It is unfortunate, but I am afraid an operation on the fast bowler's foot will be necessary.'

Leicestershire were disappointed about Larwood's absence, having expected a record gate for what was their opening match of the summer. On Saturday 13 May, the opening day of the game, the *Daily Sketch* printed an exclusive article entitled 'Arthur Carr on Larwood'. The opening paragraph ran: 'As one who knows him better than most, I should say Harold

Larwood is just about the most worried man in the world. Even those who feel he should not have spoken must realise after reading the Larwood statement sent out by the President of Nottinghamshire County Cricket Club, the predicament he found himself in when he realised his position – especially in regard to his colleagues of the tour. I know that he had no deliberate intention of stealing a march on any of them, and I know he has been so worried and upset about the whole wretched business that he has hardly known whether he has been standing on his head or his heels.'

Carr scored 87, the highest innings on either side in what turned out to be a drawn match. On the final morning of the game, the *News Chronicle* published the first instalment of extracts from Harold Larwood's forthcoming book *Body-Line?* Nottinghamshire travelled that evening to Hove for their three-day game against Sussex. Larwood was included in the side. Mr Hogarth, having inspected the foot, pronounced that no operation was necessary. Sussex scored 445, Larwood did not bowl; Nottinghamshire collapsed 227 all out and were forced to follow on. Carr was despondent announcing: 'This is the first time I can remember since I played for the team twenty-two years ago, that Nottinghamshire have ever followed on in a County Championship match.' It was a harsh coincidence that it should be Carr's thirty-ninth birthday, noted the *Nottingham Journal*. Nottinghamshire lost the game by ten wickets.

There was a drawn match away to Worcester in which Larwood batted at number six made 52 not out in the second innings. Nottinghamshire moved on to Fenner's. Carr hit 123 in 155 minutes with two sixes and fourteen fours and Nottinghamshire at last recorded victory. This clearly encouraged the side – the fifth away game brought another victory, this time in the Championship against Middlesex at Lord's. Nottinghamshire were 127 behind on first innings. Sam Staples dismissed Middlesex for 118 and Nottinghamshire required 246 in 255 minutes. Carr opened the innings but played very carefully, giving Nottinghamshire a sound start; Larwood and Arthur Staples added 101 for the fourth wicket before Larwood fell for 43. 34 more were required; young Joe Hardstaff had the satisfaction of hitting the winning run.

The Surrey Whitsun game on 3, 5 and 6 June was next on the fixture list. It had been arranged that the proceeds of the Larwood and Voce Shilling Fund should be presented to the two players on Bank Holiday Monday. 18,000 spectators came to see the celebration. DR Jardine was Surrey's captain and at close of play Larwood, Voce, Jardine and the Lord Mayor Seely Whitby of Nottingham, plus other dignitaries, assembled on the upper deck of the West Wing Stand. Larwood and Voce each received £388 and a silver salver. Larwood's book was also launched during the game, which was drawn.

However, behind the scenes Carr was unhappy with the medical treatment Larwood was receiving and the people controlling that treatment. On 25 May, Carr wrote from his mother's house at Hemingford Park, St Ives, to HA Brown:

Dear Brown,

Enclosed receipt for money received. This is the most awful team I have ever had, the batting is awful and the bowling, my God. I have not got a bowler, Voce can hardly move and you know what the rest are like. We shall not win a match until Larwood is right. Its [sic] most disheartening and I am feeling it very very much. If anyone would like to take on my job they can have it. I wired Hogarth suggesting Larwood should see a specialist in London, he replies nothing can be done without the sanction of the MCC I will see Findlay. He must be operated on at once or he will never bowl again. Will you arrange for a Selection Meeting next Thursday? I shall have a lot to say. I hope it rains for the rest of the season.

Yours, Arthur Carr.

The letter was copied and sent to AW Shelton, who immediately telegrammed Carr, who was playing for Nottinghamshire against Cambridge University: 'To Fenners Cricket Ground, Cambridge. Hearty congratulations on your fine century. When sending your telegram to Hogarth on Thursday did you then know that he was acting professionally for and on behalf of the Marylebone Club as regards Larwood's foot. Kindly reply at once. AW Shelton.'

Carr responded, 'To Shelton, King St, Nottm. Did not know Hogarth was acting for MCC. Anyhow Larwood is not better than when in Australia. Carr.'

Shelton sent this to Hogarth, who wrote to AW Shelton on May 27:

I am much obliged to you for your letter and for sending me Mr Carr's reply to your wire. All I can say that it isn't correct. Mr Carr knew perfectly well that I was acting on behalf of the Marylebone Cricket Club in Larwood's case – perfectly well, I have told him several times, and not only that there was a public official statement on Larwood made by me on their behalf. It is ridiculous of him to say he did not know, and it is quite ridiculous also to say that our Committee don't know. They most certainly do. At the present moment Larwood is under my professional care, acting on behalf of the Marlebone [sic] Club, and I am responsible to them for what treatment he has and for what he does. If you or any other member of the Nottinghamshire County Committee want to send him to see someone else, well I suppose that is a private matter altogether, but it doesn't quite seem to me to be the proper way to do things. The injury to Larwood's foot, the nature of which is not in doubt, has been discussed by me with many of the most eminent surgeons in England, and the line of treatment adopted is the one generally suggested. It isn't true to say that Larwood's foot is as bad as it was when he was in Australia – that is an untruth. When he came back here he couldn't run or play golf or walk on it much. By treatment I got it so much better that he was able to play cricket and even to bowl. Then I thought it advisable that he should have a rest from bowling for a time.

How can he be as bad as he was in Australia, when he made over 60 the other day and is playing cricket. Surely you must see that that is an untrue statement. When I see Larwood again, which I suppose will be next Wednesday, I will decide what is the best thing to be done with him, and it is quite possible I may deem an operation advisable then. It is ridiculous to suppose that I am not as interested as anyone else that Larwood should be made well as quickly as possible and available as a bowler for our county. When you told me the other day that the whole position was obscure to you and that you did not understand what the position was as regards to Larwood, I was very much surprised. I suggest to you that the position has never been obscure in any way and I cannot understand why you, as the President of our Club, did not understand the position, and if you did not understand it, why didn't you come to me and ask me exactly what the medical position was? I am sorry to have all this bother – I think it is a great pity and bad for our Club, and my desire is always to cooperate and help in every way I can to further its interests.

Yours sincerely, RG Hogarth.


Carr's original comments are lost, but presumably they followed his note during the Leicester match when Larwood was unfit to play. It is baffling that AW Shelton claims he was completely in the dark. Shelton assiduously attended Committee meetings and as President he chaired those meetings. In addition he seems to have spent more time on the Trent Bridge Ground than almost anyone else. It was not until July that both Carr and Hogarth were present at a Nottinghamshire CCC Committee meeting.

At the Committee meeting on 14 June, two items relating to Larwood were raised. He had written to the club to state that he did not believe he had broken his agreement with Nottinghamshire by writing about the Australian tour. The Committee agreed that Larwood had in fact not broken any agreement and the club had no objection to him writing about the tour. In a separate minute Hogarth was thanked for the great amount of trouble he had taken over Larwood's injury.

On 7, 8 and 9 June there was a high-scoring draw against Northamptonshire away from home during which Carr scored a century. Northamptonshire possessed Clark, described in *Wisden* that year as 'in the absence of Larwood, England's most dangerous fast bowler'. A left-hander of Voce's ilk, he was also known to employ leg theory tactics. The *Nottingham Journal* reported on Carr's innings: 'Clark might have been a slow bowler for all the respect Carr showed him, the Nottinghamshire captain walking out of his crease on several occasions to drive the left-hander to the boundary and lashing him through the covers with impunity. In his first 60 Carr had ten fours – all drives – and after completing 101 out of 158 in two hours and ten minutes he hit Cox for two sixes – one a pull sending the ball over the football embankment.'

Larwood did not play, being seen by specialists in London. The press reported on the visit to Harley Street, the upshot of which was that Larwood was free to play but should not bowl again during the season. Carr was asked to comment and said, 'I think I shall have to get some special fielding shoes while we're in Northampton.' It was not made clear whether these were for Carr or Larwood!

To the relief of all came two successive Nottinghamshire victories. Nottinghamshire were languishing thirteenth in the Championship table on 10 June, ten days later the county had moved up to ninth. Sam Staples took eight wickets to be the principal architect of a victory over Hampshire, whilst his brother Arthur took eleven wickets versus Derbyshire in the second win. In the latter match Carr hit 137 not out, he then declared Nottinghamshire innings closed at 408 for four. Larwood played in both games as a batsman. At this point Carr stood seventh in the overall first-class batting averages with a statistic of 50.53.

The match between Nottinghamshire and Yorkshire at Trent Bridge lost much of its usual intensity as it clashed with the first Test against West Indies at Lord's; four Yorkshire players were in the England team. With Voce very much out of form due to his winter's efforts and Larwood only used as a batsman, there were no Nottinghamshire players picked. Jardine retained his place as England's Test captain. England won by an innings, due to the spin bowling of Robins and Verity.

On the first day of the Yorkshire match at Trent Bridge, Nottinghamshire reached 241, the highest scorers being Larwood 59 and Voce 61, the pair adding 117 for the seventh wicket. Bowes took seven for 89. Nottinghamshire then dismissed Yorkshire cheaply with young Butler picking up five for 36, probably much helped by Voce bowling leg theory at the other end. Harold Butler, from the small village of Clifton near Nottingham, was to become Nottinghamshire's main strike bowler and played for England against South Africa in 1947 and the subsequent series of 1947/48 in West Indies.

Back in 1933, Nottinghamshire obtained a lead of 86 over Yorkshire. In the second innings Bowes, clearly retaliating to Voce's attack, resorted to a frequent use of bumpers, one of which hit and knocked unconscious Walter Keeton – a photograph shows him carried off the field by Carr, the not out batsman. Nottinghamshire ended the second day with a lead of 204 with four wickets in hand. Nottinghamshire had not beaten Yorkshire at Trent Bridge since 1891, but on the last afternoon the pitch became much easier and despite a declaration by Carr, Yorkshire through Wilfred Barber (109*) batted out time.

It would be tedious to go match by match through the rest of the season, especially since Larwood's bowling was not employed and Voce's figures continued to be modest. Of the games in this second half the most impressive was against Sussex at Hove. Sussex were then in second place in the table.

Nottinghamshire gained a first innings lead of 148 due to the success of an unknown amateur, Ramsay Cox, in taking five wickets for 36 and dismissing Sussex for 157. Nottinghamshire went on to win by nine wickets and briefly rose to fifth place. Cox played some matches for Cambridge University, though he was not awarded a blue. He was destined to play occasionally for Nottinghamshire until 1954 and captained the county's second XI. He was a major force in local club cricket.

There was much press interest when Leicester came to Trent Bridge and were told that Carr and the visiting captain Dawson had agreed that no head high bumpers should be bowled in the match. EHD Sewell, a former Essex cricketer and now well-known journalist with the *Daily Mirror,* thought the idea pretty silly. Carr defended his agreement in his *Daily Sketch* column, saying that someone will be killed and suggesting that Larwood was the only bowler capable of 'safe' leg theory bowling, due to his accuracy. Voce employed leg theory a week later when Nottinghamshire played Surrey at The Oval – Hobbs was hit by Voce, but still managed a century.

Jardine's tour book, *In Quest of The Ashes,* came in for much praise by the Nottinghamshire press. It had been published during the Old Trafford Test in late July when Jardine, captaining England, scored 127, despite the leg theory bowling of both Martindale and Constantine. Both these players were certainly fast, it was their lack of accuracy that made them relatively ineffective. On 18 August, when Yorkshire beat Nottinghamshire at Park Avenue, Bradford, the White Rose County secured the Championship title. Carr scored a valiant 97 not out in a vain attempt to save the match. During Nottinghamshire's next match against Lancashire at Old Trafford, Voce was offered £30 per week to sign for Accrington and quit county cricket – he declined the offer.

Shortly after Nottinghamshire's victory at Worksop against Northamptonshire, a couple of unusual letters appeared in the

*Nottingham Guardian:* 'Dear Mr Carr – We, the undersigned, Members of Nottinghamshire County Cricket Club, are of the opinion that we are expressing the views not only of the members, but of the cricketing public in general, in thanking you most warmly for the splendid loyalty you have shown to the Club, and the wonderful way in which you have captained the county eleven, with only one rest of three days, during what must have been one of the most trying seasons ever known. We consider that your example on the field has been an inspiration to the side and could not have been equalled by any other county captain. We hope you will remain the county's captain for several years longer and can ensure you of our entire support and gratitude.'

Two days later a letter to Carr from the Nottinghamshire professionals was published in the same paper: 'Sir – Having seen the letter in yesterday's *Guardian* to Mr AW Carr, which was signed by over one hundred members of Nottinghamshire CCC, we, the professionals of the County XI, would like to express our very deepest appreciation and gratitude to our "Skipper" for the splendid and untiring way he has captained the side this year. No man could have done more than he has done, and older members of the side especially, know what anxiety and worry this has entailed during what has been a most difficult season – a period of team building. We all thank Mr Carr from the bottom of our hearts for his guidance, counsel and friendship, and hope that he may be spared many more years to continue as the county's captain.' Carr had a suitable reply thanking members published in the paper the following day.

The final county game at Trent Bridge against Kent at Trent Bridge ended in a draw, with Keeton completing 1,061 runs, average 81.53 during the month of August there followed a last draw against Somerset at Taunton; Nottinghamshire ended in eighth place in the Championship, though the county only lost three matches.

The *Nottingham Guardian* review described the season as one of the leanest and anxious that the club has ever experienced, but in dealing with individual players its praise for Carr is unstinting: 'No one deserved better of the county's followers than AW Carr, who showed himself a real captain in every sense of the word. Worried though he must have been on many occasions, weighed down by the cares and troubles of leading a team which he knew to be inadequate to the demands of the moment, the amateur strove by advice, encouragement and personal example to restore confidence and give inspiration. His handling of the depleted bowling resources could not have been bettered; in the field he set an example of keenness and efficiency which was magnificent; and at the wickets his efforts to pull the game round, when not infrequently matters were going wrong, were heroic.'

A confidential letter was sent to each first-class county at the beginning of November 1933 stating that a meeting of the Advisory County Cricket Committee and the Board of Control would be held at Lord's on 23 November and asking that each county should be represented by both their captain and their usual delegate to ACCC meetings. Nottinghamshire sent AW Carr and Dr Gauld. No less than fourteen counties were represented by both their captain plus their usual representative. The three other county captains were unavailable but sent a delegate.

The following decision was agreed relating to leg theory bowling: no alteration in the present Laws was required. It was agreed that any form of bowling which is obviously a direct attack by the bowler upon a batsman would be an offence against the spirit of the game. It was decided to leave the matter to the captains in complete confidence that they would not permit or countenance bowling of such type. This declaration was to play a vital role in the future of not only Carr as captain, but also the Nottinghamshire County Cricket Club Committee as it stood.

By 1934 Carr was beginning to show his age

# 14

# HEART ATTACK

## 1934

Despite Carr's letter to HA Brown in May 1933 and the consequent rather unpleasant correspondence with RG Hogarth, the following paragraph appeared in the Annual Report of the county club on 1 March 1934: 'Special tribute was due to Mr AW Carr who led the side with all his special skill and to SJ Staples who bowled untiringly [Staples took ninety-seven wickets for the county and topped the bowling table]. It was hoped that Larwood would be completely restored to fitness at the beginning of the season and that, together with Voce, who had benefitted by a winter's rest, would help restore the club to its proper place in the world of cricket.' AW Shelton retired as President but Sir Julien Cahn proposed that he be made an honorary life member of the Committee to mark his fifty years of valuable service to the club. The proposal was carried unanimously.

MCC had sent a team to India in the close season. Jardine continued as the captain; it was the first tour by English cricketers to the subcontinent that included official Test matches. Sutcliffe and Hammond, the two leading batsmen on the previous winter's trip to Australia, declined invitations to go; two more of the party, Ames and Wyatt, were selected but withdrew. No Nottinghamshire players were asked. In the absence of Larwood and Voce, 'Nobby' Clark, Northamptonshire left-armer, and Morris Nichols, of Essex, opened the bowling in all three Tests. MCC won two, the other was drawn.

The Nottinghamshire players, including Carr, reported for the 1934 pre-season net practice on Monday 16 April. Unusually, the Trent Bridge gatemen were on duty and only officials and players were admitted, simply because Larwood was present and expected to bowl. In the event the ground was considered too wet for him. He did, however, bowl in the nets three days later. By coincidence Bert Oldfield, the Australian wicketkeeper who had been hit on the head by a ball from Larwood during the 1932/33 series, came to Nottingham to order 400 bats from Gunn and Moore for his own sports shop and spent an hour or two chatting to Larwood.

Carr's thoughts on the coming season just prior to Nottinghamshire's opening match were: 'Were all our fellows fit and well and we could be sure of regularly commanding their services, we should have the best side in England. The trouble is that we cannot be absolutely certain of taking the field at full strength and that the Test matches may exert a prior claim upon some of the team. We are all right in batting. Bowling is likely to be the problem.'

The forthcoming Ashes series between England and Australia and whether Larwood would be fit enough to be selected for England was the main topic of sporting discussion in April, but equally important was the question of the England captaincy. Jardine had remained in India when the tour ended and had informed MCC that he would not be available, and at the same time announced that he would not take part in Championship cricket for Surrey.

In the course of a long article in the *Nottingham Journal* Carr named six possible candidates as England's new leader. Although he thought Maurice Turnbull of Glamorgan the best choice, Carr felt that the selectors would choose Wyatt of Warwickshire, whom Carr thought was a great cricketer but not a particularly good leader. His other possibilities were APF Chapman and BH Valentine (both Kent), CF Walters (Worcestershire) and BH Lyon (Gloucestershire).

The Nottinghamshire season opened against Somerset on 4 May at Trent Bridge – the Australians had already completed their first county match at Worcester, Bradman scored 206. Nottinghamshire opposed Somerset, who elected to bat, after the start was delayed until lunch by a wet outfield. The visitors found Larwood, though not at his fastest, too much – in a spell of six overs he took three wickets at a cost of five runs and finished with four for 31 in 13.1 overs. Somerset were all out for 156. Larwood bowled to a conventional field of three slips. In contrast Voce bowled round the wicket to three leg slips; he took three for 39 off fourteen overs. Nottinghamshire were 18 without loss at the close.

On the second day Nottinghamshire gained a first innings lead of 76, but when Somerset started their second innings, Larwood, to much alarm, left the field having bowled three overs for seven runs. This might appear a minor matter, but some idea of the interest in Larwood's fitness can be gauged by the reaction of the *Daily Telegraph* cricket correspondent, Thomas Moult. He was reporting on the Australians v Leicestershire match at Aylestone Road and continued his report with: 'I have just returned [to Leicester] from Annesley Woodhouse where he [Larwood] lives. I travelled forty miles by fast car with a message of sympathy from the Australian cricketers.' The *Daily Mirror* managed to interview Carr, who said, 'He has bruised his left foot, but as far as we know, it is nothing to do with the old trouble. His doctor is away today, but Larwood will see him tomorrow.' There was no play on the final day of the Somerset game due to rain, though Larwood reported on the ground in the morning and said he would play if required.

There was a three-day gap before Nottinghamshire entertained Warwickshire at Trent Bridge. Larwood was in the eleven but did not bowl with much fire and failed to take a wicket, not being called upon at all in the Warwickshire second innings. Butler opened in his place and took six for 39 as Warwickshire, set by Carr's declaration 130 in two hours, collapsed to 105 all out. Nottinghamshire therefore obtained a surprise win by 24 runs.

Larwood was not in the eleven for the Whitsun match against Surrey. Surrey, batting first, tore the home attack to pieces and with only young Joe Hardstaff (78 and 63 not out) really flourishing for the home county, Surrey won by an innings. Carr's old friend, Percy Fender, took ten wickets in the match, including dismissing Carr for a duck in the first innings. Fender ended top of the Surrey 1934 bowling averages but was no longer Surrey's captain; rather than going back to Fender the county selected a new leader, Errol Holmes, in place of the retired Jardine. Holmes played in five Tests for England and had a fragmented county career spread over no less than thirty-two years, 1924 to 1955.

The *Sunday Dispatch* of 20 May, the day after the Surrey game began, had the headline 'Larwood will not play in Test. Cannot Stand The Strain of Fast Bowling.' This was followed by a long article from their 'Special Correspondent' in Nottingham. Prior to the first Test at Trent Bridge, a Test trial had been arranged for 2, 3 and 4 June. On 16 May, invitations were sent out to fourteen players, including Larwood, to 'hold themselves in readiness' for the trial. Larwood replied informing the selectors he did not feel himself fit enough to play. When the match took place, Clark, the bowler most likely to fill Larwood's shoes, retired injured after bowling nine overs on the first day. Essex amateur fast bowler Ken Farnes and Bowes were two other England possibilities, they returned figures of one for 132 and one for 81 respectively. The selectors announced on 4 June a squad of fourteen players for the Trent Bridge Test, both Farnes and Bowes were included; Wyatt was chosen as captain.

Australia won the game by 238 runs by declaring their second innings closed and setting England a target of 380 in just under 300 minutes. England never looked like approaching the target but battled to try to reach a draw. Australia, through spinner O'Reilly who took seven wickets, won with ten minutes to spare. England's most successful bowler was Farnes, with five wickets in each innings. Despite the fact that Nottinghamshire played Leicestershire at Aylestone Road then Sussex at Horsham during the Test Match, Carr chose to stay in Nottingham and report the game for the *Nottingham Journal*. That newspaper previewed Carr's reports with the announcement: 'Mr AW Carr, the popular captain of the Nottinghamshire county cricket team and former England captain, will attend the Test match each day and will write a special description and criticism of the play for the *Nottingham Journal*. Mr Carr is as fearless as a critic as he is versatile as a cricketer and his special criticism each day will be read with the keenest interest, not only by local patrons of the game, who admire Mr Carr as a great exponent of the national pastime, but by sportsmen far and wide.'

In his day-by-day pieces Carr praised Farnes' bowling: 'Farnes though overworked stuck to his job heroically, but while he was bowling himself to death in the cause, the Australian tail made such light of the others that the advantage was slowly frittered away. With another fast bowler to back up Farnes, how different things might have been.' Reporting on the last day's play, Carr's main comment on England's team was the lack of all-rounders, too many specialists, and the poor fielding in comparison with Australia. The Trent Bridge Test ended on 12 June; the second Test, at Lord's, was scheduled for 22 June.

Apparently Carr had some sort of argument with TA Higson, the Lancashire chairman and Test selector, who attended the Trent Bridge Test in his latter capacity. The incident occurred on the second day, 9 June. Higson complained to AW Shelton who promised to investigate. Shelton later replied to Higson, having consulted Dr Gauld and Douglas McCraith (Chairman of the Nottinghamshire Club and Ground Committee). Shelton wrote: 'We personally regret that you should have any cause to complain of unpleasantness at Trent Bridge, but we consider that it is wholly a personal matter between Mr Carr and yourself. Mr Carr was present at the Test match, not in any official capacity, but we believe was representing a group of newspapers. We cannot see how, in these circumstances, the Committee can be held responsible for what he says and does. Incidentally, and for your personal information, may I say that I had a personal word with Mr Carr on the subject last week. He gave me his personal assurance that he had no intention whatever of insulting you and was merely "pulling your leg".'

Carr's version of the event, as noted in his book, read: 'As frequently with him, he was wearing no hat, and I jokingly said to him, "For heaven's sake where's your hat? You ought to hide your face and be ashamed of yourself for having only one fast bowler in the team". Higson replied: "Well, I rang up Lord Belper and asked him what the Trent Bridge wicket was like and if it was any good for fast bowlers. Lord Belper told me that it was no good to them and that we should pick spinners." "Good Lord," I remarked, "What does he know about it?" Lord Belper was an ex-President of Nottinghamshire and a member of the County Club Committee, but as for consulting him as an expert on the choice of an England team.'

Higson had been a modest cricketer at county level with a few games for Derbyshire and even fewer for Lancashire. He was on the Lancashire Committee for forty-nine years and chairman for many years, indeed still in that post when he died in 1949. From 1931 to 1937 he served as a Test selector. Politically astute, he was not the type of person for whom Carr would have much time.

Ben Lilley took Carr's place as Nottinghamshire captain for the two matches that clashed with the Trent Bridge Test. in the first, against Leicestershire on 6, 7 and 8 June, Larwood took five for 41 in the first innings, Leicestershire were all out 103 in response to Nottinghamshire 351. The follow on was enforced and Leicestershire ended the day six for no wickets. On the third day Larwood took four for 43 and Nottingham-shire won by an innings and 53 runs – unusually Voce bowled his spinners in the second innings and took four wickets. At Horsham for the second match, on a pitch designed to keep Larwood and Voce quiet, Sussex spent all day making 285 for four, Voce taking three wickets; on the second day Larwood picked up four wickets as the rest of the batting collapsed – only 27 more runs for six wickets. A century from Charlie Harris produced a first innings lead for Nottinghamshire, then the match dribbled to a draw. In the two games Larwood had taken 14 wickets at 11 runs apiece.

Nottinghamshire, with Carr back in charge, went to Chalk-well Park, Westcliff and scored 371, of which Carr made 107, and had Essex 29 for three at the end of the first day. On the second day Larwood ended Essex's first innings with an-other five wickets. Significantly Percy Perrin, the former Essex player and current Test selector, watched the play. On 15 June, Nottinghamshire won the match by 145 runs, Larwood had another four wickets – now a total of twenty-three in three matches, still at 11 runs apiece.

On Saturday 16 June, with the Lord's Test just six days away, Nottinghamshire were back home, opposing Lancashire at Trent Bridge. On the morning of that game, Carr wrote an article in the *Nottingham Journal*: 'A new anti-leg theory war has started. Certain counties are reported to have gone to the extent of threatening discontinuance of fixtures with Nottinghamshire unless leg theory is banned altogether. Another rumour with a semi-official flavour has been published which declares that one particular county will go to the length of walking off the field if leg theory is bowled against them. All these rumours are coincident with the return to fitness of Harold Larwood and I should like to say at once they are deplorable. There has been a general outcry that Larwood should be included in the next England team to meet the Australians at Lord's on Friday. DR Jardine has written in the highest praise of Larwood and has gone so far as to say that he must play without bond or fetter if England is to win. Sir Stanley Jackson, the Chairman of the Test Selectors, in response to this demand, has declared that Larwood will be invited to play unconditionally. So far no invitation has been received by Larwood.'

Lancashire batted first, Larwood and Voce opened the bowling. Voce took the first two wickets and the pair were briefly rested. Coming on for a second spell, Larwood returned figures of 6-4-14-6 and Lancashire plunged to 67 for eight. A slight revival produced a final all out total of 119 and Larwood's complete figures were 17-4-51-6. By the close Nottinghamshire had a lead of six runs with four wickets in hand.

The newspapers the following morning changed everything. The *Sunday Dispatch* published an article signed by Harold Larwood which began, 'It is time the public knew the truth. England's selectors meet tomorrow to choose the team for the second Test match. My friends tell me that I am certain to be asked to play. It will not matter. I have definitely made up my mind not to play against the Australians in this or any of the Tests. I doubt if I shall ever play against them again – at least in big cricket.'

Further on in the same article, Larwood continues: 'Lancashire – who used leg theory long before I was born – have threatened to cancel their fixture with Nottinghamshire. I am amazed to learn that Mr Higson's name is associated with the Lancashire protest. For this Mr Higson is one of the Test selectors, who are so wary about committing themselves in regard to leg theory.'

Carr also had an article in the same edition of *Sunday Dispatch* as Larwood's piece. He wrote: 'I believe Larwood is right in not playing for England when the rulers of the game have so completely deserted him. It will be a big wrench for the boy. He is the most unassuming and undemonstrative player I have ever known in cricket, but he will give up the excitement and glamour of Test matches for the sake of a principle ... Lancashire are supposed to keep on protesting about leg theory, but the laugh is with Larwood. He bowled to a circle of slips and had all the batsmen, either playing to leg or timidly stepping out across the bat. In several matches Larwood has proved without a shadow of doubt that batsmen cannot play fast bowling. Larwood has told me that he has offered to give up leg theory in county cricket. I have been told that it may be advisable to do so. But I shall give no order to Larwood. He can go on bowling leg theory in Nottinghamshire matches until the Committee step in and call a halt. I am not going to dictate to my bowlers. I believe the full Committee of the Nottinghamshire Club is going to meet on 28 June to discuss the problem. Until then I am taking no action. It is up to the MCC to show a little moral courage and give a definite ruling on that point.'

There was a meeting of the Nottinghamshire Committee on 28 June, but two days prior to that meeting a special meeting of the Committee was called in order to settle two matters.

Carr had written to the club stating that he wished to resign as captain under certain conditions – no copy of the actual letter has been located. The second matter was a letter from Lancashire stating that the county would not be renewing fixtures with Nottinghamshire in 1935. Dealing with Carr's letter (he withdrew from the room to allow members to discuss it), the Committee told Carr that they were not prepared to agree with the condition Carr laid down. After further consideration, Carr agreed to withdraw his letter.

The Nottinghamshire Committee had met members of the Lancashire Committee, who made it clear that they no longer wished to play Nottinghamshire because the Lancashire players had objected to the dangerous bowling used by Voce and Larwood. The Nottinghamshire Committee decided that the next step was to ask permission of MCC to talk to the two umpires in the match concerned, George Beet and EJ Smith. The press were anxious to know the outcome of the meeting, but both HA Brown and Captain Howard (the Lancashire Secretary) refused to make any comments and members of the Nottinghamshire Committee also declined to speak to the press. When the usual monthly meeting was held on 28 June only formal business was discussed, with no items relating to Carr or to Lancashire in the minutes.

Returning to the Lancashire match at Trent Bridge on 16, 18 and 19 June, Nottinghamshire obtained a first innings lead on the second day of 147 due to a tremendous innings of 80 by Larwood, batting at number ten. Lancashire then turned the game upside down, reaching 357 for six by the close, Ernest Tyldesley and Lister adding 182 in two hours. On the third day Lancashire set Nottinghamshire 248 in 165 minutes. The Nottinghamshire batting failed and last man Butler was dismissed off the first ball of the last possible over. Duckworth, who it was reported had complained about Nottinghamshire's dangerous bowling in the first innings, scored 26 not out in the second.

With the second Test at Lord's clashing with the next two Nottinghamshire matches, Carr was unavailable to play and the captaincy went to Sam Staples, now recovered from the illness that had beset him at the season's start. Nottinghamshire beat Gloucestershire by an innings at Trent Bridge, Larwood took eight wickets bowling to an orthodox field; Voce took six and was described as at times unplayable. The county then went to Worcester. Larwood obtained seven wickets in the first innings, but rain deprived Nottinghamshire of victory. In the Lord's Test, outstanding bowling by Hedley Verity, who took fifteen wickets for 104, provided England with an innings victory inside three days.

Carr returned to the team for the home match against Kent starting on 27 June with Nottinghamshire now standing a respectable fifth in the Championship table. The pitch suited spin from the opening day; Nottinghamshire batted first and were fortunate that Freeman was absent injured. With fifties from Keeton and Arthur Staples the total reached 230; Kent were 134 for three at stumps. The fact that the erratic George Vernon Gunn took two of those wickets, including that of Frank Woolley, told its own story. Voce bowled spinners. On the second day Kent were dismissed for 206, Larwood failed to take even one wicket. With Keeton hitting a century in the second innings, Kent required 288 to win in 285 minutes. Carr did not field in the Kent second innings, with Lilley taking over the reins. The Kent reply had not long started when the county's opener was hit on the head by a ball from Larwood: Ashdown had expected a bumper which didn't materialise and had ducked into a normal delivery. Ashdown retired. He recovered from his knock on the head and was able to return to the crease at the fall of the seventh wicket. Valentine, the Kent amateur coming in at number six, was hit on the elbow by Voce and retired hurt, but also resumed his innings later.

Nottinghamshire won by 20 runs, Voce took five for 91; the *Nottingham Journal* noted: 'In view of Voce's accuracy of length and new energy, it was poetic justice that he should round off the innings by bowling Lewis (Kent's last man) and I cannot recollect a match this season when his bowling has been seen to greater advantage.' The game which followed, at Headingley against Yorkshire, was chosen by Maurice Leyland as his benefit. No less than 30,000 were present on the opening day and saw Nottinghamshire score 246 with Charlie Harris carrying his bat for 117. Yorkshire were 61 for one at the close. Carr was batting much lower in the order in recent games than formerly and in this game was at number eight. He hit two sixes but his nemesis, Bowes, had him bowled for 23. The game drifted to a draw, neither side going for quick runs and the pitch, supposedly doctored to counter any of Larwood's fast stuff, made batting on the last day academic.

It was during Nottinghamshire's next match, when Middlesex were beaten by eight wickets at Trent Bridge (Larwood six for 73, Voce eleven for 128) that the press finally picked up on Lancashire declining to play Nottinghamshire in 1935. Carr was quoted as saying that Lancashire batsmen just didn't like fast bowling and seem to have forgotten the exploits of their own fast bowler Macdonald (once of Australia).

On 7 July, whilst the third Test was being played at Old Trafford – the game ended in a high-scoring draw – Nottinghamshire travelled to Edgbaston and scored 442 for eight declared against Warwickshire; the home side were 17 for one on Saturday evening. It was a very hot day which had begun badly for Carr. He had only just left Bulcote Manor for Birmingham when his car started playing up. He returned home and transferred to his wife's car before driving to Edgbaston. He stated in his autobiography that he felt odd when he came out to bat and for once was relieved when he was dismissed, making 25. After a bath and a change he left the ground at the close of play to drive to his sister-in-law's house, The Chace, Upper Welland, near Malvern. Going through Worcester he took the Malvern Road and suddenly felt exceedingly ill.

Carr told the story of what happened next:

> Suddenly I saw ahead of me three lights in a distant shop window – the red, green and yellow bottles still used by some old-fashioned chemists. 'If I can only get there,' I said to myself. How I managed to do so I do not know, but I do remember being able to drive as far as the lights, pulling up the car, staggering into the shop and saying, 'I am dying – ring Malvern 163.'" Then I went completely out.
>
> The friendly chemist – Mr Lunn by name – saved my life. He saw how ill I was, immediately injected something with the hope of restoring me, and sent for a doctor. I was told that my heart actually stopped beating for about four minutes, and that if Mr Lunn had not been so skilled and prompt as he was I should have died in his shop ... It was an awful experience, but I must say this: I know that directly I fell unconscious in Mr Lunn's shop I felt as happy as a king. I had no terror, no pain, no regrets. If death, when it comes, is really like this I have no fear of it.

Mrs Vera Stevenson, Carr's sister-in-law, was interviewed by the press on the following Monday and confirmed that Arthur was at her home and ill in bed. She ended by stating, 'Mr Carr is as well as can be expected, but he won't play again this year.' Carr wrote in his autobiography that he was examined medically in the autumn and passed as being one hundred per cent fit.

A special general committee meeting of the Nottinghamshire County Club was held on 18 July, sixteen of the eighteen on the committee attended, Carr was obviously missing, the other non-attendee was Lionel Kirk, who apologised but also protested against a meeting being held on other than a Thursday. Sincere sympathy was sent to Mr and Mrs Carr, with the hope that Mr Carr would soon be restored to good health. The question of a replacement for Carr as captain was left in the hands of the selection committee.

A series of articles had been appearing in the *Sunday Dispatch* under Larwood's name. The Committee agreed that in writing these articles he was breaking the terms of his agreement with the club and the Chairman and Honorary Secretary should explain the matter to Larwood and also obtain Larwood's release from any contract he had entered into with the *Sunday Dispatch*. It was also agreed to speak to Staples and Voce regarding any articles which appeared under their names in the press. The meetings duly took place and Larwood agreed not to contribute any more articles and the *Sunday Dispatch* also agreed not to print any further articles under Larwood's name.

Despite the statement that Mrs Vera Stevenson had made about Carr not playing again in 1934, the *Nottingham Guardian* of 27 July reported that Carr was now back at Bulcote Manor. The reporter spoke to Carr by phone, the Nottinghamshire captain responding with: 'I am naturally weak as yet, and I easily tire, but I can walk about now, whereas a week or two ago I could not even shave myself. From what the doctors have told me, I am very hopeful of being able to play again in the last four matches.' He hoped to come down to Trent Bridge in the next week or so.

At the end of the fateful Edgbaston match, Nottinghamshire stood third in the Championship behind Sussex and Lancashire, but Sussex had played one more match and Lancashire two more than Nottinghamshire. In fourth place came Yorkshire, though they also had played more matches. On paper Nottinghamshire's prospects were set fair, however the team seemed totally put out by Carr's brush with death and his absence from the eleven. Of the next eight games, two were lost by an innings, four were drawn with first innings points lost. Only one was won and in the other first innings points were gained. On 11 August Nottinghamshire had fallen to seventh, no less than sixty-seven points behind the leaders Sussex.

The solitary win was certainly dramatic. Against Hampshire at Trent Bridge, Nottinghamshire were 97 behind on first innings and were seven down in their second innings and just 50 ahead. Voce came to the crease and in three quarters of an hour hit 65 out of 70. Hampshire still only required 126 to win. Voce switched his bowling styles from leg spinners to fast in-swingers, taking four of the first five Hampshire wickets that fell (Hampshire were then 48 for five). Boyes threatened to turn Hampshire round, but George Vernon Gunn bowled to some effect and Voce resumed his in-swingers to bring a most welcome win.

Larwood was employed purely as a batsman in the Hampshire match, having strained a tendon in the game before against Yorkshire. Nottinghamshire went south to play Surrey in the August Bank Holiday fixture; Hardstaff hit a much applauded hundred, Larwood again appeared just as a batsman; thence to Canterbury where Kent won with ease, Larwood again did not bowl.

The Nottinghamshire team returned to Trent Bridge to meet the Australians on 11, 13 and 14 August. The press report on the morning of the game noted: 'Larwood has been examined by the doctor for an injury to his left ankle and has been certified quite unfit to play.'

The report in the *Sunday Dispatch*, written by John Robertson, describes the first day's play: 'For weeks Nottingham has awaited the Australians. Despite the absence of Harold Larwood, exclusively forecast in the *Sunday Dispatch* a month ago, the tourists were not spared the dreaded legtheory. Majestic William Voce, on a wicket that gave him no assistance, secured eight of the ten victims. None of the Australians ever looked comfortable against him. Voce unfortunately had little backing at the other end, or the 10,000 crowd might have been in ecstasies. As a bowling partnership Larwood and Voce have no equals. Can the selectors, who have deliberately ignored Voce all the season, now leave him out of the Oval Test? In this column we have hammered all along at Sir Stanley Jackson and Co for their ostrich-like methods with Voce. It is only another proof that England and the politicians have tried to present the Ashes to the tourists. Voce made no bones about using legtheory yesterday. He had three leg-slips, a short square leg, a long leg and a mid-on. Brown was hit on the shoulder. A section of the crowd applauded. There was no protest by the Australians. As a left-hander, legtheory is natural to Voce and I know that the club officials have always thought his field legitimate.'

The Australians were bowled out on the first day for 237. Larwood did not attend the match but Carr was present, though he did not have lunch with the Australians. The tourists spent Sunday with the Lord Mayor of Nottingham, John Farr, at his residence, Worksop Manor, where they viewed the Lord Mayor's racehorses. Monday proved to be one of intermittent rain. Most of the Nottinghamshire batsmen got off to reasonable starts but, apart from Hardstaff, struggled against the spin of Clarrie Grimmett – the county were all out for 183, scored in 205 minutes. When the Australian openers, Woodfull and Brown, began Australia's second innings, Voce bowled two overs of leg theory, bad light then ended play for the day. Voce had bowled a number of deliveries that bounced head height.

After the players had left the field the Australian manager went to see the Nottinghamshire Secretary, HA Brown, and protested against Voce's bowling of those two overs. Later that evening the Australian manager met Dr Gauld, the Nottinghamshire Honorary Secretary. The following morning, Voce was called to the Secretary's office where he was examined by

Dr Gauld. It was not until the Nottinghamshire team walked on to the field that the spectators noticed the absence of Voce – a young groundstaff player, Frank Woodhead, fielded as substitute. There were cries of 'Where's Voce?' from some of the crowd and an announcement was made shortly afterwards: 'Voce was suffering from a recurrence of his sore shin problems and on medical advice will not play today.'

The Australians scored 230 for two and declared. Sections of the crowd gave the Australians a rather adversarial reception as they came out to field for Nottinghamshire second innings. The match was drawn, though Nottinghamshire got a bit of a scare when Grimmett and Fleetwood-Smith took early wickets. Lilley, captaining the county, batted out the final half hour with Ron Taylor.

Carr was interviewed by the press about the absence of Voce. His pronouncement, that if he had captained the side Voce would definitely have played and bowled, caused headlines the following day. These were hardly negated by the fact that Voce was in the Nottinghamshire team for the county match which was scheduled to start the next day in Southampton.

The controversy over why Voce was absent from the third day of the Australian match built a good head of steam, further fuelled by the fact that the selectors were due to meet to pick the England side for the fifth Test at The Oval. On 17 August, a statement was published from the Australian captain, Woodfull, saying that he would lead his team off the field if Voce was picked and bowled as he had done at Trent Bridge. Dr Tinsley Lindley, a well-known Nottingham barrister who had played for Nottinghamshire in four first-class games in 1888 and for Cambridge University, aired his views: 'Larwood and Voce are two of the finest sportsmen playing cricket today and it is utter tosh to suggest that their bowling is calculated to either lame or intimidate the batsmen. So far as this unhappy controversy is concerned I blame the MCC and Nottinghamshire

County CC for not being absolutely candid with the whole of the cricketing world. They have failed to place their cards on the table face upwards.'

On 18 August, in the *Nottingham Journal*, Carr wrote a very long article on the matter in hand – as an amateur he was not subject to the professionals' agreement with the County Cricket Club regarding articles in the press. After wondering what had happened behind the scenes to cause Voce to be withdrawn and casting doubts as to whether the truth would emerge, Carr concluded: 'For my own part I would rather finish with cricket altogether than to be a party to any alterations to the rules, which I knew had been conceived with the object, not of improving the game, but with the idea of ensuring the continuance of the Test matches to make money, especially if such alteration means that our best players are to be thrown on to the scrapheap. Whatever the result of the Oval Test, the English team cannot be said to be representative of the best players available. To all intents and purposes the Australians have been allowed to pick both sides.'

In fact, though Voce was in Southampton with the Nottinghamshire side, he was left out of the final eleven. Despite the absence of both Larwood and Voce and that Lilley, the acting captain, had to leave due to a poisoned hand (Taylor kept wicket), Nottinghamshire battled through for first innings points in a high scoring draw. Joe Hardstaff hit his highest score to date, 153, in a total of 495 for eight.

Voce was definitely fit for the annual match at Ilkeston. He took nine for 90 in the match but the Derbyshire fast bowlers, in particular Copson and Alf Pope, also exploited the favourable conditions. Stan Worthington made 93 for the home side; no Nottinghamshire batsman even managed to reach fifty, so Derbyshire won by a large margin.

Nottinghamshire's season closed at Lord's where Voce's leg theory was clearly on view for the cricket authorities who were about to discuss the issue. Voce hit Len Muncer on the head, knocking him unconscious. Muncer took no further part in the game; Robert Beveridge received a blow on his arm, but resumed after going to hospital for a check up.

The final Test match at The Oval was to be timeless since the rubber was tied on one win each. Voce was not included but Nottinghamshire's Walter Keeton, who had played in the fourth Test, was in the squad, although the selectors preferred Sutcliffe in their final decision. Australia won the toss, chose to bat, Ponsford and Bradman both scored double hundreds, the pair adding 451 for the second wicket; Australia made 701 and England were completely outplayed – Australia won by 562 runs.

Carr's article in the *Nottingham Journal* of 25 August began: 'England's inevitable defeat in the Test match this week virtually marks the end of one of the most unpleasant and turbulent cricket seasons within my twenty years experience as a county cricketer. I saw the humiliation of England's bowlers at The Oval last Saturday when Bradman and Ponsford began their record-breaking stand and need hardly tell you how amazed I was when Clark was permitted to bowl leg theory. This very form of attack, it must be remembered, had been made the excuse for the exclusion of Larwood and Voce from international cricket this summer. This was the bowling which led to all the friction and nearly severed relationships between the two countries.'

Carr completed his long piece with: 'If this should prove to be my valediction I can only say that in all my years as leader of Nottinghamshire I have always acted in what I considered to be the best interests of the side and if I have earned the gratitude of the professionals and the public in the stand I have made in defence of our two fast bowlers, Larwood and Voce, I shall have no regrets.'

In reviewing the Nottinghamshire season of 1934, the press described Nottinghamshire after Carr's heart attack as 'a ship without a man at the helm'. Lilley led the team in most of the matches when Carr was absent, but he was the first to admit that he could not fill Carr's boots.

Although Carr had seemingly recovered from his illness, it was thought most unlikely that he would be appointed captain for 1935; the differences between Carr and the Committee, not only on leg theory but a number of other issues, were now too great to paper over. Although there was theoretically a sub-committee that selected the Nottinghamshire team, Carr in reality had run the side as his fiefdom and his understanding of the players meant that they felt a tremendous loyalty to him. The position which he himself created as the only amateur with ten professionals was not unique, Yorkshire tended to be the same but in their case, between the retirement of Lord Hawke and the rise of AB Sellers, the amateur captains were mostly of little consequence, lacking the knowledge that Carr, and indeed the ability that Carr acquired over many seasons.

In the aftermath of the Nottinghamshire v Australians match, the Nottinghamshire Committee held a meeting. The Australian match was a specific item on the agenda and the minute reads: 'Dr Gauld reported upon the recent county match with the Australians in which he stated that contrary to the many reports published in the public press, he withdrew Voce from the match on the third day on medical grounds. Mr Carr stated that he refused to believe that Voce was withdrawn because he was unfit. The Chairman [AW Shelton] at once called upon Mr Carr to either withdraw or apologise for that observation or leave the meeting. Mr Carr having refused, Major Birkin moved that Mr Carr should either withdraw his remarks or withdraw from the meeting. Mr Carr refused to withdraw his remarks and left the meeting. This was seconded and carried. It was resolved that a vote of confidence in Dr

Gauld, the Hon Secty, be placed in the minutes. This was carried, one member not voting. Mr Goodall proposed and Mr Alcock seconded and it was resolved that a letter be sent to Mr Carr stating that this Committee, having seen statements in the public press attributed to Mr Carr and repeated at this meeting, seriously reflecting upon the veracity of statements made by Dr GO Gauld, the Hon Secty, are unanimously of the opinion that such statements should be withdrawn. It was resolved that no good purpose would be served by issuing any further statement to the press than that which has already been issued.'

There was not another Committee meeting until October, during which meeting a letter of resignation from the committee written by Mr Carr was read out and his resignation accepted.

At their Committee meeting of 30 November, it was agreed to set up a special sub-committee to 'go into the question of the Captaincy for 1935'. The sub-committee comprised Lord Belper, Sir Julien Cahn, Major PA Birkin, Dr GO Gauld, Mr AW Shelton and Mr JK Lane. This sub-committee reported back on 21 December, stating first that Carr should not be nominated, and suggesting that Messrs SD Rhodes and GFH Heane be appointed. The suggestion was approved with one dissentient.

When this information was released to the press, John Mac-Adam of the *Sunday Dispatch* rang up Lord Belper:

'Don't you think Voce and Carr have been let down?'
'I refuse to discuss the matter.'
'There is a definite feeling that you didn't support your own men, and rather sided with the MCC against them'
'I cannot discuss the matter'.
'You are likely to be the next MCC President?'
'I don't know anything about that.'
'You are being blamed for all this trouble you know'.

'I don't mind that.'

The subsequent article by MacAdam is volcanic:

> Political influences were determined to placate the Australians at all costs. They, through the MCC got their way in the end. The MCC had friends in Nottingham. Lord Belper, the President of the Nottinghamshire Club, is also a prominent member of the MCC Lord Belper has never played first-class cricket. He is an enthusiast, but his knowledge of the technicalities of the game is limited. He was one of the principal agents in bringing about the surrender.
>
> The crowning piece of folly was the manner in which Carr went. It showed rank ingratitude and bad manners. The name of Nottingham cricket is dragged in the mud by discourteous treatment towards one who has served it well. Nottingham supporters cannot be proud of a committee which casts aspersions on the methods of its own players. No communication was sent to Carr informing him that he was no longer captain. That was left to the newspapers. Carr has not received a letter of thanks for his wonderful services in captaining the team for fifteen [sic] years. He had the longest service in post-war cricket as captain and gave up much valuable time. Carr had played cricket for Nottinghamshire since 1910 without a break except for the war years, when he served his country. Now he is treated like a dishonest employee.

Carr sits with the 1934 Nottinghamshire team –
the last he would captain and play with

# 15

# UP IN ARMS

## 1935-1939

On 3 January 1935 the Nottinghamshire Secretary, HA Brown, received a communication signed by twenty-six members of the County Cricket Club requesting a special general meeting. They wanted to question the actions of the Committee in regards to the Nottinghamshire v Australians match during which Voce was withdrawn, and the attitude of the Committee towards Bodyline bowling. The communication also set out a specific item for the agenda of the meeting: 'That this General Meeting of Members the Nottinghamshire County Cricket Club has no confidence in the present Committee of the Club and calls on it to resign en bloc.'

It was agreed that a meeting should be held at 2.30 pm on Wednesday 16 January at the Albert Hall in Nottingham, with Alderman E Huntsman in the chair. As an aside, it was agreed that an organ recital should be given by Mr L Gordon Thorpe immediately prior to the meeting taking place.

The principal promoter of the opposition group was Mr H Seely Whitby. He it was who produced the unexpected bomb-

shell that clearly influenced the members. Mr Seely Whitby
held up and then read out the following:

> January 11, 1935
> I, William Voce, of Nottinghamshire County Cricket Club, here-
> by state that on the Tuesday of the Nottinghamshire v Australians
> match at Trent Bridge, I was fit and willing to play.
> Any statement to the contrary is untrue.
> Signed W Voce
> Witnesses: H Seely Whitby, Harry M Woolley.

Some 2,500 members attended the meeting during which
both sides spoke bluntly about the matters under discussion.
Committee members, in particular Mr Douglas McCraith and
Dr Gauld, explained their viewpoint. Mr Seely Whitby and
Mr AC Adams spoke, proposing and seconding the motion
that the Committee should resign en bloc. Mr GA Spencer
(Nottinghamshire Miners' Industrial Union) appealed to Mr
Seely Whitby to withdraw his motion (cries of 'no' accompanied this) and then asked that the Committee should rescind
its decision to remove Carr from the captaincy (to applause
and cheers).

Carr then stood up to a tumultuous welcome and the sing-
ing of 'For he's a jolly good fellow'. He said that he had no
intention of saying anything about himself, except that he did
not mind in the least being dropped from the captaincy. He
continued: 'I am here to stand by Bill Voce. I was not going to
speak about the Lancashire match at all, but now it has cropped
up I will tell you my version of it. Before the match started I
got out of my car and walked across the ground and walked
into Peter Eckersley, the Lancashire captain, I said, "You and I
have known each other for a long time; what is going to happen in this match?" He said, "Arthur I can tell you this, I have
been told to object in this match [i.e. to Voce's bowling]. I am
not going to." I said "Right" and went into the pavilion and

into the Lancashire professionals' room and said, "I am very sorry to hear you are going to object against us." They all said, "Mr Carr it isn't us." I said, "Well, who is it?"'

There were cries of 'Higson' from the body of the hall. Carr continued: 'I'll leave you to guess. During that match Larwood got six wickets and I have never seen such exhibitions of funk in all my life. There were five of our men on the off side. In the second innings they made 400 runs and won the match. The only person hit was Peter Eckersley and he was hit upon the leg and never above the belt. It is absurd to say my bowlers were unfair. They got an absolutely fair deal. I have always said my bowlers could bowl exactly as they liked for the simple reason I swear that neither of those fellows bowled against a man. We then come to the Australian match. Bill Voce bowled magnificently in the first innings and got eight wickets for 60-odd runs. A really marvellous performance. What happened during the tea interval? Two Committee men here (I think they were Mr Alcock and Mr Kirk) will agree with me, that Mr Bushby came to the tea room and said, "Haven't you got any control over your bowlers?" (Laughter). That goes to prove that they were going to get Voce out of that match on the Saturday, by fair or foul means. When he bowled his two overs (in the second innings) he bowled according to the MCC rules. What is a fast bowler for?'

Carr went on to detail what happened on the Tuesday morning when Voce was withdrawn.

Douglas McCraith summed up the Committee's case and the Chairman reminded the meeting of the motion before them, before calling for a vote by a show of hands. The motion calling on the Committee to resign was carried by about two to one.

A special Committee meeting was held the following day, with sixteen members present, AW Shelton taking the chair. All the members of the Committee announced their resignation, though Mr Shelton did so separately as he had been appointed an honorary life member of the Committee. The local press representatives were then invited into the meeting and told of the Committee's decision, which would take place at the AGM, the Committee would continue with the ordinary business of the club until that date.

Carr, who was interviewed by the *Evening Post,* was asked: '"What do you think will happen?" he replied, "I don't know. I must not say any more, you know there are some jolly decent fellows on the committee – white men you know – and I shall be sorry if their services are lost."'

When asked about the statement issued by Lancashire refuting Carr's comments, the former captain replied: 'They were bound to deny it. I don't wish to say any more, please leave me out of it. I don't tell lies. Everything I have said is true and I stick to the statement I made at the Albert Hall.'

This information duly appeared in the press on 19 January, together with a statement from Seely Whitby and Woolley who stated they were taking steps to obtain nominations for a new committee. Sir Harold Bowden, Managing Director of Raleigh Cycles, stated he would be willing to stand for the new committee.

On 30 January, Yorkshire County Cricket Club held their annual general meeting. Lord Hawke, for nearly half a century the effective controller of Yorkshire cricket, presided over the meeting and chose to direct part of his opening speech at Arthur Carr and his allies. Hawke accused Carr of going back on the pledge he and the other captains made when they met at Lord's not to operate a direct attack on opposing batsmen by the use of Bodyline.

The press interviewed Carr for his reaction to Hawke's remarks. The Nottinghamshire captain replied: 'I have always maintained that neither Larwood nor Voce ever has bowled at the batsman. This complaint about direct attack on batsmen simply does not concern us, for our bowlers have never been guilty of such a practice. Any suggestion that I am in favour of bowling of that kind is ridiculous. There is nothing contradictory in my attitude. It has never varied. At no time have I supported a type of bowling that could be fairly described as a direct attack on the batsman. Legitimate leg theory bowling is quite a different thing.'

The usual Committee report and notice of the annual general meeting was dispatched to members on 7 March. The Committee included with each report a detailed account of their actions and the reasons behind them concerning the events of the 1934 season.

The meeting was held in the Albert Hall on 21 March, but unlike the last meeting only 1,200 members attended. The meeting effectively rescinded the decision at the previous meeting when the Committee were to resign en bloc and, despite Mr Seely Whitby's opposition, a vote to apologise to Dr Gauld was passed by a substantial majority.

After the meeting the ballot papers were dispatched containing thirty-five candidates for eighteen places, the members having six days in which to return their voting slips. The total number eligible to vote was 3,720. 2,456 votes were returned, of which forty were void. Of the fourteen 'opposition' candidates only two, Arthur Carr and Sir Harold Bowden, were elected. Both AC Adams and HM Woolley, the chairman and vice-chairman of the opposition, failed. The *Sunday Dispatch* correspondent, John Robertson, campaigned for the opposition, but he appears to have been a lone voice. When interviewed the various failed opposition candidates stated that they accepted the results of the ballot box and were pleased that peace had now returned to the club.

Mr Seely Whitby, though not standing, stated: 'My object in drawing public attention to the matter was in order to clear the air. There is not the slightest doubt that, with the experience of the past, no committee will do other than take the members into their confidence. If this had been done previously there would have been no necessity for an extraordinary general meeting. Now the air has been cleared it is up to all of us to stand by the new Committee and give the members of it our whole-hearted support.'

The first Committee meeting after the votes had been received was held on 15 April 1935. Fifteen members attended, but both Carr and Bowden were absent. Carr was still elected to be a member of the selection sub-committee under the chairmanship of Lionel Kirk – Kirk had topped the poll for the General Committee, his 2,086 votes being more than 200 above second-placed Douglas McCraith; Carr received 1,488 Sir Harold Bowden 1,337.

Two items that related directly to the turmoil of the winter were discussed. It was agreed that the whole of the Nottinghamshire First XI should attend the next Committee meeting and be addressed by the chairman; separately Bill Voce would be interviewed by the chairman and vice-chairman to explain his actions during the controversy.

Arthur Carr did attend the next Committee meeting on 8 May. The players were called into the meeting and addressed by the chairman, but the minute book does not reveal what was said or if any other Committee member spoke. Similarly there is no mention of the Voce interview.

A second point at the 8 May meeting read: 'It was resolved that during the progress of a county match, no one be permitted in the professionals' rooms at Trent Bridge except medical men in the discharge of their duties and the Secretary.' It should be remembered that the amateurs' rooms were what are at the present time the lower dressing rooms used by the visiting team and the professionals occupied the rooms above, each set of rooms had separate showers, baths and toilets. If that instruction was adhered to then the chairman of the selection committee and indeed the coach, Jim Iremonger, would communicate any messages only through the amateur captain.

The Committee had appointed SD Rhodes and GFH Heane to lead Nottinghamshire in 1935 after the 'sacking' of Carr. These two amateurs were employed by Sir Julien Cahn and, although both had played regularly for Cahn's team, Heane's experience of County Championship cricket amounted to four matches while Rhodes had played seven. Neither had appeared since 1931. Heane was an all-rounder, Rhodes a batsman. Both captains appeared in the nets for the first practice session of 1935 on 15 April. All the main professional staff also reported including Larwood and Voce.

At the beginning of May the Nottinghamshire professionals invited Arthur Carr to a dinner in appreciation of his captaincy over the past sixteen years. The talk during the meal made it clear that the players would have preferred Carr to remain as captain and were none too happy with the way matters had evolved. An article in the *Sunday Dispatch* of 19 May noted: 'The members [of the County Cricket Club] voted Carr into the Committee, but he is not *persona grata* with the diehards, who still remember the severe rebukes he administered to them for their hush-hush tactics over Larwood and Voce. Although he is the most accomplished amateur at the disposal the club, the Committee have made no attempt to include Carr in the team. Even if he is not made captain Carr should be in the team, for he has the confidence of the players and that counts for a great deal. Percy Fender lost the Surrey captaincy but he is still asked to play. Surely if a man is good enough for the Committee he is good enough to play, provided his cricket is of the required standard, and that is not questioned in the case of Carr.'

The first match of 1935 was staged at Trent Bridge on 11, 13 and 14 May with the eleven reading: SD Rhodes, Harris, Walker, Hardstaff, A Staples, GV Gunn, Lilley, GFH Heane,

Larwood, Voce and Butler. Keeton had been seriously injured in a road accident in January and was still not fit to play, otherwise, apart from Carr's non-selection, the side was at full strength. Due to the weather – a snow storm – the game was drawn. Carr was a member of the Nottinghamshire selection committee; unfortunately the minutes of their meetings are no longer extant so it is not possible to discover how many of these sub-committee meetings Carr attended or how often this committee met. Carr rarely seems to have attended the monthly full Committee meetings.

Carr did watch Nottinghamshire's home matches, at least in the early part of the summer. On 29 May, the first day of the Hampshire match, Carr was reported to the Nottinghamshire Secretary for swearing at the umpire, Fanny Walden. Carr later apologised, but this incident doesn't appear to have been leaked to the press. Looking at the first day's score, it is difficult to understand what Carr could be angry about. Nottinghamshire scored 420 for four with Hardstaff ending the day unbeaten on 154. Hampshire were a weak side and, in desperation, gave Stan Fenley his first match – he had retired from the Surrey team six years previously. He qualified for Hampshire because, leaving Surrey, he had opened a cricket school in Bournemouth. Two of the Hampshire players were injured on the first day and couldn't bat, whilst captain RH Moore was taken ill with scarlet fever and also did not bat, so Hampshire batted with eight men and were all out for 221 and 37.

In the same meeting during which Carr was reprimanded for his treatment of Walden, on 4 June, a sub-committee of Sir Julien Cahn, AW Shelton, Douglas McCraith and RG Hogarth was set up to 'consider the question of the form of a testimonial to AW Carr'. On 24 October 1935, a two-page leaflet was sent to all Nottinghamshire members detailing the intention of a presentation to Carr at the 1936 AGM and requesting contributions to the cost of a proposed casket and other articles. The leaflet stated that individual contributions should be a minimum of 1/- and a maximum of 20/-.

Alderman John Alcock, a solicitor from Mansfield, was re-elected to the Committee during the rancorous election but died shortly after. It was agreed at the 4 June meeting that he should be replaced by Hyman Silverberg, a Nottingham stockbroker and Nottinghamshire Second XI player. Silverberg had the most votes of those who failed to get elected and had been part of the opposition group of fourteen.

Jack Hobbs had retired from county cricket in more amiable circumstances in 1934. *The Star* proposed a grand dinner at the Dorchester in Park Lane, to which the public was invited to buy tickets, but the great and the good came as guests – *The Tatler* features the dinner in its pages and shows photographs of HDG Leveson Gower, APF Chapman, PGH Fender, MJ Turnbull and others, but there is no sign of AW Carr.

Carr was, however, involved in a series of articles published in the *Sunday Dispatch*, the final article appearing on 9 June 1935. Although under Carr's name and by the tone largely dictated by him, it seems that his ghostwriter was John Robertson, the reporter who had supported Carr's cause in the dispute with the Committee. Within weeks of the articles, Carr's *Cricket With The Lid Off* was published by Hutchinson and Co. Clearly a rushed production – the printed edition does not even include the year of publication – its layout patently shows it to be based on the newspaper articles plus full newspaper extracts giving the detailed accounts of the Nottinghamshire County Cricket Club meetings of 1934/35. Mrs Carr kept scrapbooks of newspaper cuttings featuring Arthur and these had most probably been mined as the best, or at least the easiest accessible source material.

Hutchinson and Co had published in exactly the same format, even to the green cloth-boarded covers, Jardine's *In Quest Of The Ashes* in 1933 and there is a brief foreword by Jardine, who comments on the 1933 Whitsun match when he made presentations to Larwood and Voce. Carr's book hardly mentions the 1932/33 tour – Carr simply stated, 'It would be stale now to enter into the pros and cons of leg theory bowling as practised on that tour.' He did record the meeting of himself, Jardine, Larwood and Voce at the Piccadilly Hotel, which Jardine did not – his book omits any mention at all of Carr! Carr's book dates the Piccadilly Hotel meeting as 1931. Although no figures as regards number of copies sold seem to be extant, the book was reprinted the following year, so it must have had a reasonable circulation.

John McKenzie, a cricket book specialist, came across a copy of Arthur Carr's book which contains an intriguing dedication, written in Carr's hand, on the title page: 'To Lavender, With Best Wishes from Arthur. I should like to say more but I'm frightened of Bill!' Both Lavender and Bill are unknown. The words could be merely a flippant comment, or much more. Perhaps someone reading this will reveal its meaning? Although Carr was not particularly handsome in the conventional sense, it seems that the ladies were attracted to him. Further comment at this juncture is unnecessary.

Carr made one appearance in first-class cricket during 1935, his final first-class game. He was invited to play for Sir Lindsay Parkinson's XI v Leicestershire at Blackpool in mid July. Sir Lindsay Parkinson was a great patron of cricket and of Blackpool CC in particular. Stanley Park where the game was played was given to the local cricket club by the Parkinson family, who ran a successful building contractors business.

First-class games had been played on the ground since 1904. Parkinson assembled a motley crew for this game, including two other Test cricketers who had retired from the county game, Percy Holmes of Yorkshire and Ted McDonald, the Australian fast bowler now in local league cricket. Carr did not distinguish himself, scoring 7 and 0. Although Sir Lindsay died in 1936, it was through the Parkinson family that Harold Larwood was to become the Blackpool professional in 1939.

The first half of the season was disappointing for Nottinghamshire. On 10 July the county stood eleventh in the table and never looked likely to challenge for the title. The race was primarily led by Derbyshire and Yorkshire, the former topped the table for three weeks but Yorkshire took over on 6 July and remained in first place until the end. Nottinghamshire had a much better second half, finishing in fifth place with ten victories. Voce headed the Nottinghamshire Championship bowling figures with 133 wickets at an average of 21.19; Larwood came second with 98 at 22.46. Hardstaff, Walker, Harris, Gunn and Staples all exceeded 1,000 runs with averages above 33. Although Lancashire had refused to play Nottinghamshire, not one of the other counties took such a drastic step. A paragraph in the *Wisden* review of the summer reads: 'Having declared their future policy, Nottinghamshire resumed their old friendly associations with the counties, all of whom will be met next season. Leading cricketers stated publicly their pleasure that the correct attitude of the committee had received such strong endorsement.'

The annual general meeting of the county club was held at Albert Hall on 20 January 1936. After the usual formal business had been dealt with a presentation was made to Arthur Carr. This comprised a casket executed in etched crystal glass with bronze mounts standing on a marble base. The casket contained an illuminated address designed by the Nottingham College of Art. Sir Julien Cahn, the retiring President, made the presentation and after reading out the illuminated address which detailed Carr's career, Cahn continued: 'At the zenith of his career as a cricketer and captain, Mr Carr himself would not have realised, as he did now, what records he was making and what a splendid tradition he was building. There had been floodtides of controversy, which had surged up to Trent Bridge and which might for a moment have hidden those things from members' eyes, but it was a long and brilliant innings that was now being applauded. An innings full of dash, courage and daring. Had Mr Carr lived in the days of ancient Rome he would have had a statue erected to him (laughter). I don't suppose he would have been any more afraid of the lions than he was a couple of years ago of the kangaroos. The meeting was showing admiration for a great cricketer whose name would be for all time enshrouded in the annals of the county.'

Arthur Carr was loudly applauded when he stood up to respond. He thanked the Committee and members for the gifts and continued: 'As a boy I had three ambitions in life. The first was to captain a county cricket team, the second was to captain England and the third was to win a steeplechase. I have achieved all three. Perhaps I was lucky, but the fact remained that in the steeplechase there were seven starters and all but one fell (laughter). Whatever career a person took up, there were ups and downs. I have had mine, but I have loved my cricket at Trent Bridge and my one ambition has been to do my best for the county club. My whole heart has been in the game. Before I met her, my wife knew nothing about cricket, but I took her to Trent Bridge and she has been here ever since. I thank her for her companionship. May I end by saying that I wish my cricketing career at Trent Bridge was starting all over again.'

In addition to the crystal casket, Carr received the cricket bat he had used in his final county match at Trent Bridge with a suitable silver mount. Mrs Carr received a silver salver from the Committee and members and another gift from an anonymous donor.

Three days later the first Committee meeting of the New Year was held. Carr 'expressed his warmest thanks for the presentations made to him at the AGM'. The various sub-committees were chosen and Carr was included on the selection committee with Lionel Kirk as chairman.

After a gap in 1935, Lancashire resumed matches with Nottinghamshire, the first being at Old Trafford on 20, 22 and 23 June. Nottinghamshire won by five wickets, Larwood took ten for 62 and Voce six for 78. The Nottinghamshire Secretary received a telegram the following day and this was read out at the meeting on 25 June: 'Please convey my heartiest congratulations to your Committee on your splendid victory. Delightful pleasant match. Tommy Higson, Chairman Lancs CCC.' Nottinghamshire responded: 'Committee thank you sincerely for your very kind telegram. Hope to have many more matches in future. Brown.'

At the following month's Committee meeting it was resolved to invite twelve members of the Lancashire Committee to Trent Bridge for the return match in August. Carr attended both these General Committee meetings, one can visualise steam coming out of his head, although the minutes do not state that he spoke!

Nottinghamshire were captained throughout the season by George Heane. His joint captain in 1935, Rhodes, left county cricket though continued with Cahn's team. With Harold Larwood in splendid form, Nottinghamshire flourished and in mid-season briefly led the Championship table. In the end they settled for fifth place with eight victories against three defeats. Larwood had been awarded a benefit and chose the match at Trent Bridge against Yorkshire in mid-July. Financially the match was a great success.

LV Manning of the *Daily Sketch* offered Larwood £2,000 to report on the forthcoming Australia v England Tests scheduled for the winter of 1936-37. Larwood had discussions with Manning, accompanied by HA Brown and Douglas McCraith, but on the advice of McCraith he declined the offer on the grounds that he was under agreement with Nottinghamshire that he would not write any articles for the press whilst employed by the county club. The MCC wrote to the county club asking permission for both Hardstaff and Voce to join the MCC tour to Australia. Permission was granted. Larwood was granted permission to take up a coaching post in India during the winter.

Carr was re-appointed to the selection sub-committee for 1937; the only General Committee meeting he attended during that year was a special meeting called with regard to Larwood's recent behaviour. Larwood had been asked by the Secretary to attend net practice at Trent Bridge in order that his match fitness could be assessed, but the fast bowler did not turn up.

It was not an isolated incident, either. A month earlier the Nottinghamshire captain reported that Larwood was drunk on the first day of the Nottinghamshire match at Northampton. The match had begun on time but rain ended play after ninety minutes with Northamptonshire 60 for one. The players therefore spent the rest of the playing time confined to the pavilion. Ironically the sun came out in the evening and, at 9.30, three Nottinghamshire players decided to go for an evening drive. Voce led the way in his car, Flight Sergeant Rowley of RAF Bicester followed in his car with Larwood as one of the passengers, Arthur Staples was in the rear in his car. About two miles out of Northampton, the cars met a bus coming in the opposite direction over a bridge. Voce passed safely but Rowley's brakes jammed, he collided with the bus and the car somersaulted down a deep ditch. Staples pulled up in time. Rowley was thrown clear of the wreckage but Larwood and another passenger were injured. An ambulance was called and ferried the three injured parties to hospital. In addition a motorbike and sidecar collided with the back of the bus as it stopped suddenly – the rider and passenger also required hospital treatment. Fortunately Larwood's injuries only comprised a badly cut hand and a strained back. He reported at the ground for the second day's play, but clearly couldn't take any part in the action. At 11.45, Arthur Carr arrived in his car – he had been contracted to broadcast the afternoon's play for the Midland region of the BBC. According to the press report, Carr instructed his chauffeur to take Larwood back home.

Even though Carr attended the special meeting to discuss Larwood's behaviour and was at least partially involved, he was not part of the sub-committee asked to interview Larwood and report back – that sub-committee comprised Messrs McCraith, Kirk and Rushworth – interestingly neither McCraith nor Rushworth were members of the selection committee which normally dealt directly with the first XI. Two days later the three members of the sub-committee reported back to General Committee (fourteen members came, including Carr) and Larwood was suspended for the rest of the season (two matches remained) for a 'breach of discipline'. According to Duncan Hamilton's biography of the player, Larwood had gone on holiday to Skegness when he should have been at the Trent Bridge nets.

The minutes of both these meetings do not describe in detail who said what and about whom. They proved to be the last meetings Carr ever attended. Reading between the lines and being aware of Carr's character and his affinity to the players, particularly Larwood, one would be entitled to believe that Carr had his say in defence of Larwood. Possibly he criticised the new captain in the process and, having his point of view brushed aside, decided he had had enough of the intrigues of county cricket. He resolved then to finish with the Committee, but did not formally resign until the following January – Carr was not a great letter writer at the best of times.

This biography commences with Carr's official letter of resignation. Having finished with cricket, with which his summers were totally occupied since the end of the First World War, the question must be asked: what did someone as active as Carr do with his summer months? Hunting occupied his win-

ters. He wished to become Master of the South Nottinghamshire Hunt but needed a substantial addition to his income
to do the job in style. He went to see his mother at Hemingford Park. She declined to help and so his dreams of being
Master were crushed. Sir Julien Cahn was also a hunt enthu-
siast and had wanted to join the Quorn Hunt of which Carr
was a member, but he failed to be elected, perhaps because he
was Jewish. Cahn joined the Burton Hunt and was elected as
Master. After some obscure disagreements, Cahn resigned and
took up the Master's role with the Woodland Pytchley Hunt.
Sir Julien's home was at Stanford Hall, whose estate adjoined
that of Rempstone Hall, Carr's former home. In Miranda Rijks' *The Eccentric Entrepreneur,* a biography of her grandfather
Sir Julien Cahn, there is only one passing reference to Arthur
Carr. One imagines that the relationship between Cahn and
Carr was no more than a grudging acceptance, one to another
despite their common interests in both cricket and hunting.

Arthur Carr, his wife Ivy, and son Angus lived in the style of
a lord of Bulcote Manor. According to an essay by Joan Allen,
which appeared in the *Bulcote Village Newsletter* of June 1992,
the Carr's domestic staff comprised a butler, cook and several
maids; the outside staff included three grooms to look after the
horses and several gardeners. She notes that two of his horses
in 1935 were named Nottinghamshire Forever and Bodyline.
Apart from his interest in horses, Carr was keen on greyhound
racing; he mentions watching races in South Africa in his autobiography. Sir Home Gordon, in *Background to Cricket*, relates
the following yarn: 'Arthur Gilligan and I were in Nottingham
for the Sussex match. Nothing would do but that we should
motor after close of play some ten miles to see his [Carr's] dog
run, assuring us that it would romp in an easy winner ... His
dog was unplaced in the fourth race, so we lost our money and
arrived back towards ten, at the Victoria Hotel for some sort

of meal. The owner only grumbled at his dog having kept him so late from his bed.'

One of Carr's relatives, who knew Arthur's brother Gordon better than they knew Arthur, stated that the two brothers were only interested in three things in the late 1930s: horses, dogs and women – in which order it was difficult to say. Several press photographs of the Nottinghamshire players at Trent Bridge in the late 1920s and early 1930s depict Carr with one of his dogs, as does the official team photo of 1934, with Fido sitting on the grass in front of his master. Carr's niece, June Prescott, recalls visiting Bulcote Manor around that time and being overwhelmed by Spinach, whom she describes as a large woolly animal. Talking some thirty years ago to some of the Bulcote villagers who lived in the terrace of cottages next to Bulcote Manor, they remembered Carr returning from Trent Bridge with fellow cricketers and celebrations occasionally carrying on well into the early hours.

Nottinghamshire recorded a poor season in 1937; the county ended tenth in the table, the worst position since the resumption of cricket in 1919. Voce missed half the Championship matches, he played in one of the New Zealand Tests but latterly suffered a serious knee injury, Larwood played in eighteen games and no longer seemed to have the bite that he had managed to rekindle in 1936. Nottinghamshire's close fielding was described as quite abysmal. To an extent Harold Butler filled the fast bowling gap, though he was never going to fill both Larwood's and Voce's boots; of the rest of the attack, no one averaged under 30. The strong batting line up of Hardstaff, Keeton, Harris and Gunn made Nottinghamshire difficult to beat, with Hardstaff's overall record earning him a place as one of *Wisden's* five Cricketers of the Year.

Arthur Staples had been awarded a benefit that season and among the fixtures arranged for him was one at the beginning of May on The Forest, the original home of Nottingham cricket before the opening of Trent Bridge, where Nottingham-shire played PGH Fender's XI. Carr was a member of Fender's side and, batting at number five, scored 11 runs. The newspaper report comments: 'AW Carr, who had a cordial greeting, was taken by Harris off Gunn after a couple of characteristic swipes.' Carr also bowled, taking one wicket for 15 runs, his victim being no less than Harold Larwood, who was caught by HR Cox for 54. On 4 May Carr attended a dinner at the Black Boy, given by the Nottinghamshire Committee for the playing staff.

1937 was George Heane's second season in sole command. The official county cricket club report of the season hands him some praise but the *Nottingham Journal* is not particularly forthcoming. This was in strong contrast to their comments on Carr's captaincy in every one of his sixteen seasons when, whatever the team's performance, his leadership qualities and fielding were always commended. Heane would remain forever in Carr's shadow, although it would not be until 1946 that the players quietly revolted against his style of leadership. Frank Woodhead was so disenchanted that he quit county cricket, but returned as soon as he discovered that Bill Sime was replacing Heane for the 1947 season. The Committee had been forced to make a change. George Heane farmed in Lincoln-shire and played for that county from 1947 to 1950.

With Carr out of the picture the 1938 Nottinghamshire cricket season passed by without controversy. The Ashes series was similarly devoid. There had been some discussion on the captaincy of England but this was solved when Walter Hammond, the Gloucestershire cricketer and outstanding batsman of 1937, changed hats and moved from professional to amateur. Len Hutton, the Yorkshire opener, amassed the record Test score of 364 in the fifth and final Test at The Oval. England tied the series by gaining victory in that game, though Australia were severely handicapped, only batting with nine men in each innings due to Bradman and Fingleton both being injured. Bradman naturally dominated the headlines through the summer, just as he had done in 1930 and 1934.

1938 was not only an Australian year, it was the centenary of Trent Bridge. Sir Julien Cahn paid for a centenary book to be published and a copy sent to every member of the club. *A Hundred Years of Trent Bridge* was edited by EV Lucas, a well-known writer of the day. The main content is a forty-three-page history of Nottinghamshire cricket by Lucas with six subsidiary essays. There are twenty-eight full-page photographs, mainly individual portraits. The book is a prime example of how bitterly Carr divided Nottinghamshire cricket. There are portraits of the four captains who immediately preceded Carr – Alfred Shaw, Sherwin, Dixon and Jones – but not of Carr, though he lasted longer than any of them. The famous professionals who served under Carr; John Gunn, George Gunn, Larwood, Voce and both Joe Hardstaffs, all have portraits, and most of the ten listed above have reasonable narrative pieces.

Arthur Carr was reduced to two small references. On page 39, 'When the game was renewed after, however, many tragic losses, in 1920 [sic] Mr AW Carr was Nottinghamshire's captain, holding the post until his retirement in 1934. One of Mr Carr's greatest matches was against Sussex at Brighton in 1922, when he scored 104 out of 133 in ninety minutes.' On page 63, 'The Test of 1926 was what might be called the period of the "Trent Bridge deluge". AW Carr did his duty in winning the toss.' Carr, it might be said, was almost air-brushed out of Nottinghamshire history!

AW Shelton worked tirelessly to gather memorabilia and have it displayed in the pavilion Long Room. Saturday 28 May was set as the day on which the centenary of the ground would be celebrated. Nottinghamshire were scheduled to play Hampshire on the ground that day and the following Monday and Tuesday. The BBC arranged for a special broadcast from Trent

Bridge on the evening of 30 May. The Committee suggested the following take part in this broadcast: Sir Douglas McCraith (chairman), HA Brown (secretary), Walter Marshall (former player, coach and groundsman), GFH Heane (captain) and WAS Oldfield (representing Australia). The BBC then insisted that Harold Larwood, Bill Voce and Joe Hardstaff be added to the group. The Committee agreed on condition that the Committee approved the players' speeches beforehand, it was also suggested that George Gunn be asked. Despite the fact that Carr had been broadcasting for the BBC in 1937 and the former England and Nottinghamshire captain was on paper the most obvious choice for such a programme, the BBC would not suggest him because of the 1934/35 controversy.

A curiosity of 1938: George Duckworth, the Lancashire and England wicketkeeper, had taken over Arthur Carr's spot as cricket writer on the *Empire News*. Directly prior to the Trent Bridge Test match of 1938, Duckworth's weekly column featured Jardine, Larwood and Bodyline bowling. In a piece that runs to some 2,000 words, nowhere is Carr even mentioned. The rawness of the incident with TA Higson and Carr, in which Duckworth, the Lancashire wicketkeeper, was involved, remained an open sore.

In December 1938, Mrs Amy Lewin Borton, Carr's mother-in-law and step-mother of Ivy, died in Upton-on-Severn, Worcestershire, aged eighty. She had been a widow for fourteen years and lived latterly not too far from Mrs Vera Stevenson, her other daughter. Arthur Carr's mother remained at Hemingford Park and encouraged her children and grandchildren to come and stay. Gordon's son, Philip Montague, was a permanent resident with the Wendells and their two children, Jac and June. June recalls Uncle Arthur as a man of few words who would listen to the family discussions and now and then contribute a pithy comment accompanied by a knowing smile.

When Nottinghamshire cricketers reported at Trent Bridge for net practice prior to the start of the 1939 season, there was a massive change in comparison with previous post-war springs. James Iremonger, coach since 1921 and mentor of Larwood and Voce, had retired. He was replaced by two former internationals, DJ Knight of Surrey and England and Alan Fairfax of New South Wales and Australia. Both had their salaries as coaches paid for by Sir Julien Cahn.

The players were addressed by Douglas McCraith, club chairman, prior to their initial practice session. He emphasised that fielding practice and physical training were the top priorities. Major TP Barber, the new club president, was also present together with eight members of the Committee. The club captain, GFH Heane, and Joe Hardstaff were absent still on their way home having toured New Zealand with Sir Julien Cahn's team.

The final pre-war season finished with Nottinghamshire in twelfth place, identical to 1938. The attack relied largely on Butler and Voce, neither of whom played in the Test series versus West Indies, however Nottinghamshire's two principal batsmen, Joe Hardstaff and Walter Keeton, both represented England, the former scoring 94 in the final Test. The declaration of war caused some September first-class fixtures to be cancelled and the West Indian touring party left England for home earlier than planned. Hardstaff joined the Army and was to serve in India, where he also managed to fit in a few first-class matches between military duties.

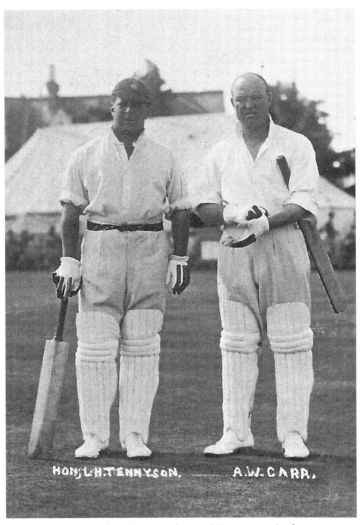

At his peak – Carr with Lord Tennyson before
the 1928 Gentlemen v Players match

# 16

# BACK TO WAR

## 1939-1963

Being an Army reservist, Arthur Carr found himself, like quite a number of his generation who survived the Great War, called to arms for the second time. His regiment, the 5th Royal Irish Lancers, was sent to serve in India when he left them in 1920. They merged with the 16th Queen's Lancers in 1922 and returned to England in 1926 before going back to India in 1936. They came home in 1940 and Carr was ordered to Catterick Camp near Richmond in Yorkshire.

Arthur Carr's move to Catterick gave him a chance to renew his cricketing skills. The report in the 1940 winter annual of *The Cricketer*, written by no lesser person than Capt Hedley Verity of 10 for 10 fame, noted, 'Arthur Carr is still hitting very hard, as mid-off knows to his cost.' The only match score printed in that magazine, a game between the Catterick Garrison and 123rd OCT Regiment, credits Carr, coming in first wicket down, with just a single. He was dismissed by AB Lavers, the Essex off-spinner. Verity was the sole success for the Garrison team in that game, taking seven wickets and making the highest score, 51.

Sometime before this game, most probably during the winter of 1939/40, Carr had spent an evening at a local dance. Here he met Beryl, a forty-two year old who was separated from her husband, Lieutenant Colonel Frank William Sopper.

Born in 1880, Frank Sopper had been educated at Marlborough and Sherborne. He was commissioned as a second lieutenant in the 8th Hussars in 1900 and promoted to captain in 1909. His first marriage took place at St George's, Hanover Square, in 1912 to Yvonne Temperley; she died in 1918 aged thirty-seven. He married Beryl in York on 2 April 1921; she was seventeen years his junior. There were no children. Sopper served in South Africa during the Boer War and in France during the First World War. After the war he retired, granted the rank of lieutenant colonel and placed on the reserves until 1934 when he attained the age limit of liability. The colonel was exceedingly wealthy with a large Scottish estate at Easter Aberchalder, Gorthleck, Inverness-shire, as well as a London residence at 126 Sloane Street, SW1. His father had died in 1911 with an estate worth nearly £400,000, the majority of which was shared between Frank and his brother.

Beryl Margery Whitehead was the second child of the Rev George Talbot Whitehead, who was educated at Charterhouse and Cambridge, and his wife, Margaret Louise, nee Begbie. Beryl was born on 25 March 1897, at Flanders Hall, West Burton, Bishopsdale, off Wensleydale.

Beryl later recounted meeting Arthur Carr. The band were playing the Cole Porter number 'I've Got My Eyes On You', a popular melody in 1940. Being of a romantic nature, Beryl bought Arthur a cigarette lighter with an eye engraved on each side, commemorating that first meeting, or maybe dance. The pair 'clicked' almost at once and the colonel was seemingly happy to divorce his wayward and feisty wife. The undefended divorce took place in the Court of Sessions in Edinburgh on 15 August 1941, with Arthur cited as the co-defender. The couple had signed into an Edinburgh hotel under the names Mr and Mrs Carr in June 1941, Beryl having previously notified her husband's lawyers that she and Arthur Carr would be staying two nights at the hotel.

Colonel Sopper may have been content to finish his marriage and see his wife co-habiting with Carr, but Carr's own wife was certainly not content, nor was his mother. Whilst Arthur Carr had been rather too busy at Catterick, Ivy Carr had been making her contribution to the war effort by organising a canteen for troops stationed in the Bulcote area. She managed to acquire a few extra rations to stock the kitchen and feed these soldiers some home treats. Ivy flatly refused to divorce Arthur, an act which had financial repercussions since Arthur's father's legacy to Arthur and Ivy had been split between each of them.

With the breakdown of the Carr marriage and the subsequent Sopper divorce, Ivy Carr moved from Bulcote to London. Her new address was given as 26 Kensington Court off Kensington Church Street, W8. Moving with Ivy was a favourite maid and companion from Bulcote Manor. The marriage between Arthur and Ivy had not been a particularly happy arrangement, their only real link being their son, Angus. Like too many couples in the inter-war period they had rubbed along together. Ivy had taken an interest in cricket but she had little interest in either horses or dogs. When Beryl arrived, definitely interested in horses and dogs, that sounded the end for Arthur's marriage. His mother did not approve and never allowed Beryl to visit Hemingford Park. She would never mention Beryl's name and when it was necessary to refer to her, Mrs Carr senior simply called her 'that woman'.

Ivy Carr received a second, tragic blow during the war. Her son, Angus, had been educated at Marlborough where he proved a useful cricketer but did not obtain a place in the eleven. From Marlborough he went on to Sandhurst and he received his commission in 1939. At the outbreak of war he was a lieutenant in the South Nottinghamshire Hussars. On 18 January 1940, his regiment was ordered to travel to Palestine. They went by ship from Southampton to Cherbourg then by train to Marseilles, Another ship took the troops across the Mediterranean to Haifa, arriving there on 29 January. In *The South Nottinghamshire Hussars: The Western Desert 1940-1942* there is a description of some cricket being played, but no specific mention of Angus Carr on the cricket field. On 25 June 1940 the regiment moved to Mersa Matruh. They had a successful campaign against the Italian forces and retired back to the Suez Canal. In the meantime the Afrika Corps, led by General Rommel, arrived in Tripoli. The South Nottinghamshire Hussars were ordered back to defend Tobruk. In the spring of 1942, Carr's regiment advanced from Tobruk and reached a crossroads, nicknamed Knightsbridge. Here they were caught without any tank or infantry support and ordered to fight to the last man.

Lieutenant Angus Carr was killed on 27 May 1942, aged twenty-four. It was the first day of the prolonged German attack which would more or less wipe out the South Nottinghamshire Hussars in the area, either killed, wounded or captured. His obituary notes that he was a fine horseman and, like his father, rode to hounds with the South Nottinghamshire, Quorn and Belvoir Hunts. On the same day another South Nottinghamshire Hussars fatality was Major Philip Birkin. Nine years older than Angus Carr, Major Birkin was the son of Major Philip Austen Birkin, member of the county cricket club Committee from 1926 to 1937, who suddenly resigned due to a disagreement with Sir Julien Cahn over the manner in which an appeal for funds had been handled. Philip Austen Birkin had taken responsibility of the work done by the head groundsman at Trent Bridge and used to visit the ground on almost a daily basis to check on any matters of moment. In the internal committee wrangling on Arthur Carr's suitability as captain, Birkin usually sided with the skipper. In 1935 Arthur Carr had given Birkin a copy of *Cricket With The Lid Off* specially inscribed and with a reference to their times as drinking companions.

Another direct connection between the defeat of the Hussars in May 1942 and the county club was Sergeant Charles 'Jim' Ward. He was captured by the Germans and spent the rest of the war as a prisoner. Ward, a keen member of Wollaton Cricket Club, was on the county cricket club Committee from 1980 to 1987 and president from 1993-94.

Shortly after his divorce and before Angus's death, Arthur Carr retired from the Army. The press report of Angus's death gives the address of his next of kin as Ivy's flat in Kensington; on the paperwork it is shown as the residence of both Ivy and Arthur though, of course, the latter never lived there. Instead, Arthur's whereabouts during the rest of the war are rather nebulous. In 1943 he was apprehended by a police constable for riding a bicycle after dark without lights. Instead of apologising politely, Carr began arguing with the officer, saying that he ought to have more important duties to perform than to worry about Arthur's lack of lights. The matter ended at court where Carr was fined and admonished by the magistrate. The incident occurred in Guiseley, a few miles outside Leeds, with Carr's address also being given as in Guiseley. According to an old inhabitant of Rempstone, speaking some forty years ago, after retiring from the Army Carr took a job as a taxi driver in Leeds. What is more certain is that he made several visits to see his mother at Hemingford Park and attempted reconciliation, but 'that woman' was a permanent stumbling block.

Arthur's brother, Gordon, had been discharged from the Army in 1918 as unfit for service so, unlike his sibling, was not recalled to the colours. On the outbreak of hostilities he was living in Sussex Gardens, Bayswater, and it was here that he caused a minor stir in the press under the headline 'Midnight Flat Scene Costs Man £20'. Gordon had been charged with causing grievous bodily harm to a lady in Strathern Place, round the corner from his flat. In the magistrates' court the charge was reduced to common assault. The lady in question, Mrs Clare Rhodes, claimed she had been kicked on the head but, at least in the press reports which appeared on 15 December 1939, seemed more concerned that her £250 fur coat had been dumped in the bath. Gordon was fined £5 with 15 guineas (£15.75) costs – he claimed in mitigation that the widow was helplessly drunk at the time of the alleged attack.

Gordon had worked for the family stockbroking business, but it seems that he retired from the firm under a cloud, though the date of his retirement is unclear. Following his problems with law, evacuated himself to the West Country for the duration.

Arthur's sister Eileen was also living in Bayswater in 1939, with her husband Jac Wendell and their two children, Jac junior (born 1924) and June (born 1927). Jac was now at Eton. A talented cricketer, he would play in the Eton v Harrow match of 1942. The house where the family lived was destroyed in an air raid in the Blitz. Fortunately no one was in residence at the time. Eileen travelled from Hemingford to inspect the damaged premises and to rescue what personal possessions she could, but a great deal was lost. She and the children were to stay with Arthur's mother, Louisa, for the rest of the war.

Louisa died on 16 April 1946 at her home in Hemingford Abbots, Huntingdonshire. The will was published on 22 October of the same year. The estate was valued at £41,671.1.4d from which had to be deducted estate duty of £7,757.14.9d. The contents came with a bitter pill to both of her sons, Arthur and Gordon – they were omitted entirely. Living in sin with Beryl was something that Louisa clearly could never forgive. Aside from some small personal bequests, the bulk of the estate was simply divided between her daughter, Eileen, and her grandson, Philip Montague, though the latter's share would be in trust, with him receiving only the interest until he attained the age of twenty-five and a lump sum of £2,000 at twenty-one – he was nineteen at the time of Louise's death. The executors of the will were Jacob Wendell and Eileen (both given as residing at Hemingford Park when the will was made in November 1945), a third executor was the family solicitor.

To embarrass Arthur further, a legacy of £50 was left to Ivy Carr. The only other family members named were Louisa's Scottish relatives, sister Lizzie Donald and niece Dorothy Donald. It was another member of the same Donald family, Grahame, born two years before Arthur Carr, who had the sort of career that Carr's might have been if he had had a different temperament. Donald was educated at Dulwich where he, like Carr, excelled at sport. He played both cricket and rugby. He was in the college rugby XV and the cricket XI, topping the bowling averages in his final summer. Sherborne never played Dulwich so the two cousins don't seem to have met on the cricket field. Grahame Donald managed to go to Oxford University and in 1914 represented Scotland at rugby. He joined the Royal Navy in 1914, but transferred to the Royal Naval Flying Corps in 1916, which was absorbed into the RAF in 1918. He remained in the RAF, ending as Air Marshal and being awarded a knighthood. There is one later pattern that mirrors Carr – Donald's only son, Ian, went to Dulwich College and RAF Cranwell. He was killed during the Battle of Britain on his debut in action, his plane being shot down by a Messerschmitt 109 and crashing in Dover; he was twenty-two. The family home was in Tilford, Surrey, and he is buried in the churchyard there. Sir Grahame Donald died in December 1976.

As neither Eileen nor Philip Montague could afford to buy the other out, Hemingford Park and most of its contents were sold. In 2009, when the property came on the market again, it was valued at £4,500,000 and was described as a Grade II listed hall with a thatched lodge, cottage, coach house, stables, cattle barns and seventy-one acres of timbered parkland. The cricket ground had closed with the death of Louisa Carr and the rather sumptuous pavilion was a bungalow. The village team still survives, though now playing in Hemingford Abbots itself – two of Philip Montague Carr's sons, now in their fifties, used to play in the team in the 1980s.

Arthur Carr and Beryl lived in a flat in Harrogate in the late 1940s. Arthur, ever a lover of sport, took up squash and legend has it that he beat the club professional who taught him, most probably at the Majestic Hotel. Two squash courts still exist there, no longer used for squash, but as gyms. A press report of a race meeting at Thirsk, 10 April 1954, contains the note: 'Other firm supporters of racing in the country noted at this meeting were Mr TL Taylor (President of Yorkshire CCC) Colonel Chaytor, Chief Constable of the North Riding, Mrs Arthur Carr, Lady Wingate Saul with Miss Crookenden, etc, etc.' 'Mrs Arthur Carr' was Beryl, rather than Ivy, who now lived in London.

It was not until 23 November 1955 that Ivy Carr died, still residing in her flat at Kensington Court. The cause of death was liver cancer; her sister, Vera Stevenson, was in attendance. Ivy was sixty-three years of age. Two months later Arthur Carr and Beryl, who had been living as man and wife for more than ten years, married in Chelsea Register Office by special licence. Jacob Wendell, Carr's brother-in-law, was one of the witnesses. Carr is described as 'of independent means'. Both bride and groom gave addresses in Chelsea but were now living in a semi-detached cottage in the small village of West Witton in Wensleydale.

Beryl's former husband, Lieutenant Colonel Sopper, had died on 3 May 1950, having recently returned from a world cruise. He was eighty at the time of death and left over £300,000. In the same year the death was recorded at Flanders Hall, West Burton, of the Rev George Talbot Whitehead, Beryl's father. Currently Flanders Hall is used for holiday lets.

Although Arthur Carr's interest in cricket was no longer acute, his interest in horse racing remained very strong. The advantage of living in West Witton was that the village lay not far from Middleham, a major centre of racing stables and in particular in the 1950s and 1960s of the trainer Sam Hall. Carr still owned racehorses, although his financial situation would seem to indicate that he may not have been the sole owner. He is reported to have spent many hours at Sam Hall's stables, keeping an eye on the horses under training. A letter to John Hall, the former Nottinghamshire cricketer who also had more than a passing interest in racing circles, read:

> Clumber Cottage, West Witton, Leyburn, Yorks
> April 29

My dear John,

Enclosed two vouchers for York as you will be certain to be coming. We shall win some races all right as the horses are just coming to hand. Winscale is very fine and Joe Sime fancies him very much but for myself I just doubt if he will come up the hill. I have only got a little on him. Joe thinks he's certain to beat all those he beat at Thirsk.

I could not go to the dinner, my back was bad again. I cannot get rid of those bloody East winds. I think both my two-year-olds will win later on. Looking forward to seeing you,

Ever,
Arthur.

Joe Sime, a well-known jockey, raced from 1941 to 1969; his best season was 1960 when he finished second to Lester Piggott in the jockeys' table. It comes as no surprise that Sime was also interested in cricket; Sam Hall, the trainer, had well over 1,000 winners in his career and had been based at the Brecongill stables in Middleham from 1949 when he obtained his own licence. Beryl's niece, Lady Leticia Inge, who was born at Swinithwaite Hall on the outskirts of West Witton, recalls going to York races with Arthur Carr as a teenager. She was allowed to pass the day at the racecourse whilst Carr dealt with his own interests and met his friends. Beryl's great-nephew, Adrian Thornton-Berry, resides at Swinithwaite Hall and was given the bat Arthur Carr used on his last appearance as captain at Trent Bridge. This bat and other cricket memorabilia was left by Carr in his will to Beryl.

When not at the Middleham stables or away at the races, Carr passed much time in the local West Witton pub, just a few yards away from Clumber Cottage. It was at this pub that Fred Trueman, the England bowler, met Carr when researching his book on the Yorkshire Dales. The book includes a photograph of the pub – the Wensleydale Heifer – but fails to mention what the two old Test cricketers discussed. Was it horse racing or cricket, or maybe just the weather? We shall never know! The pub now boasts a very good restaurant which has won a variety of awards as well as en-suite accommodation.

In the 1950s, after years in exile, Arthur Carr received invitations to attend the Test matches at Trent Bridge – the exact year of his return is not known as detailed correspondence to the Secretary during that period is no longer extant and no one presently at the cricket ground remembers him. Those with whom he had very serious disagreements had passed on; Dr GO Gauld died in 1950, Sir Douglas McCraith in 1952, RG Hogarth in 1954 and Lord Belper in 1956. Sir Julien Cahn had passed away in September 1944.

Arthur Carr had a heart attack and died whilst clearing snow on the road adjacent to his cottage in West Witton on 7 February 1963 – the 1962/63 winter was a particularly severe one with heavy falls of snow, with the Yorkshire Dales severely affected during January and February. His death certificate describes Carr as a retired Army officer. The informant on the certificate is his widow, Beryl. A private cremation took place at Darlington Crematorium. His will, published in August, valued his effects as being worth £11,492 12s. Beryl was the beneficiary. The one unusual note on his will is the fact that he is described as 'Carr, Arthur William OBE'. A search of the records printed in the *London Gazette* fails to provide a date for the awarding of the OBE.

The principal Nottingham newspaper of the time, the *Guardian Journal*, published an obituary on 16 February 1963, but it was disappointingly bland, as was the brief notice in the *Playfair Cricket Monthly*.

John Arlott's obituary of Carr, published in *The Cricketer*, contained a better description of the former Nottinghamshire and England captain: 'Tall, wide-shouldered with a high forehead, eyes constantly narrowed – as if in approval – strong mouth and firm jaw, he took his cricket grimly as though it satisfied some hugely combative streak in him.' The anonymous writer of obituaries in *Wisden* commented: 'Of somewhat stern appearance, but kind and generous at heart and a lover of cricket, Carr was a man of forthright views.'

The Nottinghamshire County Cricket Club Annual Report for 1963 recorded Carr's death, together with the deaths of John Gunn and Ted Alletson. The piece on Carr read: 'Arthur Carr, a former captain of the County and England, was a pugnacious batsman, who brought the same qualities of fearless aggression and uncompromising zest into his captaincy. They won him many admirers, for he was a courageous leader of men, with the ability to command and return loyalty, and a natural air of authority. He led the county XI in 1929, the last occasion they won the County Championship.'

Arthur Carr was not completely forgotten – for a period in the 1970s, a section at the back of the George Parr Stand was formed into a small area for drinks and snacks and named the Carr Bar. On 28 August 1999, one of the races held in the evening meeting at Colwick was run for the Carr Trophy. A similar race was staged in 2000. The prep school which Carr attended, Hazlewood, now awards an Arthur Carr Scholarship each year to a boy of eight or nine who has a particular sporting talent.

Beryl Carr must have made a favourable impression on the Nottinghamshire CCC officials when she had accompanied Arthur to Trent Bridge Tests since she accepted an invitation to the 1978 Test match. At that time she was living at Fold Cottage in West Witton. The death of Gordon, Arthur Carr's brother, also occurred in 1978, in Marlborough – he left his estate to charity. Jacob Wendell, Arthur's brother-in-law, died in 1983 and his sister, Eileen, in 1985. Both Jacob Wendell and Eileen were buried on the estate at Highclere. Beryl Carr died in 1987, aged eighty-nine.

The firm of WI Carr and Sons disappeared in name in 2001, now part of Investec. The Carr family had long left the firm by the time of the final merger; Gordon would seem to have been the final direct link.

Rather than close with a list of further details of Carr's extended family, I feel it more appropriate to add Cecil Parkin's brief piece published in *Cricket Triumphs and Troubles* in 1936: 'I had the greatest admiration for Arthur Carr of Nottinghamshire, as a batsman, fielder and skipper. When he got set in an innings he took the gloves off and was merciless on the bowling. Some of his hitting was like Jessop's and that was the mood everybody liked to see him in – except the poor bowlers who were wheeling 'em up to him. He was one of the strongest players I have ever seen and one of the fastest workers imaginable in attacking the bowling. As a fieldsman he was absolutely fearless and he very rarely missed a catch though he often stood dangerously close to the batsman.'

This biography began with a verse from Sir Henry Newbolt's 'Vitaï Lampada'. Given Arthur Carr's battles, both on and off the cricket field, perhaps the second verse provides a suitable finale:

The sand of the desert is sodden red –
Red with the wreck of a square that broke –
The Gatling's jammed and the Colonel dead,
And the regiment blind with dust and smoke.
The river of death has brimmed his banks,
And England's far and Honour a name,
But the voice of a schoolboy rallies the ranks:
Play up! Play up! And play the game!

# ACKNOWLEDGEMENTS

I must first of all thank Duncan Anderson for the consistent advice and help he has given me through both the long research process and the actual writing of the manuscript. It was his delvings into cricketers who fought in the First World War that persuaded Duncan that I should write this biography. I was familiar with Carr's career on the cricket field, but until I looked a little deeper, I had not realised that I would be straying into several activities of which my knowledge was slim.

Mrs June Prescott, Arthur Carr's niece, has been tremendous in helping me to provide a more rounded portrait of her uncle and the work would be that much poorer if I had had to rely solely on the written word. Other relations of the extended Carr family; Mrs Olive Carr, Adrian Thornton-Berry, Field Marshall Lord Inge and Lady Inge have also been of help. Mrs Fiona Wright forwarded a number of most interesting family photographs.

As with many of my recent books, friends and acquaintances got invited to share the problems I encountered as I built up the chapters in this volume. Quite a number burrowed into hidden corners and produced worthwhile data. The basic genealogy was ferreted out by David Gretton with specific additions by John Goulder, John Goulstone, Andrew Thomas and Duncan Anderson. The statistical detail was most carefully checked by Derek Drake and Michael Goulder, though if any errors have crept in I hold up my hand.

The following were also of help in the course of my researches: David Beaumont, Steve Bilton, Rob Brooke, Derek Clifton, Hazel Crozier, George Fish, Mark Friedberger, David Frith, John Grimsley, Aidan Haile, Duncan Hamilton, Rachel Hassell (Sherborne School archivist), John McKenzie, Eric Midwinter, Chris O'Brien, Tony Percival, Jo Smith, Ray Smithson, Keith Warsop (who double-checked the final manuscript), Chris Waters, Edith Wynne-Thomas and Dr Neil Young.

The extensive archives at the Trent Bridge Cricket Library have been thoroughly mined, especially the scrapbooks compiled by Mrs Herbert Roe and those of ERB Alcock.

# BIBLIOGRAPHY

Ashley-Cooper, Frederick, *Nottinghamshire Cricket and Cricketers* (HB Saxton, 1923)

Bassano, Brian, *Mann's Men: MCC to South Africa 1922-23* (McKenzie, 2001)

Blaxland, Gregory, *Golden Miller* (Constable, 1972)

Blew, William, *The Quorn Hunt and Its Masters* (JC Nimmo, 1899)

Bowes, Bill, *Express Deliveries* (Stanley Paul, 1948)

Briscoe, Basil, *The Life of Golden Miller* (Hutchinson, 1944)

Byrne, Ciaran, *The Harp and Crown* (Lulu, 2008)

Carew, Dudley, *England Over* (Secker, 1927)

Carr, Arthur, *Cricket With The Lid Off* (Hutchinson, 1935)

Darling, Major JC, *20th Hussars in the Great War* (self published, 1923)

Gibson, Alan, *The Cricket Captains of England* (Cassell, 1979)

Gordon, Sir Home, *Background of Cricket* (Arthur Barker, 1939)

Gourlay, A.B., *A History of Sherborne School* (Sawtells, 1971)

Hamilton, Duncan, *Harold Larwood* (Quercus, 2009)

Hart, Peter, *The South Notts Hussars 1940-42* (Pen and Sword, 2010)

Haynes, Basil & Lucas, John, *The Trent Bridge Battery* (Collins Willow, 1985)

Herbert, Ivor & Sanyly, P, *The Winter Kings* (Pelham, 1968)

Jardine, Douglas, *In Quest of the Ashes* (Hutchinson, 1933)

Larwood, Harold, *Bodyline?* (Elkin, Mathews and Marrot, 1933)

Lemmon, David, *Percy Chapman: A Biography* (Queen Anne, 1985)

Lucas, Edward, *A Hundred Years of Trent Bridge* (privately published, 1938)

Parkin, Cecil, *Cricket Triumphs and Troubles* (C.Nicholls and Co, 1936)

Perkins, Kevin, *The Larwod Story* (WH Allen, 1965)

Rijks, Miranda, *The Eccentric Entrepreneur* (History Press, 2008)

Robertson-Glasgow, RC, *More Cricket Prints* (Werner Laurie, 1948)

Root, Fred, *A Cricket Pro's Lot* (Arnold, 1937)

Swanton, Ernest, *Gubby Allen: Man of Cricket* (Hutchinson, 1985)

Thomas, Andrew, *Pears 150* (self published, 2014)

Warner, Pelham, *The Fight for the Ashes in 1926* (Harrap, 1926)

Waugh, Alec, *The Loom of Youth* (Dodo, 1917)

# STATISTICS

The Nottinghamshire County Cricket Club scorebooks are extant for every season in which Carr represented the county except for 1933, however for that season the detailed scores, taken from the scorebook, were published in the Nottinghamshire Club Yearbook. The statistics relating to Carr's county career have been compiled from these scorebooks, plus that one Yearbook. Carr's figures for non-Nottinghamshire matches are derived from the ACS Match Score Books plus the books compiled by Jim Ledbetter containing first-class match scores. The author has been much assisted by Derek Drake in the compilation of the various tables included in this section.

## Batting and Fielding
## Nottinghamshire matches only

| Year | M | Inn | NO | Runs | HS | Avg | 100s | 50s | 0s | 6s | Ct |
|---|---|---|---|---|---|---|---|---|---|---|---|
| 1910 | 1 | 2 | 0 | 1 | 1 | 0.50 | - | - | 1 | - | - |
| 1911 | 3 | 6 | 1 | 116 | 47 | 23.20 | - | - | 1 | - | 2 |
| 1912 | 5 | 8 | 0 | 136 | 44 | 17.00 | - | - | 1 | - | 1 |
| 1913 | 8 | 12 | 0 | 431 | 169 | 35.91 | 1 | 2 | - | 1 | 7 |
| 1914 | 5 | 9 | 0 | 176 | 68 | 19.55 | - | 1 | - | 1 | 7 |
| 1919 | 14 | 20 | 1 | 640 | 114 | 33.68 | 2 | 4 | 1 | 7 | 17 |
| 1920 | 20 | 32 | 1 | 698 | 105* | 22.51 | 1 | 4 | 2 | 2 | 12 |
| 1921 | 25 | 43 | 1 | 1115 | 204 | 26.54 | 2 | 5 | 7 | 3 | 18 |
| 1922 | 26 | 36 | 1 | 1331 | 124 | 38.02 | 3 | 5 | 2 | 15 | 24 |
| 1923 | 24 | 38 | 2 | 1205 | 165 | 33.47 | 4 | 6 | 4 | 16 | 24 |
| 1924 | 27 | 41 | 6 | 1321 | 134 | 37.74 | 5 | 3 | 3 | 4 | 30 |
| 1925 | 24 | 39 | 4 | 1864 | 206 | 53.25 | 7 | 7 | 1 | 42 | 27 |
| 1926 | 21 | 35 | 0 | 1110 | 138 | 31.71 | 2 | 7 | 1 | 27 | 22 |
| 1927 | 29 | 41 | 2 | 742 | 59 | 19.02 | - | 4 | 4 | 15 | 25 |
| 1928 | 31 | 42 | 5 | 1442 | 150 | 38.97 | 3 | 11 | 3 | 29 | 21 |
| 1929 | 31 | 45 | 3 | 1410 | 194 | 33.57 | 4 | 4 | 3 | 30 | 24 |
| 1930 | 24 | 32 | 3 | 737 | 101* | 25.41 | 1 | 1 | 3 | 9 | 19 |
| 1931 | 27 | 40 | 0 | 1283 | 140 | 32.07 | 3 | 5 | 5 | 20 | 28 |
| 1932 | 30 | 43 | 3 | 1118 | 132* | 27.95 | 1 | 8 | 8 | 10 | 27 |
| 1933 | 29 | 45 | 4 | 1542 | 137* | 37.60 | 3 | 6 | 1 | 27 | 23 |
| 1934 | 12 | 21 | 3 | 437 | 107 | 24.27 | 1 | 1 | 4 | 9 | 10 |
| TOT | 416 | 630 | 40 | 18855 | 206 | 31.95 | 43 | 84 | 55 | 267 | 368 |

## Batting and Fielding
## All first-class matches

| Year | M | Inn | NO | Runs | HS | Avg | 100s | 50s | 0s | Ct | St |
|------|---|-----|-----|------|-----|------|------|-----|-----|-----|-----|
| 1910 | 1 | 2 | 0 | 1 | 1 | 0.50 | - | - | 1 | - | - |
| 1911 | 3 | 6 | 1 | 116 | 47 | 23.20 | - | - | 1 | 2 | - |
| 1912 | 5 | 8 | 0 | 136 | 44 | 17.00 | - | - | 1 | 1 | - |
| 1913 | 8 | 12 | 0 | 431 | 169 | 35.91 | 1 | 2 | - | 7 | - |
| 1914 | 5 | 9 | 0 | 176 | 68 | 19.55 | - | 1 | - | 7 | - |
| 1919 | 17 | 24 | 1 | 785 | 114 | 34.13 | 2 | 6 | 1 | 22 | - |
| 1920 | 22 | 36 | 1 | 744 | 105* | 21.25 | 1 | 4 | 2 | 13 | - |
| 1921 | 25 | 43 | 1 | 1115 | 204 | 26.54 | 2 | 5 | 7 | 18 | - |
| 1922 | 33 | 45 | 1 | 1749 | 135 | 39.75 | 4 | 8 | 3 | 27 | 1 |
| 1922-23 | 14 | 24 | 2 | 428 | 63 | 19.45 | - | 2 | 1 | 2 | - |
| 1923 | 27 | 43 | 2 | 1397 | 165 | 34.07 | 4 | 7 | 4 | 27 | - |
| 1924 | 29 | 45 | 6 | 1358 | 134 | 34.82 | 5 | 3 | 3 | 30 | - |
| 1925 | 30 | 49 | 4 | 2338 | 206 | 51.95 | 8 | 11 | 1 | 28 | - |
| 1926 | 29 | 42 | 0 | 1236 | 138 | 29.42 | 2 | 7 | 2 | 30 | - |
| 1927 | 29 | 41 | 2 | 742 | 59 | 19.02 | - | 4 | 4 | 25 | - |
| 1928 | 33 | 46 | 5 | 1600 | 150 | 39.02 | 3 | 13 | 3 | 22 | - |
| 1929 | 35 | 51 | 3 | 1575 | 194 | 32.81 | 4 | 5 | 3 | 26 | - |
| 1930 | 24 | 32 | 3 | 737 | 101* | 25.41 | 1 | 1 | 3 | 19 | - |
| 1931 | 27 | 40 | 0 | 1283 | 140 | 32.07 | 3 | 5 | 5 | 28 | - |
| 1932 | 30 | 43 | 3 | 1118 | 132* | 27.95 | 1 | 8 | 8 | 27 | - |
| 1933 | 29 | 45 | 4 | 1542 | 137* | 37.60 | 3 | 6 | 1 | 23 | - |
| 1934 | 12 | 21 | 3 | 437 | 107 | 24.27 | 1 | 1 | 4 | 10 | - |
| 1935 | 1 | 2 | 0 | 7 | 7 | 3.50 | - | - | 1 | 1 | - |
| **TOT** | **468** | **709** | **42** | **21051** | **206** | **31.56** | **45** | **99** | **59** | **395** | **1** |

# Centuries for Nottinghamshire

| Date | Inn | Pos | Sixes | Fives | Fours | Mins | Opponents |
|---|---|---|---|---|---|---|---|
| 12.8.1913 | 169 | 3 | 1 | 0 | 20 | 180 | Leics (Trent Bridge) |
| 30.5.1919 | 104 | 4 | 1 | 0 | 13 | 90 | Sussex (Hove) |
| 11.8.1919 | 112 | 4 | 2 | 0 | 11 | | Sussex (Trent Bridge) |
| 4.8.1920 | 105* | 4 | 0 | 0 | 10 | 180 | Surrey (Kennington Oval) |
| 9.6.1921 | 204 | 5 | 1 | 0 | 25 | 255 | Essex (Leyton) |
| 4.7.1921 | 102 | 3 | 0 | 0 | 15 | | Sussex (Trent Bridge) |
| 24.5.1922 | 110 | 4 | 0 | 0 | 9 | 195 | Warks (Trent Bridge) |
| 2.8.1922 | 103 | 4 | 0 | 0 | 15 | 105 | Lancs (Trent Bridge) |
| 19.8.1922 | 124 | 4 | 2 | 0 | 14 | 180 | Leics (Trent Bridge) |
| 24/25.5.1923 | 100* | 4 | 2 | 0 | 10 | | Northants (Northampton) |
| 20/21.6.1923 | 106* | 4 | 0 | 0 | 12 | | Northants (Trent Bridge) |
| 27.6.1923 | 165 | 4 | 2 | 0 | 21 | | Kent (Trent Bridge) |
| 22/23.8.1923 | 105 | 6 | 0 | 0 | 16 | | Kent (Dover) |
| 21/22.5.1924 | 111 | 4 | 0 | 0 | 15 | 160 | Glam (Trent Bridge) |
| 9/10.6.1924 | 112* | 4 | 0 | 1 | 12 | 200 | Surrey (Trent Bridge) |
| 3/4.7.1924 | 127* | 4 | 1 | 0 | 13 | | Essex (Worksop) |
| 12.7.1924 | 134 | 4 | 0 | 0 | 20 | | Middx (Trent Bridge) |
| 19.8.1924 | 101 | 4 | 0 | 0 | 13 | 150 | Derbys (Derby) |
| 11.5.1925 | 104 | 4 | 5 | 0 | 10 | 120 | Sussex (Trent Bridge) |
| 8.6.1925 | 206 | 4 | 8 | 0 | 20 | 225 | Leics (Aylestone Rd) |
| 22.6.1925 | 123 | 4 | 1 | 0 | 17 | 125 | Middx (Trent Bridge) |
| 30.6.1925 | 102* | 4 | 3 | 0 | 9 | 180 | Lancs (Trent Bridge) |
| 13/14.7.1925 | 124 | 4 | 5 | 0 | 12 | 70 | Sussex (Hove) |
| 30.7.1925 | 103 | 4 | 6 | 0 | 9 | 90 | Kent (Trent Bridge) |
| 4.8.1925 | 107* | 4 | 0 | 0 | 8 | 125 | Surrey (Kennington Oval) |
| 25.5.1926 | 115 | 5 | 3 | 0 | 13 | 120 | Surrey (Trent Bridge) |
| 19.8.1926 | 138 | 4 | 0 | 0 | 22 | 150 | Worcs (Trent Bridge) |
| 9.6.1928 | 150 | 4 | 1 | 0 | 18 | 225 | Leics (Aylestone Rd) |
| 7.7.1928 | 100 | 4 | 0 | 0 | 14 | 120 | West Indians (Trent Bridge) |
| 12.7.1928 | 100* | 4 | 1 | 0 | 15 | 60 | Northants (Northampton) |
| 11/13.5.1929 | 123 | 4 | 3 | 0 | 15 | 180 | Kent (Trent Bridge) |
| 17.5.1929 | 100 | 6 | 1 | 0 | 13 | 90 | Cambridge U (Fenner's) |
| 6.7.1929 | 194 | 4 | 7 | 0 | 20 | 235 | South Africans (Trent Bdge) |

| 3.8.1929 | 114 | 4 | 0 | 0 | 12 | 140 | Surrey (Kennington Oval) |
|---|---|---|---|---|---|---|---|
| 4/5.6.1930 | 101* | 4 | 1 | 0 | 8 | 160 | Worcs (Worcester) |
| 19.5.1931 | 140 | 4 | 6 | 0 | 10 | 160 | Northants (Trent Bridge) |
| 13.6.1931 | 102 | 4 | 2 | 0 | 9 | 150 | Middx (Lord's) |
| 24/25.6.1931 | 127 | 4 | 1 | 0 | 9 | 200 | Worcs (Worcester) |
| 13/14.7.1932 | 132* | 6 | 2 | 0 | 13 | 150 | Essex (Trent Bridge) |
| 25.5.1933 | 123 | 4 | 2 | 0 | 14 | 155 | Cambridge U (Fenner's) |
| 7.6.1933 | 125 | 4 | 2 | 0 | 14 | 165 | Northants (Northampton) |
| 17/19.6.1933 | 137* | 4 | 0 | 0 | 13 | 230 | Derbys (Trent Bridge) |
| 13.6.1934 | 107 | 7 | 2 | 0 | 12 | 150 | Essex (Westcliff) |

Note: The length of each innings is as reported in the local newspapers and therefore only accurate to the nearest five minutes, times of dismissal are not recorded in the Nottinghamshire scorebooks until after the Second World War.

# Sixes

Arthur Carr hit 267 sixes in Nottinghamshire first-class matches, a county record. The next highest total is 224 by Fred Barratt. Carr's most productive summer was 1925 when he recorded 42 sixes; Fred Barratt holds the county record with 46, scored in 1928.

In four other seasons Carr hit 20 or more sixes:

- 1926 (27)
- 1928 (29)
- 1929 (30)
- 1931 (20)
- 1933 (27)

According to Gerald Brodribb's research, Carr hit 48 sixes in all first-class matches in 1925, which was then a first-class record, but we have been unable to check all the scorebooks for Carr's appearances in non-Notts matches that summer and therefore cannot confirm that figure. A detailed article on Nottinghamshire's six hitters, written by Derek Drake, appears in the Notts Cricket Annual of 2009, pages 28 and 29.

## Bowling

| Year | Inn | Ov | M | Runs | Wkts | Avg | BB | BPW |
|------|-----|-----|----|------|------|-------|------|-----|
| 1912 | 1 | 3 | 0 | 15 | 0 | - | - | - |
| 1913 | 6 | 48 | 4 | 243 | 5 | 48.60 | 3-73 | 58 |
| 1919 | 4 | 17 | 3 | 72 | 2 | 36.00 | 2-45 | 51 |
| 1920 | 12 | 45 | 10 | 126 | 7 | 18.00 | 3-14 | 39 |
| 1921 | 6 | 17.5 | 0 | 84 | 0 | - | - | - |
| 1922 | 4 | 9 | 1 | 48 | 1 | 48.00 | 1-21 | 54 |
| 1923 | 2 | 12 | 0 | 48 | 2 | 24.00 | 2-45 | 36 |
| 1924 | 4 | 10.5 | 0 | 57 | 1 | 57.00 | 1-7 | 65 |
| 1925 | 2 | 2 | 0 | 10 | 1 | 10.00 | 1-7 | 12 |
| 1926 | 6 | 27.4 | 4 | 81 | 3 | 27.00 | 1-9 | 55 |
| 1927 | 6 | 12 | 1 | 31 | 3 | 10.33 | 2-15 | 24 |
| 1928 | 7 | 24 | 4 | 100 | 2 | 50.00 | 2-21 | 72 |
| 1929 | 2 | 7 | 0 | 34 | 0 | - | - | - |
| 1930 | 1 | 0.2 | 0 | 4 | 0 | - | - | - |
| 1931 | 4 | 54 | 10 | 162 | 4 | 40.50 | 2-37 | 81 |
| 1932 | 1 | 4 | 0 | 8 | 0 | - | - | - |
| 1933 | 3 | 9 | 2 | 27 | 0 | - | - | - |
| TOT | 71 | 302.4 | 39 | 1150 | 31 | 37.09 | 3-14 | 58 |

Note: AW Carr's bowling was, in first-class cricket, confined to Notts matches. Only the seasons in which he bowled are included.

# Record against each county, ground by ground

| DERBYSHIRE | M | Inn | NO | Runs | HS | Avg | 100 | 50 | c/s |
|---|---|---|---|---|---|---|---|---|---|
| Trent Bridge | 16 | 21 | 1 | 641 | 137* | 32.05 | 1 | 2 | 9 |
| Worksop | 2 | 3 | 0 | 139 | 75 | 46.33 | 0 | 1 | 1 |
| Home Total | 18 | 24 | 1 | 780 | 137* | 33.91 | 1 | 3 | 10 |
| Blackwell | 1 | 2 | 1 | 12 | 12 | 12.00 | 0 | 0 | 1 |
| Chesterfield | 3 | 6 | 0 | 58 | 33 | 9.66 | 0 | 0 | 3 |
| Derby | 2 | 2 | 0 | 134 | 101 | 67.00 | 1 | 0 | 2 |
| Ilkeston | 8 | 11 | 0 | 292 | 84 | 26.54 | 0 | 2 | 5 |
| Away Total | 14 | 21 | 1 | 496 | 101 | 24.80 | 1 | 2 | 11 |
| TOTAL | 32 | 45 | 2 | 1276 | 137* | 29.67 | 2 | 5 | 21 |

| ESSEX | M | Inn | NO | Runs | HS | Avg | 100 | 50 | c/s |
|---|---|---|---|---|---|---|---|---|---|
| Trent Bridge | 9 | 12 | 1 | 521 | 132* | 47.36 | 1 | 4 | 8 |
| Worksop | 1 | 2 | 1 | 127 | 127* | 127.00 | 1 | 0 | 1 |
| Home Total | 10 | 14 | 2 | 648 | 132* | 54.00 | 2 | 4 | 9 |
| Leyton | 5 | 7 | 1 | 322 | 204 | 53.66 | 1 | 1 | 4 |
| Southend | 3 | 3 | 1 | 15 | 12* | 7.50 | 0 | 0 | 4 |
| Colchester Gar A | 1 | 1 | 0 | 16 | 16 | 16.00 | 0 | 0 | 1 |
| Westcliff | 1 | 2 | 0 | 113 | 107 | 56.50 | 1 | 0 | 3 |
| Away Total | 10 | 13 | 2 | 466 | 204 | 42.36 | 2 | 1 | 12 |
| TOTAL | 20 | 27 | 4 | 1114 | 204 | 48.43 | 4 | 5 | 21 |

| GLAMORGAN | M | Inn | NO | Runs | HS | Avg | 100 | 50 | c/s |
|---|---|---|---|---|---|---|---|---|---|
| Trent Bridge | 9 | 9 | 0 | 340 | 111 | 37.77 | 1 | 1 | 15 |
| Swansea | 2 | 3 | 0 | 113 | 56 | 37.66 | 0 | 1 | 0 |
| Cardiff Arms Park | 4 | 6 | 2 | 209 | 92 | 52.25 | 0 | 2 | 4 |
| Away Total | 6 | 9 | 2 | 322 | 92 | 46.00 | 0 | 3 | 4 |
| TOTAL | 15 | 18 | 2 | 662 | 111 | 41.37 | 1 | 4 | 19 |

| GLOS | M | Inn | NO | Runs | HS | Avg | 100 | 50 | c/s |
|---|---|---|---|---|---|---|---|---|---|
| Trent Bridge | 10 | 16 | 1 | 248 | 68 | 16.53 | 0 | 2 | 7 |
| Cheltenham | 2 | 4 | 0 | 67 | 35 | 16.75 | 0 | 0 | 5 |
| Bristol City Gd | 4 | 7 | 0 | 64 | 41 | 9.14 | 0 | 0 | 2 |
| Bristol Greenbank | 1 | 2 | 0 | 79 | 53 | 39.50 | 0 | 1 | 2 |
| Gloucester | 1 | 1 | 0 | 6 | 6 | 6.00 | 0 | 0 | 0 |
| Away Total | 8 | 14 | 0 | 216 | 53 | 15.42 | 0 | 1 | 9 |
| TOTAL | 18 | 30 | 1 | 464 | 68 | 16.00 | 0 | 3 | 16 |

| HAMPSHIRE | M | Inn | NO | Runs | HS | Avg | 100 | 50 | c/s |
|---|---|---|---|---|---|---|---|---|---|
| Trent Bridge | 12 | 14 | 1 | 419 | 68 | 32.23 | 0 | 2 | 12 |
| Southampton | 7 | 12 | 0 | 268 | 84 | 22.33 | 0 | 2 | 5 |
| Portsmouth | 1 | 1 | 0 | 5 | 5 | 5.00 | 0 | 0 | 0 |
| Bournemouth | 2 | 3 | 0 | 112 | 81 | 37.33 | 0 | 1 | 3 |
| Away Total | 10 | 16 | 0 | 385 | 84 | 24.06 | 0 | 3 | 8 |
| TOTAL | 22 | 30 | 1 | 804 | 84 | 27.72 | 0 | 5 | 20 |

| KENT | M | Inn | NO | Runs | HS | Avg | 100 | 50 | c/s |
|---|---|---|---|---|---|---|---|---|---|
| Trent Bridge | 15 | 24 | 2 | 723 | 165 | 32.86 | 3 | 2 | 18 |
| Canterbury | 6 | 11 | 0 | 178 | 58 | 16.18 | 0 | 1 | 6 |
| Catford | 1 | 2 | 1 | 97 | 79* | 97.00 | 0 | 1 | 0 |
| Tunbridge Wells | 2 | 4 | 0 | 115 | 45 | 28.75 | 0 | 0 | 4 |
| Dover | 4 | 7 | 0 | 206 | 105 | 29.42 | 1 | 0 | 2 |
| Gravesend | 1 | 1 | 0 | 12 | 12 | 12.00 | 0 | 0 | 0 |
| Maidstone | 1 | 2 | 0 | 20 | 13 | 10.00 | 0 | 0 | 1 |
| Away Total | 15 | 27 | 1 | 628 | 105 | 24.15 | 1 | 2 | 13 |
| **TOTAL** | **30** | **51** | **3** | **1351** | **165** | **28.14** | **4** | **4** | **31** |

| LANCASHIRE | M | Inn | NO | Runs | HS | Avg | 100 | 50 | c/s |
|---|---|---|---|---|---|---|---|---|---|
| Trent Bridge | 14 | 22 | 2 | 640 | 103 | 32.00 | 2 | 3 | 11 |
| Liverpool | 1 | 2 | 0 | 34 | 24 | 17.00 | 0 | 0 | 0 |
| Old Trafford | 14 | 22 | 0 | 448 | 67 | 20.36 | 0 | 3 | 16 |
| Away Total | 15 | 24 | 0 | 482 | 67 | 20.08 | 0 | 3 | 16 |
| **TOTAL** | **29** | **46** | **2** | **1122** | **103** | **25.50** | **2** | **6** | **27** |

| LEICS | M | Inn | NO | Runs | HS | Avg | 100 | 50 | c/s |
|---|---|---|---|---|---|---|---|---|---|
| Trent Bridge | 15 | 23 | 1 | 812 | 169 | 36.90 | 2 | 2 | 20 |
| Loughb'h Park Rd | 1 | 1 | 0 | 60 | 60 | 60.00 | 0 | 1 | 2 |
| Aylestone Road | 13 | 22 | 0 | 868 | 206 | 39.45 | 2 | 4 | 12 |
| Away Total | 14 | 23 | 0 | 928 | 206 | 40.34 | 2 | 5 | 14 |
| **TOTAL** | **29** | **46** | **1** | **1740** | **206** | **38.66** | **4** | **7** | **34** |

| MIDDLESEX | M | Inn | NO | Runs | HS | Avg | 100 | 50 | c/s |
|---|---|---|---|---|---|---|---|---|---|
| Trent Bridge | 17 | 27 | 2 | 847 | 134 | 33.88 | 2 | 4 | 13 |
| Lord's | 15 | 27 | 1 | 961 | 102 | 36.96 | 1 | 9 | 17 |
| **TOTAL** | **32** | **54** | **3** | **1808** | **134** | **35.45** | **3** | **12** | **30** |

| NORTHANTS | M | Inn | NO | Runs | HS | Avg | 100 | 50 | c/s |
|---|---|---|---|---|---|---|---|---|---|
| Trent Bridge | 11 | 10 | 2 | 434 | 140 | 54.25 | 2 | 1 | 8 |
| Worksop | 2 | 4 | 0 | 95 | 67 | 23.75 | 0 | 1 | 3 |
| Home Total | 13 | 14 | 2 | 529 | 140 | 44.08 | 2 | 2 | 11 |
| Northampton | 11 | 18 | 4 | 709 | 125 | 50.64 | 3 | 3 | 7 |
| Kettering | 1 | 2 | 0 | 36 | 36 | 18.00 | 0 | 0 | 3 |
| Away Total | 12 | 20 | 4 | 745 | 125 | 46.56 | 3 | 3 | 10 |
| **TOTAL** | **25** | **34** | **6** | **1274** | **140** | **45.50** | **5** | **5** | **21** |

| SOMERSET | M | Inn | NO | Runs | HS | Avg | 100 | 50 | c/s |
|---|---|---|---|---|---|---|---|---|---|
| Trent Bridge | 7 | 8 | 1 | 150 | 48 | 21.42 | 0 | 0 | 8 |
| Taunton | 4 | 5 | 0 | 148 | 72 | 29.60 | 0 | 1 | 4 |
| Bath | 1 | 2 | 0 | 73 | 37 | 36.50 | 0 | 0 | 0 |
| Away Total | 5 | 7 | 0 | 221 | 72 | 31.57 | 0 | 1 | 4 |
| **TOTAL** | **12** | **15** | **1** | **371** | **72** | **26.50** | **0** | **1** | **12** |

| SURREY | M | Inn | NO | Runs | HS | Avg | 100 | 50 | c/s |
|---|---|---|---|---|---|---|---|---|---|
| Trent Bridge | 16 | 27 | 2 | 743 | 115 | 29.72 | 2 | 2 | 4 |
| Oval | 16 | 24 | 2 | 900 | 114 | 40.90 | 3 | 5 | 14 |
| v The Rest | 1 | 2 | 0 | 97 | 91 | 48.50 | 0 | 1 | 1 |
| **TOTAL** | **33** | **53** | **4** | **1740** | **115** | **35.51** | **5** | **8** | **19** |

| SUSSEX | M | Inn | NO | Runs | HS | Avg | 100 | 50 | c/s |
|---|---|---|---|---|---|---|---|---|---|
| Trent Bridge | 14 | 21 | 3 | 705 | 112 | 39.16 | 3 | 0 | 15 |
| Hove | 8 | 11 | 0 | 426 | 124 | 38.72 | 2 | 1 | 6 |
| Hastings | 4 | 8 | 0 | 135 | 32 | 16.87 | 0 | 0 | 3 |
| Horsham | 2 | 4 | 0 | 22 | 11 | 5.50 | 0 | 0 | 0 |
| Eastbourne | 2 | 2 | 0 | 20 | 16 | 10.00 | 0 | 0 | 1 |
| Away Total | 16 | 25 | 0 | 603 | 124 | 24.12 | 2 | 1 | 10 |
| **TOTAL** | **30** | **46** | **3** | **1308** | **124** | **30.41** | **5** | **1** | **25** |

| WARKS | M | Inn | NO | Runs | HS | Avg | 100 | 50 | c/s |
|---|---|---|---|---|---|---|---|---|---|
| Trent Bridge | 7 | 10 | 0 | 273 | 110 | 27.30 | 1 | 1 | 7 |
| Edgbaston | 4 | 4 | 0 | 75 | 38 | 18.75 | 0 | 0 | 3 |
| Coventry | 2 | 2 | 0 | 58 | 58 | 29.00 | 0 | 1 | 1 |
| Away Total | 6 | 6 | 0 | 133 | 58 | 22.16 | 0 | 1 | 4 |
| **TOTAL** | **13** | **16** | **0** | **406** | **110** | **25.37** | **1** | **2** | **11** |

| WORCS | M | Inn | NO | Runs | HS | Avg | 100 | 50 | c/s |
|---|---|---|---|---|---|---|---|---|---|
| Trent Bridge | 11 | 13 | 2 | 458 | 138 | 41.63 | 1 | 3 | 11 |
| Worksop | 1 | 2 | 0 | 16 | 14 | 8.00 | 0 | 0 | 2 |
| Home Total | 12 | 15 | 2 | 474 | 138 | 36.46 | 1 | 3 | 13 |
| Worcester | 11 | 17 | 1 | 583 | 127 | 36.43 | 2 | 2 | 9 |
| Stourbridge | 1 | 2 | 0 | 14 | 14 | 7.00 | 0 | 0 | 0 |
| Dudley | 1 | 1 | 0 | 64 | 64 | 64.00 | 0 | 1 | 0 |
| Away Total | 13 | 20 | 1 | 661 | 127 | 34.78 | 2 | 3 | 9 |
| **TOTAL** | **25** | **35** | **3** | **1135** | **138** | **35.46** | **3** | **6** | **22** |

| YORKSHIRE | M | Inn | NO | Runs | HS | Avg | 100 | 50 | c/s |
|---|---|---|---|---|---|---|---|---|---|
| Trent Bridge | 14 | 21 | 1 | 400 | 62 | 20.00 | 0 | 3 | 8 |
| Headingley | 5 | 10 | 0 | 185 | 52 | 18.50 | 0 | 1 | 4 |
| Huddersfield | 1 | 2 | 0 | 7 | 7 | 3.50 | 0 | 0 | 2 |
| Bramall Lane | 6 | 10 | 1 | 208 | 54 | 23.11 | 0 | 1 | 8 |
| Bradford Park Ave | 3 | 5 | 1 | 145 | 97* | 36.25 | 0 | 1 | 5 |
| Away Total | 15 | 27 | 2 | 545 | 97* | 21.80 | 0 | 3 | 19 |
| **TOTAL** | **29** | **48** | **3** | **945** | **97*** | **21.00** | **0** | **6** | **27** |

| OXFORD UNI | M | Inn | NO | Runs | HS | Avg | 100 | 50 | c/s |
|---|---|---|---|---|---|---|---|---|---|
| Trent Bridge | 1 | 2 | 0 | 19 | 11 | 9.50 | 0 | 0 | 0 |
| The Parks | 1 | 2 | 0 | 40 | 20 | 20.00 | 0 | 0 | 2 |
| **TOTAL** | **2** | **4** | **0** | **59** | **20** | **14.75** | **0** | **0** | **2** |

| CAMBRIDGE U | M | Inn | NO | Runs | HS | Avg | 100 | 50 | c/s |
|---|---|---|---|---|---|---|---|---|---|
| Fenner's | 9 | 14 | 1 | 633 | 123 | 48.69 | 2 | 3 | 4 |

| TOURING | M | Inn | NO | Runs | HS | Avg | 100 | 50 | c/s |
|---|---|---|---|---|---|---|---|---|---|
| Australians | 2 | 4 | 0 | 61 | 31 | 15.25 | 0 | 0 | 0 |
| South Africans | 2 | 4 | 0 | 252 | 194 | 63.00 | 1 | 0 | 1 |
| West Indians | 3 | 4 | 0 | 164 | 100 | 41.00 | 1 | 0 | 1 |
| New Zealanders | 2 | 2 | 0 | 21 | 18 | 10.50 | 0 | 0 | 2 |
| Indians | 1 | 2 | 0 | 61 | 38 | 30.50 | 0 | 0 | 2 |

| MCC | M | Inn | NO | Runs | HS | Avg | 100 | 50 | c/s |
|---|---|---|---|---|---|---|---|---|---|
| Lord's | 1 | 2 | 0 | 84 | 81 | 42.00 | 0 | 1 | 0 |

## Modes of dismissal for Nottinghamshire

| Season | Total diss | bowled | caught | stumped | lbw | run out | hit wkt |
|--------|-----------|--------|--------|---------|-----|---------|---------|
| 1910 | 2 | 1 | 1 | | | | |
| 1911 | 5 | 2 | 2 | 1 | | | |
| 1912 | 8 | 4 | 3 | | 1 | | |
| 1913 | 12 | 4 | 6 | | 1 | 1 | |
| 1914 | 9 | 2 | 7 | | | | |
| 1919 | 19 | 6 | 11 | 2 | | | |
| 1920 | 31 | 9 | 19 | 2 | 1 | | |
| 1921 | 42 | 15 | 24 | 1 | 2 | | |
| 1922 | 35 | 13 | 20 | 1 | | | 1 |
| 1923 | 36 | 8 | 21 | 1 | 4 | 2 | |
| 1924 | 35 | 10 | 18 | 2 | 5 | | |
| 1925 | 35 | 7 | 23 | 3 | 1 | 1 | |
| 1926 | 35 | 9 | 24 | | 2 | | |
| 1927 | 39 | 10 | 27 | | 1 | 1 | |
| 1928 | 37 | 8 | 26 | 2 | 1 | | |
| 1929 | 42 | 11 | 23 | 2 | 6 | | |
| 1930 | 29 | 4 | 22 | | 3 | | |
| 1931 | 40 | 7 | 24 | | 7 | 2 | |
| 1932 | 40 | 8 | 26 | 2 | 3 | 1 | |
| 1933 | 41 | 11 | 24 | 2 | 3 | 1 | |
| 1934 | 18 | 4 | 12 | 1 | 1 | | |
| **Total** | **590** | **153** | **363** | **22** | **42** | **9** | **1** |
| % | | 25.93 | 61.52 | 3.72 | 7.11 | 1.52 | 0.16 |

Note: In 1921 Carr is shown as stumped Oldfield for Notts v Australians, but caught in Wisden. The scorebook is assumed correct. In 1933 Carr is shown as caught Levett for Notts v Kent (Maidstone) in the Notts Yearbook (no scorebook can be found) but the Nottingham Journal, both in the set out score and the written description of the match, is given as stumped Levett. The Nottingham Journal is taken as correct.

## Bowlers to dismiss Carr on eight or more occasions in first-class matches

| Bowler | Type | Total diss | bowled | caught | lbw | st | Inns | Avge |
|---|---|---|---|---|---|---|---|---|
| AS Kennedy (Hts) | RM | 17 | 4 | 12 | 0 | 1 | 41 | 2.41 |
| HA Smith (Leics) | RF | 8 | 2 | 4 | 1 | 1 | 20 | 2.50 |
| CWL Parker (Glos) | SLA | 12 | 4 | 8 | 0 | 0 | 33 | 2.75 |
| AP Freeman (Kent) | LBG | 15 | 3 | 7 | 1 | 4 | 42 | 2.80 |
| JA Newman (Hts) | RFM | 8 | 2 | 5 | 1 | 0 | 23 | 2.87 |
| FE Woolley (Kent) | SLA | 18 | 5 | 11 | 1 | 1 | 53 | 2.94 |
| LF Townsend (Dby) | RM | 9 | 0 | 8 | 1 | 0 | 27 | 3.00 |
| VWC Jupp (Sx, Nrthts) | RFM/ OB | 9 | 3 | 6 | 0 | 0 | 27 | 3.00 |
| CF Root (Worcs) | RFM | 8 | 2 | 5 | 1 | 0 | 31 | 3.87 |
| FJ Durston (Middx) | RFM | 10 | 6 | 4 | 0 | 0 | 40 | 4.00 |
| W Rhodes (Yorks) | SLA | 9 | 2 | 5 | 1 | 1 | 38 | 4.22 |
| PGH Fender (Sy) | RM/ LB | 13 | 3 | 8 | 2 | 0 | 55 | 4.23 |
| JW Hearne (Midx) | LBG | 12 | 5 | 4 | 1 | 2 | 53 | 4.41 |
| G Geary (Leics) | RFM | 8 | 0 | 6 | 2 | 0 | 36 | 4.50 |
| NE Haig (Middx) | RFM | 9 | 4 | 5 | 0 | 0 | 43 | 4.77 |
| MW Tate (Sussex) | RFM/ RM | 11 | 7 | 3 | 1 | 0 | 55 | 5.00 |

Note: The 'average' is obtained by dividing the number of innings in which the bowler bowled, when Carr batted by the total of number of times the bowler dismissed Carr. This figure can only be used as a rough guide, since it is impossible to know, from the existing scorebook details, whether or not the bowler actually bowled against Carr.

## Results obtained by Nottinghamshire captains

|  | Seasons | M | W | L | D | W-L |
|---|---|---|---|---|---|---|
| AW Carr | 1914-34 | 369 | 168 | 56 | 145 | +112 |
| AO Jones | 1897-14 | 259 | 97 | 63 | 99 | +34 |
| CEB Rice | 1979-87 | 171 | 57 | 32 | 82 | +25 |
| GFH Heane | 1928-46 | 154 | 38 | 35 | 81 | +3 |
| SP Fleming | 2005-07 | 35 | 13 | 11 | 11 | +2 |
| RT Robinson | 1987-97 | 160 | 49 | 48 | 63* | +1 |
| JA Dixon | 1889-04 | 147 | 45 | 45 | 57 | 0 |
| A Jepson | 1954-59 | 34 | 8 | 9 | 17 | -1 |
| CMW Read | 2008-16 | 136 | 39 | 40 | 57 | -1 |
| JER Gallian | 1998-06 | 91 | 29 | 33 | 29 | -4 |
| J Hardstaff | 1951-54 | 27 | 2 | 7 | 18 | -5 |
| JB Bolus | 1966-72 | 52 | 7 | 12 | 33 | -5 |
| GS Sobers | 1968-73 | 86 | 15 | 20 | 51 | -5 |
| WA Sime | 1947-50 | 84 | 15 | 22 | 47 | -7 |
| AJ Corran | 1962 | 26 | 4 | 11 | 11 | -7 |
| P Johnson | 1992-98 | 46 | 9 | 18 | 19 | -9 |
| NW Hill | 1966-67 | 50 | 2 | 14 | 34 | -12 |
| JD Clay | 1961 | 27 | 3 | 20 | 4 | -17 |
| G Millman | 1962-65 | 86 | 13 | 33 | 40 | -20 |
| MJ Smedley | 1973-79 | 104 | 15 | 42 | 47 | -27 |
| RT Simpson | 1948-61 | 233 | 49 | 99 | 85 | -50 |

Note: Only includes captains since 1889 who led Nottinghamshire in twenty or more first-class matches. * denotes one match which ended in a tie.

# INDEX

# Arthur Carr

# ARTHUR CARR

**Rebel With A Cause: The Life and Times of Jack Crawford
by Keith and Jennifer Booth**

Jack Crawford, described as the greatest ever schoolboy cricketer, blazed into the Surrey team at the age of seventeen and broke a host of records: the youngest Surrey centurion and double centurion, the youngest player to achieve the double of 100 wickets and 1,000 runs in a season. He became the youngest cricketer to play for England and a Wisden Cricketer of the Year.

Yet, not long after his twenty-first birthday, he played the last of his twelve Test matches. He fell out with the Surrey committee, then with the South Australian Cricket Association and Otago Cricket Association after moving to play in the Southern Hemisphere. What went wrong?

Crawford's career raises many questions which have only been partially answered. Why did he stand up to the Surrey committee? What happened in Australia and New Zealand? Did he try to dodge the Great War? Was he a bigamist? Now, thanks to Keith and Jennifer Booth's meticulous research, the truth is fully known.

**The Champion Band: The First English Cricket Tour
by Scott Reeves**

In 1859, twelve cricketers left Liverpool to embark on the first overseas tour by a representative England side. Their destination was the place where cricket looked most likely to flourish: Canada and the United States.

It was not an easy trip - the English players experienced death on the high seas, were threatened at gunpoint and sensed unrest in the pre-Civil War USA.

Led by George Parr, the English tourists came up against the best of the New World cricketers. Some of the locals would go on to pioneer the sport that ultimately caused the death of North American cricket: baseball.

A gripping account featuring original research, THE CHAMPION BAND tells the fascinating story of the first English cricket tour.

ALSO FROM CHEQUERED FLAG PUBLISHING

### Lahore To London
### by Younis Ahmed

Younis Ahmed was a talented middle-order batsman who left his native Pakistan to forge a successful career in cricket around the globe. But he is not remembered for his vibrant batting. Instead it is for moments of controversy: an international ban for touring apartheid-era South Africa, taking Surrey to a tribunal, leaving Worcestershire under a cloud. Now Younis tells his side of the story.

Younis also describes winning the County Championship and Quaid-e-Azam Trophy, replacing Garry Sobers at South Australia at the invitation of Don Bradman, pioneering professionalism and sponsorship in cricket, taking the sport to the Middle East and playing alongside legends including Javed Miandad and Imran Khan.

This is the colourful and chequered story of how one cricketer's journey from Lahore to London took him to the top of the game, but also to the depths rejection and despair.

### The Father of Modern Sport: The Life and Times of Charles W Alcock
### by Keith Booth

A model Victorian sporting all-rounder, Charles Alcock was a prime mover in the development of both football and cricket as the world's biggest sports.

As a player, he was the first ever footballer to be ruled offside, the captain of the first FA Cup winners and played club cricket to a high standard.

As Secretary of the FA, Alcock was one of the men responsible for the first ever football international and was the driving force behind the creation of the FA Cup in 1871. In cricket, he arranged the first Test match in Britain, between England and Australia at The Oval in 1880.

Close attention to detail combined with a breadth of vision to change the sporting world – this is the definitive biography of the nineteenth century's most important sports administrator.

HOWZAT FOR A GREAT CRICKET BOOK?

Chequered Flag
PUBLISHING

www.chequeredflagpublishing.co.uk

17952356R00172

Printed in Poland
by Amazon Fulfillment
Poland Sp. z o.o., Wrocław